CREATIVITY & ART

ANDREAS STECK • BARBARA STECK

CREATIVITY & ART

NEUROSCIENTIFIC AND PSYCHOANALYTIC PERSPECTIVES

EPFL PRESS

Cover illustration: Garry Killian, © Shutterstock

EPFL PRESS is an imprint owned by the Foundation Presses polytechniques et universitaires romandes (PPUR), a Swiss academic publishing company whose main purpose is to publish the teaching and research works of the Ecole polytechnique fédérale de Lausanne (EPFL), of universities and other institutions of higher education.
PPUR, EPFL – Rolex Learning Center, CP 119, CH-1015 Lausanne, info@epflpress.org

www.epflpress.org

First edition
ISBN 978-2-88915-423-4

Printed in Italy

TABLE OF CONTENTS

PART IV

PART V

PART VI

INTRODUCTION

Taking an interdisciplinary approach, the authors discuss creative processes in art from a neuroscientific and a psychoanalytic perspective. *Creativity and Art* combines a scientific basis looking at the neural mechanisms of creativity with a humanistic point of view emphasizing a developmental and psychoanalytic perspective in a contextual relationship. We give voice to artists' own expressions of their life experiences to illustrate their subjectivity, construction of meaning, and associated feelings and emotions. This creative elaboration and attribution of signification is intimately related to their artistic production.

Nature is a major source of aesthetic encounters and awareness; human aesthetic experiences are shaped by our physical, social, and cultural environments. Nature amazes us with its richness and unbelievable diversity of forms. The forces driving creativity in the animal kingdom, but especially in humans, is staggering, our brains and thus our minds are profoundly creative. Art contains symbolic representations involving communication and promotion of survival as demonstrated, for example, in the Lascaux prehistoric paintings of hunting scenes.

We explore the relationship between the creative and aesthetic aspects of the mind and the emotional and cognitive functions of the brain. Our cultural mind is made up of mental representations derived from our own experiences within familial, cultural, and societal surroundings as well as from transgenerational transmissions. Charles Darwin in the nineteenth century recognized that emotions played an important role in our cultural practices, and now modern neuroscience is helping us understand the biological roots of human cultural endeavors by exploring the mental processes involved in creativity.

How do we perceive our environment? Evolution has endowed us with a multisensory perception system including sight, hearing, touch, smell, and taste. Vision is the most developed sense in humans, and we derive much of the information knowledge we have of the world from our sight. The study of how memory functions is at the center of the sciences of the mind. Human memory is unique because it possesses an inherent representational capacity that allows many symbolic activities characterizing our mental lives and our many skills. Memory is both conscious and unconscious, and in this stored information lies a seemingly unlimited potential for imagination and creativity.

Aesthetic judgment finds its foundation in the recognition of pleasure experienced when seeing works regarded as art and associated with the notion of beauty. A comprehensive neuroscientific theory explaining aesthetic experiences and artistic creation is not yet within reach, yet profound changes have taken place in our conception of beauty from ancient to modern times. The authors present the classical ideal of an alliance between beautiful and good in ancient Greek art, representing the harmony of soul and body. Modern art challenged the notion of "classical" beauty and culminated in anti-aesthetic movements. Contemporary art emphasizes the sociohistorical context from which art emerges and has generated new aesthetic inspiration and expressiveness. The increasing interaction, contact, and comprehension between art, psychology, sociology, psychoanalysis, and psychiatry during the twentieth century led to the recognition of the true artistic value of works from mentally ill patients. A major step was the creation of the art brut movement in France and Switzerland, eventually spreading worldwide as outsider art.

Many artists from different fields are presented here with an emphasis on how their subjective lived experiences of critical life events are expressed and reflected in their artwork. We prefer to let the reader discover them through their own words, which reflect the atmosphere they lived under and their struggle, mood, insight, and wisdom, with an acuity that we could never render ourselves.

Grief is a recurrent theme addressed by artists, finding its expression in music, literature, poetry, sculpture, or painting. Bereavement, loss, trauma, and adversities are accompanied by a crisis of meaning, and work undertaken while mourning tends to restore the signification of lived injuries. The testimonies of various artists with respect to the absence of significant family members are highlighted. Voice is given to writers, who, deported as children or adolescents, have endured the traumatic consequences of the Holocaust, and to those who describe their status as refugees as well as their situation as African Americans.

Early childhood development and its fundamental contribution to creativity are discussed. Failures in the essential early emotional relationship between infant and mother or the primary caregivers' inability for sensitive receptiveness to their infant and young child's spontaneous expressions may have a great impact on developmental structures and functions. The evolution of these processes reveals complex interactions between constitutionally determined capacities and environmental experiences.

Creative inspiration belongs to art and science, but science and psychoanalysis are distinctly different in their concept and forms of evaluation. Whereas science searches for objective truth, psychoanalysis is looking for a subject's inner truthfulness and self-integrity. Art and psychoanalysis are embedded in the lived moment and enhance self-awareness. All subjective experiences have qualitative features and unfold in time and space. Thoughts and expressions of one's self characterize a subject. Science withdraws from subjectivity, uses quantitative methods, deals with declarative knowledge, and verifies objective universalities relevant across time and space. Psychoanalytic understanding of art, human aesthetic experience, and creativity are discussed. The concept of the uncanny, its diverse manifestations and appearances, as well as its expressions in literature are described. The aesthetic experience and creativity in psychoanalytic therapy and in dreams are elaborated. Psychoanalytic therapy is associated with an opportunity for remembering, a time of thoughtful comprehension. The need to understand creates a deep introspection, reverie, and contemplation. A therapeutic session allows time to stand still, maintains a present, and allows the subject to immerse themselves in memories of the past as well as involvement into the future. A child analysis of a future artist and an adult analysis of an artist are summarized, and the lived experiences of two psychoanalysts are presented.

Creativity serves self-regulating processes leading to a better somatopsychic stability. In our societies science and technology continue their intensely creative procedures, while insight, which requires consciousness—oriented to the inner world and interested in the psychic processes determining human behavior, feelings, and personality—seems to be more and more challenged. Yet inventive and creative abilities continue to belong to the amazing resilience of human beings.

Epalinges and Evolène, Switzerland
Andreas Steck and Barbara Steck

PART I

Chapter 1

THE BEGINNINGS

Forms in nature

In the inorganic world, from minerals to plants, we can observe a multitude of forms, ranging from geometric shapes in minerals and stones, to the most exuberant arborizations found in the plant kingdom. Which rules are followed and how structures are designed by nature can be described in detail and codified by physical laws (Fivaz 1989). The formation of a crystal (Fig. 1.1) follows strict physicochemical rules, and its form, shape, and matrix are predictable if we know its molecular composition. Unless there are impurities, it organizes itself into a well-established order. The process of crystallization follows a defined pattern, dictated by forces acting at the molecular level. Although crystallization dynamics is a complex process, it can be understood and described in mathematical terms: a crystal cannot form if only two particles are present, a large number of particles are necessary for the construction of an ordered structure, and crystallization requires an exchange between the ordered structure to be built and the environment, which provides the necessary particles or molecules. The whole process is energy dependent and obeys the laws of thermodynamics, which in turn govern the overall order-disorder balance in nature.

The formation of arborizations is another example of an interesting arrangement from the point of view of the acquisition of order in nature; it is extremely common and is easily recognizable. It has various levels of complexity and can be found in the mineral, plant, and animal kingdoms. Typical examples of arborization in the physical world include lightning in the night sky, trees in the plant kingdom, and neuron dendrites in the animal kingdom (Fig. 1.2). Of course, the laws governing arborization differ greatly in these examples.

Figure 1.1 A crystal is an emerging structure: the initial state is totally chaotic, but the acquisition of order leads in stages to the perfect crystalloid form.

Figure 1.2 Examples of arborizations. Lightning in the night sky (left), cherry blossom tree (middle), cortical neurons (right).

Fractals are infinitely self-similar, repeated constructs. Fractal-like patterns occur widely in nature, in phenomena as diverse as clouds, mountains, coastlines, crystals, or leaves. Symmetry is another widespread pattern observed in nature. Animals have bilateral or mirror symmetry, as do the leaves of plants. The reason for symmetry in animals that move in one direction is quite obvious: they have head and tail ends, and the body becomes bilaterally symmetrical with a left and a right side. Other patterns are spirals, observed in plants or mollusk shells.

Figure 1.3 Vincent van Gogh. *The Starry Night* (1889). Oil on canvas.

Finally, our mineral and biological world is inherently unstable, prone to chaos. Any dynamic system will evolve according to its endogenous thermodynamic laws, but is usually contained by the environment, the meanders of a river being a classic example. A typical chaotic motion is turbulence. Turbulence is commonly observed in everyday phenomena such as surf, fast flowing rivers, storm clouds, or smoke from a chimney. The idea of turbulence was expressed poignantly in the works Vincent van Gogh[1] painted during the acute phases of his illness, while he was hospitalized in the psychiatric hospital at Saint-Rémy (Fig. 1.3).

The term "biomorphic" has been proposed to describe all organic, abstract shapes derived from biology or living organisms. In art, biomorphism has markedly influenced modern painting and architecture. It uses organic shapes of biology and elements of natural life. Abstract art—as championed by Pablo Picasso, Joan Miro, Jean Arp, and others—makes extensive use of biomorphic forms. In architecture, a well-known example of biomorphism can be found in the Sagrada Familia church, designed by the Spanish architect Antoni Gaudi (1852–1926) in Barcelona. The architecture of

[1] See chapter 7.

this church contains many elements derived from nature, such as branching columns modeled on trees.

There is so much to look at and so much to admire in nature that it is easy to be overwhelmed by its richness. Until the seventeenth century, theology taught us that the magnificence of nature is proof of God's existence and that God created humankind to enjoy all that is beautiful on earth. The Age of Enlightenment, beginning in the eighteenth century, marked the start of an intellectual movement influenced by philosophers and scientists such as René Descartes, Emmanuel Kant, and Isaac Newton. The scientific revolution led the way to a more in-depth exploration of the world by emphasizing reason, knowledge, and experience, with our study of the world being driven by factual rigor.

Living creatures

Living creatures are understood in biological terms; Linnaeus classified and separated them into species (Anderson 1997). Darwin then taught us that all life forms are connected and are produced by a selection process (Darwin 1860). According to the theory of evolution, all organisms are inscribed in a phylogenetic tree. Each creature will in the course of ontogeny develop into a unique individual. While individuation is rudimentary at the lower level of the evolutionary tree, as in the case of viruses or bacteria, it increases exponentially in the mammalian world. Let us consider some of the driving forces behind selected individuation processes, beginning at the most elementary level.

All living creatures are in constant exchange with the external world in order to maintain homeostatic control of their metabolism. Sensors adapt the opening and closing of channels to regulate the concentration of ions or nutrients. Protozoa like viruses or bacteria have no nervous system, and metabolic regulation follows the rule of their genetic endowment. Variations in their attributes are subject to environmental changes, especially when they are challenged by the immune system of their hosts. Antigenic variation, by which protozoa alter their surface protein in order to avoid recognition by the immune system, is a well-known phenomenon.

If we go up the chain of life, with the transition from unicellular organisms to multicellular ones, a new element appears: the nervous system. The snail's nervous system is very simple, consisting of about 20,000 nerve cells. This very primitive brain is, however, already capable of associative learning. When threatened, the snail retracts quickly into its shell. Whether it feels an emotion, which would imply that it possesses some kind of a representation of the self, of being its own organism, is unlikely. However, we should not consider emotion as a uniquely human or mammalian trait. Neuroscientist Antonio Damasio (1999) suggests that emotion appears very early on in evolution. He proposes that an emotion is a kind of autonomic intelligence, enabling a well-orchestrated set of alterations in the body, which increase survival abilities by dealing with danger or taking advantage of opportunities. As we further ascend the evolutionary tree, and as the primitive nervous system eventually evolves into a complex organ, instinctual behaviors and individuation processes become more complex.

Life instincts are most apparent in the development of sexual behavior. As Darwin pointed out, one primary biological function in any organism is reproduction. The instinctual behavior of reproduction has evolved to include elaborate courtships featuring rituals based on performance, movements, vocalization, and a display of beautiful ornaments.

Biological ornaments

Biological ornaments are used in courtship displays in many species. A well-known ornamentation used in courting is seen in peacocks. Male peacocks open and move their tails to attract and impress potential mates. The female chooses the peacock with the largest number of eyespots on its tail. One can argue that this sexual display and drive is only an instinctual behavior. There are also, however, arguments supporting the idea that this behavior is guided by emotion, suggesting that the male peacock is aware of his own body and possesses feelings of self-representation when engaging in pageantry behavior toward a sexual partner.

Biologists have tried to explain the paradox of exaggerated sexual dimorphism. Sexual dimorphism is the difference in appearance between male and females of the same species. Differences in color, shape, and size are commonly observed in birds. Sometimes these differences are excessive, as is the case with the elaborate peacock plumage, which appears to be incompatible with natural selection. Ronald Fisher (1930), a British geneticist, developed a theory called "runaway selection." Runaway phenomena occur above all where aesthetics come into play. This triggers breakthroughs in seemingly senseless beauty and sometimes also the ugly. Fisher explains this apparent maladaptive trait by what he calls the "handicap principle." Such an ornament is costly to produce and to display, and as such may appear to be a handicap, but at the same time it also shows the fitness of the bearer. Eventually it gives an advantage for female choice to the peacock with the most beautiful plumage, resulting in a selection advantage and thus the likelihood of having more descendants.

Representations and communications

In his book *The Story of Art*, Ernst Gombrich (1995), an Austrian-born art historian, describes how making art evolved in primitive society. He emphasizes the fact that images are not just objects to view, but that they are inner representations, charged with meaning. The first images drawn by humankind were only partially inspired by real things, even if they reproduced their appearance. These archaic human traces, abstract or not, constituted a representation of myths: they had symbolic value and were not primarily substitutes for things. The artistic creations found in the caverns of Chauvet and Lascaux in France are an attempt to humanize the external world by recreating images on rock walls. These paintings—estimated to be about 20,000 years old[2] and depicting animals and human figures—are believed to illustrate a kind of magical power; by externalizing the inner image of animals on the wall of a cave, the artist and by extension the viewer of the painting exert some kind of power over these animals. In other words, as these people were hunters and depended on hunting to survive, painting their prey would give them a form of supernatural ability to improve future hunting endeavors. An image representing a hunting scene thus provides a means of intervention, allowing an artist to influence the outside world and at the same time protect the self.

Art can be seen as a reflection of the artist's conscious and unconscious mind. Each painting amounts to a display of an experienced psychological state of mind. The inner images that the artist conveys in the painting become physical reality. It is an object that is translatable and communicable to the community. Art manifests a clear communicative structure, establishing a meaningful connection with the viewer. Accordingly, a conceptual understanding of artworks should always take place within the context of its epoch. Art is a method of communication, though it often remains opaque, establishing a metaphoric language that is highly context dependent and culturally tainted. A work of art is not only the mediator of aesthetic communication but also a mental representation, and it has often been employed as a moral carrier. In churches, paintings have been used for their ability to give rise to feelings of devotion, according to the well-known observation that representations or objects that are seen have more power than words.

From gestures to signs

Iconic gestures, that is, hand gestures carrying a meaning, were used for nonverbal communication and occurred before language. Pointing gestures as a means of natural communication are easily understood. Human gestures are intended to direct the attention of the other, as well as provide guidance and information. As humans we are all in close interaction with our physical, social, and cultural environment. Consciously or not, we develop representations of the world that are saved and stored in our brains; they are organized as a form of reasoning and eventually expressed in thoughts and ideas. The social world we live in requires a continuous cultural exchange. Over time, humankind has progressed and clarified the role of the image in the genesis of written communication.

[2] Archaeological data from Indonesia suggest a much older origin for cave painting, dating it to about 40,000 years ago and thus challenging the notion that humanity first became modern in Europe (Price 2019).

If we were able to translate languages on a graphic visual medium, it is because figures were first invested with a power of semanticization,[3] giving sense or meaning.

Writing, drawing, and painting have mixed destinies. Writing is a form of codified drawing. It refers either to a sound or to an idea. The emergence of the graphic symbol presupposes the establishment of new relationships. The vision of an image and the reading of a text lead the viewer into two distinct modes of decoding. The first mode, that of the image, leaves interpretation open and allows a free mental and sensory activity, while the second imposes on the reader a course determined by the order of the letters. Roland Barthes (1982) sees "the truth of writing" in the hand that supports signs and behaves in resonance with "the beating body."[4] Thus, as we try to substitute the reign of speech for that of the gesture, the gesture is in hindsight like an evaporated figurative trace; the stroke of the painter makes the brush move according to the body.

Barthes proposes to distinguish between the message that wants to produce information, the sign that brings a comprehension, and the gesture that produces all the rest: the gesture is the indeterminate and inexhaustible sum of reasons, impulses, and idleness that surround an act. As long as humankind has practiced manual writing, to the exclusion of print, the path of the hand was the fundamental act by which the letters were defined, studied, and classified in a codex that was perfectly worked out.

History of writing

The development of writing, a strictly human invention, is one of the most documented examples of a cultural evolution made possible by the existence of an innate cerebral predisposition. This progress may have come about as part of a genetic selection advantage. Alternatively, as societal exchanges provided a particular superiority, a culturally derived evolution could have occurred via epigenetic mechanisms, that is, through changes in the environment, eventually influencing and modulating gene expression. The idea that human evolution is in part driven by our lifestyle and the society we live in reflects the observation that behaviorally learned characteristics can be rapidly acquired (Fisher and Ridley 2013). In this case, new behavioral traits, directly stimulated by cultural innovation, can be transmitted to the next generation (Heard and Martienssen 2014). This phenomenon is particularly true for the last ten millennia, a period of rapid change in societal lifestyle and of intellectual, scientific, and artistic change. Social gains are added epigenetically to our genome, kept as cultural heritage, and further transmitted from generation to generation by tradition, arts, speech, writing, symbolic representations, and today by modern electronic means of dissemination.

3 The concept of semanticization is used in linguistics to describe the meaning of a word.

4 Barthes was very much interested in the corporality of movements and rhythms, obviously inherent in music, but also present in writing. "Beating body" refers to an imaginary body.

The emergence of modern humans was defined by their capacity to make gestures and then to speak—we were probably not fully human until we developed the ability to speak. The invention of writing occurred rather late in the history of humankind and dates only to about 3,500 years ago. The history of writing is primarily the development of expressing language, first by pictograms and marks, and eventually by letters (Renfrew 1987). The appearance of artworks, and later writing, led to enriched social and cultural exchanges, which each heralded the beginning of a new cultural era and increased human creativity. The age we call prehistoric is the time prior to the use of writing. It does not mean that we are ignorant about human history before the advent of writing, but information is more limited and depends mainly on archaeological findings.

Beyond its function to represent language, the major role of writing is to store information and communicate across time and space. Writing also allows a passage from the auditory sphere to the visual domain, giving visibility to our thoughts and acts. The graphic sign reaffirms what is individual and the signature what is highly personal, permitting identification. Early figures, marks, or signs did appear, but these representations corresponded to an object and their relationship with speech remained uncertain. With the appearance of cuneiform writing in Mesopotamia, signs become simpler and more abstract, having a triangular form (Fig. 1.4). Correspondence with the spoken language was based on logophonetic signs, with no clear sound representation as yet—this had to wait for the emergence of the alphabet. First came the Semitic alphabets, such as the Phoenician alphabet with about twenty letters, which is strictly consonantal. Vowels appeared with the Greek alphabet (Fig. 1.4). Writing went on to rapidly spread across the world; Indo-European languages are rich in vowels, while Semitic languages remain rather consonantal.

Writing was developed to store, transmit, and make available the multiple knowledges accumulated by human societies, but which had become too numerous to be kept in individual brain memories. The introduction of writing allowed the transition from oral to written culture, a huge societal change that began in Mesopotamia and Egypt in the third millennium BC. In ancient Greece, the earliest transition from oral to written culture occurred—according to records—around 750 BC. In this period, literature was passed from generation to generation, in both the ancient oral tradition of memorization and through the new methods of reading and writing. Gutenberg's invention of printing by movable type[5] in the mid-fifteenth century allowed the mass production of printed books for the first time. Another dramatic change began in the twentieth century, when the print-centric world started to evolve to the present time, in which printing co-exists with the various electronic media imbedded in the World Wide Web.[6]

5 Printing type made up of individual pieces (each carrying a single letter or other character) for free assembly.

6 The World Wide Web (WWW) is a global information system invented by the English scientist Tim Berners-Lee in 1990, while employed at CERN, Geneva, Switzerland.

Figure 1.4 Cuneiform writing (left), early Phoenician and Greek alphabets (right).

Chapter 2

BRAIN, MIND, BODY

An interwoven system

The French philosopher René Descartes (1596–1650) in his proposition of dualism, where "mind is different from the body in substance and causal relationship," declared the independency of the mind from the body (Descartes 1644/1911). If we can accept that "things" can happen to the mind and not to the body and vice versa, the idea that the mind floats above the body, being another substance, is no longer tenable. Modern neuroscientific research has taken an opposite view to Descartes, arguing that brain, mind, and body form an interwoven system that works together, with the sum of all three parts being much more than their individual components.

Obviously, our thoughts, emotions, and personality, basically all that is in our mind, originates in our brain. But our brain should not be perceived as an independent commanding organ. The brain is interconnected with the body in a very tight and bidirectional way, with brain and body interacting constantly with the outside world, both on a physical and social level. In his book *The Biological Mind*, Alan Jasanoff (2018) criticizes the modern tendency of neuroscience to take what he calls a "brain-centered view," overlooking the importance of all the many external sources shaping our brain and consequently our mind and behavior. We will discuss here some arguments presented by Jasanoff in support of his "extended mind" thesis, demonstrating that we are much more than simply our brain.

According to Jasanoff, although the brain is often compared to a computer, because it has circuits and uses electricity to conduct information, this comparison only partly explains the actual situation. The brain is very much an organic or chemical organ, containing 50% nonelectrically active brain cells, the glial cells, and more than 100 different chemical substances such as hormones, peptides, and neurotransmitters. In addition, the brain is interconnected with the body through several pathways. For example, the hypothalamic-pituitary-adrenal (HPA) axis is central to homeostasis, stress response, and energy metabolism. It comprises centers in the body and the brain (adrenal gland, pituitary, hypothalamus), as well as hormones (cortisol, corticotropin, corticotropin-releasing hormones), and the receptors for these hormones. Beyond its central role in dealing with all forms of stress, the HPA axis is involved in the modulation and regulation of behavior and cognition (Miller 2018).

The gut-brain axis is another system linking the brain to the body. What we call the enteric nervous system is a mesh of nerves present in the gastrointestinal tract, which has been called our "second" brain. The enteric nervous system uses more than thirty neurotransmitters, and 95% of the body's serotonin is found in the bowels (Kim and Camilleri 2000). Gut-brain signaling involves neurotransmission from gut sensory epithelial cells. Not only are gut signals transmitted at epithelial-neural synapses through release of the neurotransmitter serotonin, but the gut endocrine cells form glutamatergic synapses to communicate with the brain. Glutamate is the most ancient excitatory neurotransmitter. Mammalian gut use of this ancient neurotransmitter to mediate sensing suggests that it was perhaps the earliest sense to arise during evolution (Kaelberer et al. 2018), making the enteric nervous system not our "second" but our "first" brain. The popular term "gut feeling," often called intuition, has in this perspective a firm biological basis. Evolution eventually developed this into a multisensory perception system including sight, hearing, touch, smell, and taste; but the gut is the earliest sense to have arisen during evolution, allowing the brain to receive a representation generated in the body's interior. This strong coupling of the body to the brain is exemplified by the fact that when we feel an emotion, we can observe a corresponding sensation in our body. In his book *The Strange Order of Things*, Damasio (2018) states that the body and the brain are in a constant cross-talk. For him "feelings are based physiologically on hybrid processes that are neither purely neural nor purely bodily" (139). The mental experience we call feeling, is made up of intimately connected bodily and neural processes.

Perception

One of the main functions of the brain is to acquire new knowledge. All our senses are involved in obtaining information from our surroundings. As part of our interactions with the external world we assimilate sensory-motor and visual information from the outside world. Perception results from physical or chemical stimulation of the sensory organs relaying signals to the brain. Vision involves light striking the retina of the eye, smell is mediated by odor molecules stimulating olfactory receptors, and hearing involves vibrations detected by the ear. Perception is more than the passive reception of these signals, as it is also an active process shaped by learning, memory, and attention. The brain transforms this low-level input to higher-level information by extracting, for example, shapes and forms for object recognition. Perception is a process modeled by a subject's experience, knowledge, and attention.

To understand perception, a variety of techniques and avenues are needed. Psychophysics aims at quantitatively describing the relationships between the physical qualities of a sensory input and its perception. Neuroscience investigates the brain mechanisms underlying perception using computational modeling to study information processing. With respect to vision, the perceptual system of the brain allows us to see our surroundings as stable, even though the sensory information is fragmented and varies rapidly. To obtain a stable image, the brain has to reconstruct our visual perceptions. This takes place in different areas in the visual cortex and will be discussed in chapter 4. This principle of modularity applies to all the specialized regions in the brain processing various kinds of sensory information. Modules, also referred to as brain maps, are the building blocks that compose and define our perceptive capacities.

Brain maps

The brain can be looked upon as a patchwork of different maps, involved not only in analyzing visual images, but also any other information conveyed by our senses, such as touch, smell, taste, or hearing (Fig. 2.1). The somatosensory maps in the parietal cortex are organized around spatially restricted neurons that respond to specific tactile stimuli. Our sense of touch is not only a sensorial response, but it also represents a cognitive capacity. When we move, inputs from our senses such as vision, proprioception, hearing, and olfaction are used to orient ourselves in space. This spatial representation of the outside world has been called a cognitive[7] or mental map. Cognitive mapping is largely a hippocampal function. The hippocampus, a large formation in the midbrain (Fig. 2.2), functions as a hub, integrating spatial and nonspatial information. There, information for navigation is stored in "navigator" cells, such as place and grid cells, helping to orient us in space (Moser et al. 2008). These cells are specifically activated when we are in a particular location, thus encoding a cognitive representation of the space around us.

Cognitive maps in the hippocampus are not only concerned with geographical and physical space, but also social space. Social space refers to the interaction of our self with other people. In the physical space, memory coding in relation to the objects comprising our surrounding environment is called allocentric, while in the social space, when memory coding relates to objects or people in relation to one's own body, it is

7 According to Neisser (1967) the word "cognition" refers not only to the process by which a sensory stimulus is perceived and elaborated, but also to images and sensations arising in the absence of stimulation. Thus, one can consider that every psychological phenomenon is a cognitive phenomenon. Cognitive psychology can be considered as the science of the mind, while neuroscience is the science of the brain.

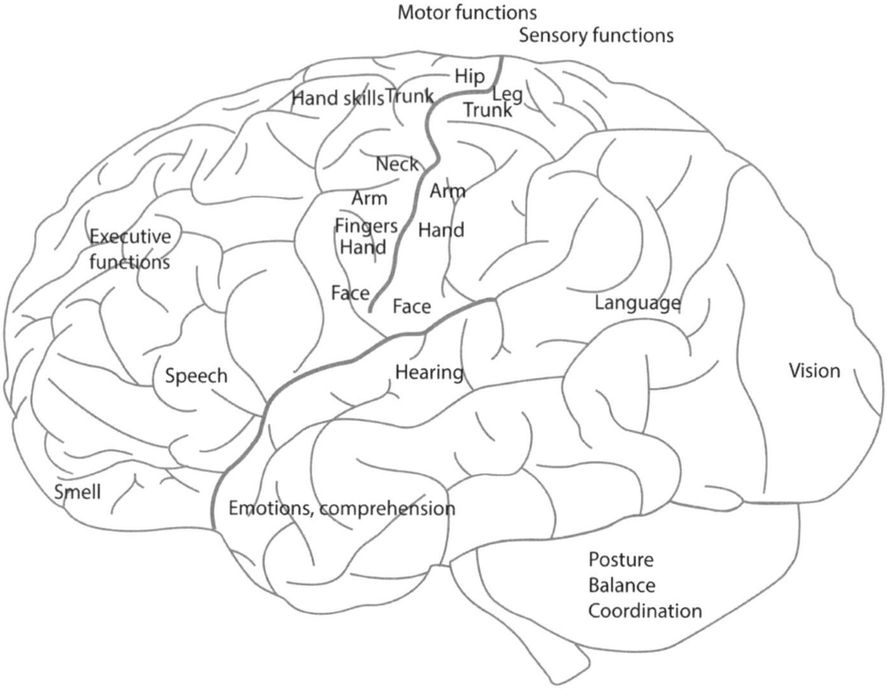

Figure 2.1 Maps in the brain and their functions.

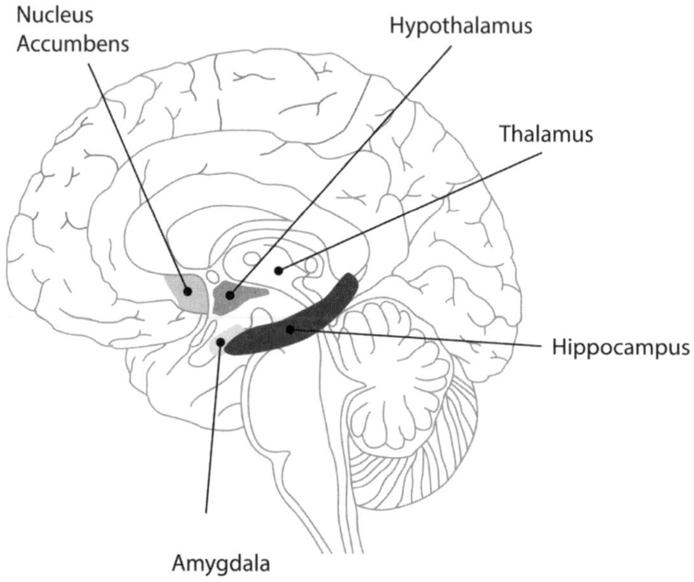

Figure 2.2 Hippocampus and other deep brain structures, also called subcortical areas, as discussed in the text.

referred to as egocentric (Eichenbaum 2015; Ribordy Lambert et al. 2015). It has also been demonstrated that the hippocampus is involved in our sense of monitoring time (Kraus et al. 2015). We can therefore conceive that the brain constructs a kind of time-space-continuum representation. This is particularly important when we consider the essential role of the hippocampus in our ability to remember—mostly memories of events or everyday facts, or what is known as declarative memory.[8] In a way this time-space continuum helps us build memory maps, a kind of timeline onto which sequential events are attached. Thus, the hippocampus, originally thought to be involved in navigating in the physical space around us, has all the attributes to guide us through much more demanding tasks and operate across the complex activities of social life.

Maps do not operate only in the hippocampus but are present in other regions of the brain, such as the medial frontal, medial parietal, and lateral temporal cortex. A network comprising these cortical areas, called the default mode network, is active when a subject is involved in thinking and planning. Many different brain maps and networks exist, which use a similar grid-like code as described for the hippocampus (Constantinescu et al. 2016). Taken together all these networks create the enormous cognitive capacities we need to solve our everyday tasks.

Emotional systems

Historically our understanding of instinctual behavior and emotional systems has been dominated by Darwin's theory, described in his book *The Expression of the Emotions in Man and Animals* (1872), where he states that emotions are part of a universal approach-avoidance system, designed to seek out pleasure and decrease exposure to pain. This idea was taken up and applied to human behavior by Freud, who described the pleasure principle as an instinctual seeking of gratification and avoidance of pain in order to satisfy biological and psychological needs.

All creatures have experiential states helping them guide their behavior. Animals have feelings of their own, though of course their mental reality is different from our own. It is appropriate to distinguish between a pattern of reflexive and sensory affects, observed in more primitive creatures, and a pattern of genuine emotional behavior that we find mostly in mammals, and in particular in domestic animals (Panksepp 2005).

Sigmund Freud, the founder of psychoanalysis, whose work and ideas will be presented in different chapters in this book, was very much interested in the nature of the driving forces behind our behavior and referred to these drives as life instincts, which also include sexual instincts. We have come to realize how much biology and psychology are interdependent, and how we can learn from both fields to better understand human nature. Instinctual drives shape our mental life, model the most diverse activities, including our need for love and attachment, and fashion the most elaborate forms

[8] The different types of memory are discussed in chapter 5.

of human activity, including artistic creation in its widest sense. The slow and gradual passage of evolution from one life form to another was accompanied by a greater complexity in the nervous system, giving rise to the increasingly broad and abstract representations of the world that characterize modern humans as they emerged some 50,000 years ago.

Emotional and cognitive processes

Objects are not only perceived but experienced and emotionally felt. The American psychologist William James (1842–1910) was one of the first to construct a modern theory of emotions. He understood that the brain had a strong connection with the body. Perceptual stimuli always trigger an activity in the autonomic nervous system, producing all kinds of emotional experiences. We understand now, as discussed below, that emotions are processed in subcortical structures, such as the amygdala (Fig. 2.2), before they express themselves in visceral and autonomic manifestations. While the role of the body was neglected in emotion studies during the first part of the twentieth century, modern studies have revealed the complete interdependence of the brain and the body, underscoring the strong interconnection between emotional and cognitive processes (Damasio 1999; Le Doux 2000; Panksepp 2011).

In modern terms, emotions are sometimes referred to as feelings, which can be considered as personal affective representations of the subject experiencing them. Mood is a more general term describing an affective state lasting for a much longer duration than an emotion. There have been numerous attempts to classify emotions. Ekman et al. (1972) describe six basic emotional states, universally recognized across different cultures: anger, disgust, fear, happiness, sadness, and surprise. These categories are derived from their studies of emotions and their relation to facial expressions. We constantly use facial expression to interpret moods and emotions of others; facial expression can therefore be considered as a readout for emotional states. In this context it is interesting to note that "face-responsive" neurons are found in the insular cortex, a region important for the representation of feelings and emotions (Dolensek et al. 2020).

In "appraisal theory," emotions are always analyzed and reflected in a given context, in other words, they are evaluated according to the events taking place (Kappas 2006). For example, if we are going to meet somebody we like, we feel joy and happiness in advance. On the other hand, if we are going to meet a person we dislike, we are beset with bad feelings. Unfolding emotional moments will always include a cognitive appraisal. There are commonalities in the processing of emotions and forms of cognition, making it difficult at times to detangle emotion from cognition: our way of perceiving, reasoning, and thinking cannot be easily dissociated from our feelings. Even the most rational decisions are consciously or unconsciously influenced by our feelings (Damasio 1994). Support for the idea that considers emotion as part of a cognitive process comes from neurobiological studies. The theory of assigning emotions solely to subcortical structures and cognition to the neocortex has been challenged. While it remains correct that centers such as the amygdala (Fig. 2.2) are closely related to emotion, emotional processing is now considered to involve parallel cortical and subcortical structures. The amygdala also projects to the anterior insula, a cortical area involved in conscious awareness of bodily sensation (Craig 2009), as well as to structures of the prefrontal cortex involved in decision making. The amygdala is a hub connecting the visceral brain, including the hypothalamus and the autonomous nervous system, to all the major sensory areas of the cortex involved in vision, smell, touch, and audition. In essence, the neural processing of emotions cannot be separated from the neural processing of cognition. It is well known that there are no purely disembodied cognitive processes: if you perform a cognitive task, such as consulting your checking account and notice a negative balance, you automatically "feel bad," while if the balance is positive, you "feel good." This suggests a primacy of feelings, even when making the simplest reason-based assessment.

Feelings, affects, emotions, and cultural endeavors

In everyday language we often interchangeably use the terms "feelings," "emotions," and "affects," though affects may be a more general term. Emotions can be considered as the direct more or less complex reactions of the body to certain stimuli and represent mostly unconscious behavioral components. Feelings describe various sensations, and they represent a vast number of states that can be categorized, such as pleasure or pain, urges like thirst or hunger, emotional states like fear and anger, as well as aspirations such as needs, wishes, or sexual desire. Feelings are unique in their nature, since they are one of the most exquisite products of the embodied mind, in other words they represent individual instances of subjective, conscious, or unconscious experiences taking place in the whole being of an individual.

We follow here the concept proposed by Damasio (2018) who states that feelings are "mental experiences of body states," which arise as the brain interprets emotions. In this definition, feeling refers to the subjective experience of an emotion. "Feelings disturb what might otherwise be an indifferent mental flow. … Feelings motivate, and feelings check the answers provided by reason and creative intelligence. … Feelings are mental stirrings, troubling or glorious, gentle or intense. They can stir us subtly, in an intellectual sort of way, or intensely. … Even at their most positive, they tend to disturb the peace and break the quiet" (12). Feelings are much more than experiences and representations of the body. Feelings are elaborated in the brain and may not always directly result from a bodily stimulus as, for example, when we feel sympathy or love for someone.

Freud underscored the importance of unconscious mental processes, in which an important role is played by emotions and feelings. He developed a model that explains our behavior, in which he emphasized the roles of drives, such as desire, pleasure, and aggression. These drives are life instincts, and this energy has been referred to by Freud as libido, as he believed that sexual drives are an important part of our unconscious mental life.

The neuroscience of emotions states that feelings have an important function in helping us make decisions, rejoining here the Freudian notion of drive. Although primary emotional systems including categories such as "seeking," "lust," "rage," "fear and panic," and "separation distress" have been localized in animal studies in subcortical brain regions (Fig. 2.2) (Panksepp 2011), as mentioned before, it would be a mistake to hold that emotions and feelings are solely the construct of subcortical brain regions. Rather, emotional experiences are always part of an integrated system involving bodily states reflected in deep brain regions together with higher-level brain sensory and associative functions, spanning large cortical areas such as the frontal, insular, and parietal cortex.

If we consider the biological roots of human cultural endeavors, feelings play an important role in our cultural practices, serving as motives and monitors. Our cultural mind is made up of mental representations derived from our own experiences as well as narratives or images transmitted by the society we live in. But this more cognitive processing is constantly updated by feelings and emotions, giving it its true dimension. Conscious and unconscious feelings play a fundamental role in the way we act. A critical dimension is given by our capacity to transform the elementary sensations of pleasure or pain into feelings of joy or sadness. Artistic experiences and activities translate or express positive or negative feelings. Feelings mobilize our cognitive capacities and for better or worse have elevated our intellect away from ever present genetic control. Artistic creations represent a subjective inner, often unconscious process that eventually results in a conscious project affirming itself in the collective space. Feelings are at the heart of our cultural endeavors, such as in music, visual arts, poetry, and writings.

Chapter 3

HIERARCHIES OF CONSCIOUSNESS

Philosophical and historical aspects

Descartes, in *The Principles of Philosophy* (1644/1911), identified the mind with consciousness and, in his proposition of dualism, argued that the mind is independent from the body. Descartes used the term "conscientia," which in modern terms means primarily moral conscience. Neuroscience, as we discussed in the previous chapter, puts aside Descartes' dualistic distinction between mental and physical entities and proposes a monist solution to the mind-brain problem, calling to an end of the division between mind, body, rationality, and emotion.

In a personal communication, Kent Baldner of the Department of Philosophy at Western Michigan University stated the following about consciousness: In philosophical terms it is widely held that the immediate object of conscious experience (including, but not limited to sense perception) is some kind of mental entity, such as an "idea," "perception," "appearance," or "mental representation." One should always keep in mind the inherent subjective nature of the experience of consciousness. When perceiving an object, we "see" a mental content that may correspond to an external object. In this situation, our experience is veridical. Consciousness however cannot be reduced to the perception of external objects. We are constantly aware of ideas or sensations in our mind, and this happens autonomously. What we know is mind dependent: we can only know how things appear to us and not how they are in themselves. Consciousness can be understood as the awareness of mental representations. This is in line with Kant,[9] who claims that we only know "appearances" and not "things in themselves." On the face of it, this seems to clearly endorse the idea that we are only

[9] Immanuel Kant (1724–1824) was an influential German philosopher of the Enlightenment.

directly aware of mind-dependent entities: we only know how this reality appears to us (due to the subjective and constructive nature of consciousness), and not how it is in itself. The problem, philosophically, is that once we claim that we are directly aware only of what exists solely in our minds, it becomes increasingly difficult to justify claims that we can know anything about any reality outside of our minds, including the belief that such a realm even exists. The functioning of the brain tells us what it is to perceive an object, but not what object "it is" that we perceive.

Consciousness defined broadly, has a clear sociocultural dimension. We live with our memories, past and present, and plan for the future. Our mental abilities and moral sentiments are unique features that neuroscience may explain biologically, but cannot exclusively account for, if we want to escape a reductionist approach to the mind-brain problem. Our tremendous capacities in terms of memory, language, reasoning, imagination, and creativity made possible the development of culture, ideas, and customs. Within this sociobehavioral context, we can go beyond the limits of all possible experiences and knowledge, transcending our material existence. This ability is something not entirely set by our biology, dependent from the social-cultural system we live in; it can be enhanced and further developed.

Modern philosophers, especially phenomenologists, emphasize that we should leave to neuroscientists the task of finding out what the human mind is made of (Bakewell 2016). Philosophy should instead consider what "the mind does and how it grasps its experiences." We should approach the mind in terms of its "intentions." "Our thoughts are invariably about something: in love something is loved, in hatred something is hated, in judgment something is affirmed or denied. Even when I imagine an object that is not there, my mental structure is still one of 'aboutness,' except in deepest sleep, my mind is always engaged, it has intentionality" (44–45). This concept of intentionality has been expressed as "all consciousness is consciousness of something" (47).

For the French philosopher Jean-Paul Sartre (1905–1980), philosophy is not just a profession, it is life itself. He put this principle into the following slogan: "Existence precedes essence." "I go on to create my own definition (or nature, or essence) in a way that never happens with other objects or life form. … I create myself constantly through action and this is so fundamental to my human condition from the moment of first consciousness to the moment when death wipes it out" (Bakewell 2016, 6). As the English novelist E. M. Forster declared (in Bakewell 2016, 325): "We grow up immersed in the 'imponderable bloom' of life and relationships. This 'bloom' of experience and communication makes possible the living, conscious, embodied beings that we are." The study of consciousness—as philosophy teaches and engages us—is to place sociality into a central position in our "being-in-life."

Historically, consciousness was defined by the English philosopher John Locke (1632–1704) as "the perception of what passes in a man's own mind." This definition is still valid today and emphasizes the most important aspect of consciousness; it is always about us and by definition subjective. Consciousness is achieved by our brain and gives us a sense of self awareness. Another remarkable feature of consciousness is the incredibly wide spectrum of feelings, images, representations, and narratives that can go through our mind at any moment. Finally, consciousness is unified: our mental life is not composed of bits or pieces of sensory information or images, but our mental world is highly organized and integrated. Where and how consciousness emerges in the brain and how a unified mind takes place has been intensely studied and is presented below.

Developmental theory of the mind

Swiss psychologist Jean Piaget (1896–1980) developed a cognitive developmental theory of the mind (Piaget 1953). He distinguished four main stages of development: a sensory-motor stage, lasting from birth to two years, during which infants start to explore the world with their five senses, but also discover their motor capacities; a preoperational stage from two to seven, during which children develop language and start using mental symbols; a concrete operational stage, from seven to eleven, when children gain the ability to think logically and begin organizing the information they are learning; and finally an operational stage, where adolescents start to think in more abstract forms.

The innate and genetically shaped development of intelligence proposed by Piaget has been considerably updated since his original empirical proposal. It is now considered that instead of stages, cognitive development proceeds as a continuous process. By focusing on child cognition only, Piaget did not sufficiently recognize the role of emotional and social interactions between children and caregivers for mental development. Modern child developmental theories emphasize the importance of the relation between the social world and cognitive development. We live in a world where we constantly interact with other people. We are dependent on others from birth onward. The kind of social interactions we entertain as adults is formed in infancy and the relationship and attachment between an infant and parents will shape behavior into adulthood. Lev Vygotsky (1896–1934), a contemporary of Piaget, emphasized social interactions as crucial for cognitive development: a child's learning always occurs in a social context in cooperation with someone more skillful (Cole and Wertsch 1996). Social interaction is essential, providing language opportunities and play—both sources of imagination and creativity.

Philosophers such as Merleau-Ponty (1908–1961) underscored the role of initial developmental stages and early life experiences in the building of our perceptive capabilities (Toadvine 2019). We learn the skills of interpreting the world in early childhood: our first perceptual experiences in observing the world will remain with us for the rest of our life. We learn to recognize a pastry and at the same time how good it tastes. Thus, the sight of pastry will always evoke an anticipatory pleasure. Perception mostly functions when all senses work together in a holistic way. We touch and grasp things in order to understand them. We analyze the texture of an object by taking it in our hands. When we pay attention to a particular scene, we not only engage our senses, such as vision, but also make "calculations" in order to understand the world around us. We explore our surroundings as a whole rather than in separate bits and pieces. Thus, "in the movement of the branch, from which a bird has just left, we read its flexibility and its elasticity" (Bakewell 2016, 232).

The different states of consciousness

Consciousness evolves with the overall arousal state of the brain. The brain is in a constant state of change, fluctuating between continuums of wakefulness, drowsiness, and sleep cycles. Consciousness in the awake state is obviously different from consciousness in sleep where mentation occurs in the form of dreams. From a neuropsychological viewpoint we refer to the level of consciousness, distinguishing different states such as alertness, somnolence, or deep sleep. As we fall asleep, the level of wakefulness decreases and as a consequence, awareness of the environment is diminished.

Wakefulness is critically determined by a subcortical arousal system, called the ascending reticular activating system (Fig. 3.1). This system extends from the brain stem to the thalamus and consists of a network of different pathways and nuclei, which activates the cortex, thus fulfilling a crucial role in maintaining an arousal state. This network also carries the sensory information from all the sensory organs necessary for achieving a conscious state and distributes this information to the different regions of the cortex. Consciousness, meaning the ability to feel and experience a subjective point of view, is dependent on the cerebral cortex.

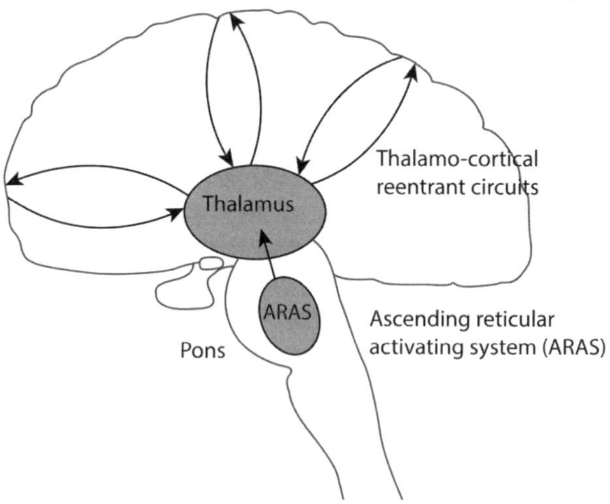

Figure 3.1 Consciousness and the thalamocortical system. Consciousness depends on the activation of the thalamus—by the ascending reticular activating system (ARAS)—and on the thalamo-cortical reentrant circuits. Conscious experience requires rapid bidirectional interactions among distributed neuronal populations.

Conscious perception

There is not one place in the brain where consciousness in the full sense of the term can be localized. Full consciousness can only be accomplished from the combined operations of many brain systems. Baars (1988) proposed one of the first models of consciousness. He described a "conscious access hypothesis" in a framework called the "global workspace" (Fig. 3.2). In this theory, a number of brain components momentarily integrate sensory stimuli with conscious and unconscious images, ideas, and thoughts to constitute a conscious spotlight. This theory was conceived mainly from a cognitive psychological point of view and initially had little impact because the evidence was indirect and did not rely on anatomical or physiological bases. However, modern developments in neuroimaging techniques broadly support this hypothesis. In order to become conscious a perception has to be processed and transmitted via long-distance axons to many cortical processors, enabling locally available information to be brought into consciousness (Dehaene et al. 2006).

The following illustration helps us understand how conscious perception works (Fig. 3.3). When we see a word, for example, the visual cortex is activated. If this information remains in the visual cortex and eventually disappears, it will remain unconscious. To become conscious, the information has to be amplified and broadcasted to parieto-frontal areas. In order for a word we see for a few seconds to be kept in our mind and consciously reported, the information has to reach the global workspace, reverberating between the many cortical areas involved in language, naming, and understanding percepts and concepts.

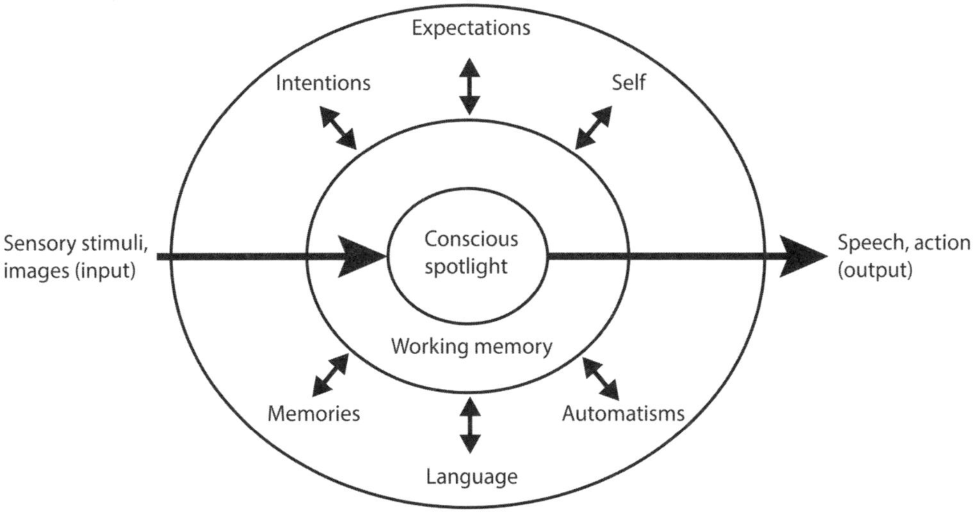

Figure 3.2 The global workspace theory of Baars consists of a cognitive architecture and is based on the principle that conscious brain events evoke widespread cortical activity.

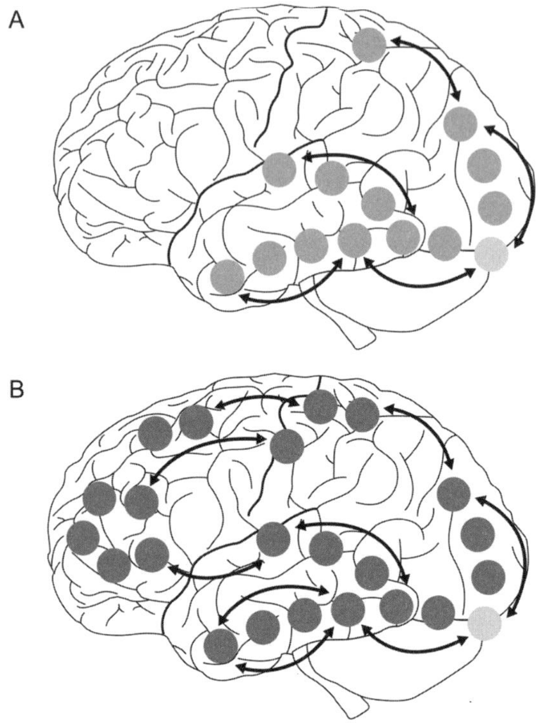

Figure 3.3 (A) Unconscious perception: activity in the visual cortex vanishes before reaching higher brain regions. (B) Conscious perception: higher brain regions become activated and the visual information becomes conscious. (Adapted from Dehaene et al. 2006).

Much progress has been made in the question of how we become aware of our sensory world. A constant flow of images, or auditory or tactile impressions, goes through our mind and we are conscious of this flow except when we sleep. Our brain constitutes our mind by constructing visual, auditory, and tactile maps. Mental experiences would, however, not be possible without the participation of memory holding regions, described in chapter 5. We are aware of our selves independently of what we immediately perceive. This self-consciousness can be understood as an "inner" conscious state.

Expanded consciousness, self-consciousness

The cognitive model of consciousness emphasizes reportability as a key property of conscious representations, and a mental state is considered conscious when it is verbally reportable and accessible. However, our brain constantly works unconsciously. Not only do we process sensory information about our surroundings unconsciously, but much of our intrinsic brain activity is independent of external sensory drives. Consciousness is a subjective functional state, modulated rather than generated by the senses.

It is accepted that the bulk of what we consider mental activity occurs outside of awareness. Neuroscientists are looking at how unconscious processing operates and how deep it goes. Freud was one of the first to try to fill the gaps in our inquiry of the unconscious phenomena of consciousness. He underscored the fact that our mind is largely unconscious. He described our mind as having conscious and unconscious components, and he emphasized the role of instincts that are outside our awareness but are motivating forces influencing our behavior. He highlighted the role of two opposite instincts, a self-preservation and sexual drive, and a self-destructive and aggressive drive.

In neuroscientific terms, we distinguish what is affectively or emotionally unconscious from what is cognitively unconscious. Much of what Freud attributes to as being unconscious refers to "unrepresentable" thoughts, what we nowadays would refer to nondeclarative memory (Paulson et al. 2017). Our mind needs to render many processes unconscious in order to keep order and control of our conscious life and avoid being reduced to an instinctual life. Another aspect to be considered is the fact that our conscious cognitive capacity is limited, so there is a need to constantly remove content out of consciousness as rapidly as possible in order to use our mind efficiently. We therefore automatize problems once they are solved and put them in the cognitive unconscious. There is, however, a lot of information in our mind that concerns unsolved problems. We also automatize these unsolved problems as "non-solutions" (this process starts in infancy). Comparing the cognitive and the Freudian unconscious, we can say that the former consists of problems that are automatized, accessible, and updatable, while the latter includes items that are automatized very early in childhood and stored in a preverbal nondeclarative mode and consequently are not easily updatable. They will often repeat themselves in an irrational way at later periods during the life of an individual.

Consciousness cannot be narrowly defined; it is an ongoing process and experience with an objective and a subjective dimension. The combination of these dimensions is often called expanded consciousness. For subjectivity to take place, we constantly create a personal perspective of the images going through our mind. We generate a complex mix of these images, constructing our own set of subjective images. These images become representations and include feelings, affects, or instincts.

Expanded consciousness registers the state of the subject, principally an affective subject, aware of their needs (for example, instincts such as hunger, sex, play, or thirst) through their feelings. Affects play an important role in the constitution of subjectivity. Affects also represent a value system, in which pleasurable feelings signal a state of the body that enhances the chances of survival and reproductive success, and in which unpleasurable feelings signal the opposite. Only the affective subject is able to experience perceptual and cognitive representations. There can be no objects of consciousness without a conscious subject to experience them (Solms 2017).

François Jacob (1920–2013) was a French biologist who, together with Jacques Monod, helped unravel the mechanisms of gene regulation and expression. For this scientific discovery, he shared the 1965 Nobel Prize in Medicine with Jacques Monod and André Lwoff. He is the author of an autobiography *La Statue Intérieure* that has drawn wide attention in France and also in the United States in its English translation *The Statue Within* (Jacob 1988). In this autobiography, Jacob recounts an event: when watching a movie without great interest late on a Sunday afternoon with his wife he confusedly perceived associations that formed ideas, moved him and suddenly led to the glare of the obvious. He wrote that if "day science advances in light and glory, conscious of her approach, proud of her past, sure of her future. … Night science, on the contrary, wanders blindly, hesitates, stumbles, recedes. What guides the mind then is not logic, it is instinct, intuition" (in Jacob 2001, 126).

We come back to Freud's view of the interplay between the conscious and the unconscious, a perspective that was taken up by Damasio who points out that the cognitive revolution of past decades, which has yielded cognitive neuroscience and artificial intelligence, has been, in fact, too cognitive, too rationalist, and not concerned enough with the role that affects play in the operation of our mind (Damasio 2018). The brain has the capacity to bring together and bind multiple entities and representations to construct and achieve what we call expanded consciousness. The cognitive unconscious and the Freudian unconscious, including all the personal feelings making up our subjective self must be intimately integrated to realize this kind of unique consciousness that we experience as a singular subject and individual. The current move toward embodied theories of mind proposes that brain and body are linked together forming an intimate partnership.

Layered theory of consciousness

For Damasio the theory of consciousness is based on a hierarchy of stages leading to self-consciousness (Damasio 1999). The basic element is core consciousness, consisting of maps of the body's interior and used as a kind of "primary self-reference." This reference must be very stable; it is in essence the "interior milieu" of our body. Our brain is tightly bound to the body and receives a constant flow of information from bodily sensations, constituting a continuously evolving emotional state of consciousness. There is a seamless continuity between brain and body throughout life.

Core consciousness can be viewed as a nonconscious collection of representations of the multiple dimensions of the current state of the many parts of our body. When out of this background emotional state our brain generates a conscious representation or a cognitive conscious state, we have, according to Damasio, "extended consciousness." It consists of an autobiographical self, containing our memories, past, present, and future. Extended consciousness still bears a relationship with our bodily parts and environmental stimuli, but by incorporating the biographical self, we are aware of a large collection of entities and events and have the ability to generate a sense of individual perspective or ownership. We can only fully "own" our mind when non-conscious inputs combine with conscious inputs resulting in a unique conscious experience. A conscious mind is a mind with a self. This endeavor requires the interplay of the multiple neural components supporting consciousness, involving higher-order cortical representations and lower-order subcortical circuits. How they combine in a temporal and hierarchical sequence remains to be understood.

The autobiographical self can be regarded as a construction built on past memories and memories of the projects or strategies we have developed; it is the lived past and the anticipated future. The autobiographical self allows reasoning, imagination, creativity, and language to evolve and mature, and eventually permits us to develop the various human undertakings involved in culture, religion, art, and science. It is within this broad scenery that arises an individual mind that is not only set by our biology, but by the sociocultural world that we have shaped and in which we live.

Neuroscience still struggles to address the brain-mind divide well enough to be able to convincingly erase the dualistic distinction between mental and physical entities and to explain how the organic material of the body and the brain gives rise to consciousness. In our quest to understand how the brain produces a subjectively unified conscious mind, let us see in the next chapter how visual information is transformed into a conscious experience.

Chapter 4

THE VISUAL BRAIN

Visual consciousness

The study of how visual information is processed in the brain is helping us to understand how the brain constructs conscious experiences. Semir Zeki, a neuroscientist who specialized in studying the visual brain, proposed dividing visual consciousness into two different levels (Zeki 2003). The *first level* is called micro-consciousness and can be best explained by considering how the brain processes visual perception for color and motion. Color is processed in the occipital cortex of the brain in the V4 complex, while motion is processed in the V5 complex (Fig. 4.1). These two complexes are geographically separated and have different interactions, resulting in our perceiving color before motion. A lesion in area V4 produces achromatopsia, the inability to see colors, while motion-vision remains intact. Conversely, a lesion in V5 produces akinetopsia, an inability to see motion, while color-vision remains unaffected. However, in spite of these clear anatomical and functional differences, the visual world we perceive is integrated. The distinct attributes of visual perception such as color and motion are perceived as unified; they are bound together and constitute what Zeki calls *the second level* or macro-consciousness. Micro-and macro-consciousness eventually lead to a final unified consciousness of the perceiving subject. This capacity of the brain to integrate clues across different lines of information is defined as "binding" (Treisman 1999). The unity of conscious perception originates from the combination of the activity of different neuronal populations. Eventually the brain chooses the correct sensory data to represent an object and not some illusory reconstruction of its features. The conscious experience of seeing an object is rarely limited to just seeing its color or its motion, but a visual experience will mobilize many additional features such as form and texture stored in different brain maps. Thus, a perceptual visual event is recombined in a broader conscious experience.

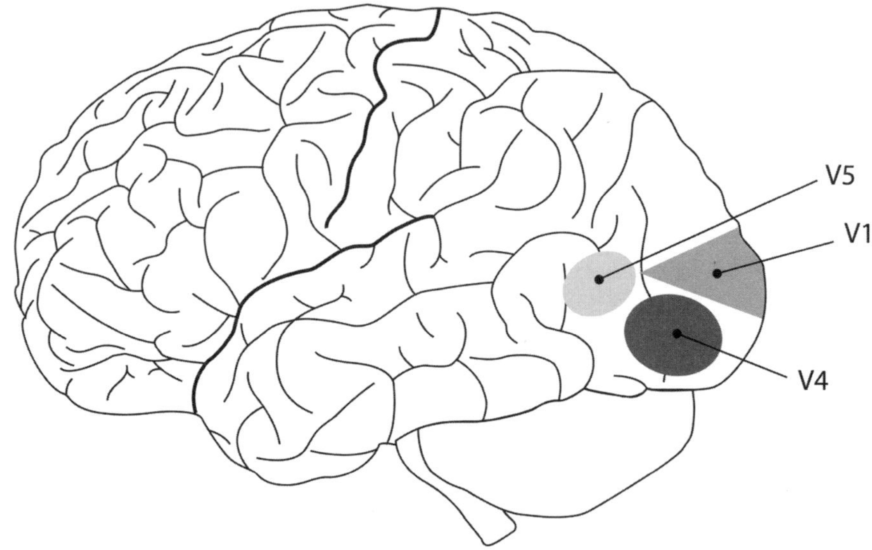

Figure 4.1 Representation of primary visual area V1 and specialized visual areas V4 (color) and V5 (motion) of the human brain. Localizations are schematic as the organization of the visual cortex is complex and includes as many as twenty visual areas (Kaas 1989).

It should be noted that seeing an object is not the same as identifying it; to correctly identify an object we must collect all the different attributes of this object and compare it with pre-stored "models" of the same type. This takes place more or less implicitly within a very short time scale of a few milliseconds and involves two pathways called the ventral "what" and the dorsal "where" pathways,[10] connecting to parietal and frontal areas. A full conscious experience is only possible when the widely distributed information in these different pathways is integrated, allowing a unity of conscious perception. How do we understand the neurobiological correlates underlying the unity of perception and how do we solve the integrating or binding problem? We have in the previous chapter discussed how a full conscious experience requires the activation of widely distributed population of neurons. To explain this highly integrated neuronal activity, Edelman and Tononi (2000) actualized the "global workspace" model proposed by Baars (1988), and renamed it the "dynamic core." This new model proposes that the activity of a given group of neurons contributes to conscious experience if it is part of a "functional cluster." This functional cluster consists of neurons that are much more interactive among themselves than with the rest of the brain. The dynamic core typically includes posterior-cortical-thalamic regions

[10] These pathways are discussed later and represented in Figure 4.3.

involved in perceptual categorization together with anterior regions involved in concept formation. The rapid integrating activity of the dynamic core is made possible by reentrant thalamo-cortical pathways, allowing connection within the cortex and between the cortex and thalamus (see Fig. 3.1). These reentry processes are thought to facilitate the coordination of neuronal firing in anatomically and functionally segregated areas. This helps the formation of cross-modal sensory features by synchronizing and integrating patterns of neural activity in different brain regions. Such a principle can be applied to the visual system and to all sensory and motor modalities and to conscious perception in general.

Since images are so important in our mental life as inner representations or external experiences, we will now discuss some key neurobiological aspects of vision.

Perception of the visual image

We are profoundly visual beings and our ability to see, interpret, and perceive our surroundings is essential for our interaction with the outside world. What matters most is to get a coherent view of our environment. In order to characterize objects, recognize people or landscapes, or analyze artworks, we need to capture a constant and lasting characteristic of the shape, color, or texture of the objects that surround us. In reality, objects are observed under different angles, distances, and light conditions, and are often moving. The brain has therefore to subtract these continuous changes in order to gain the necessary information to categorize objects in a meaningful manner. The acquisition of visual information by the brain is a very sophisticated and complex process leading to mental representations that are part of our internal reality. Vision is an active process and seeing is a creative process, involving not just the visual brain, but many more brain areas with which the visual system is connected (Zeki 1999).

An image of the external world is produced by the excitation of two types of neurons in the retina of the eye; cones are sensitive to bright light and rods respond to dim light. The visual information captured by the cones and rods are compressed to fit the limited capacity of the optic nerve. The information from the retina is projected to the brain in a very specific way: after being relayed through a large center, the lateral geniculate nucleus, it reaches the primary visual cortex (Fig. 4.2). The mechanisms involved in the construction of a visual image have been unraveled in an unprecedented way, making the visual system the most understood among sensory systems. A large number of cells in the different cortical areas in the visual system have to collaborate in a hierarchical way to render vision fully colored and three-dimensional.

The light captured by the eye reaches the retina after it has been focused by the lens. Human vision perceives only a small portion of the electromagnetic wave spectrum of light, extending from about 400 to 700 nanometers. While for centuries light was believed to have no color, the seminal wave optic experiment by the English physicist Isaac Newton (1643–1727) demonstrated that the colors we see are the

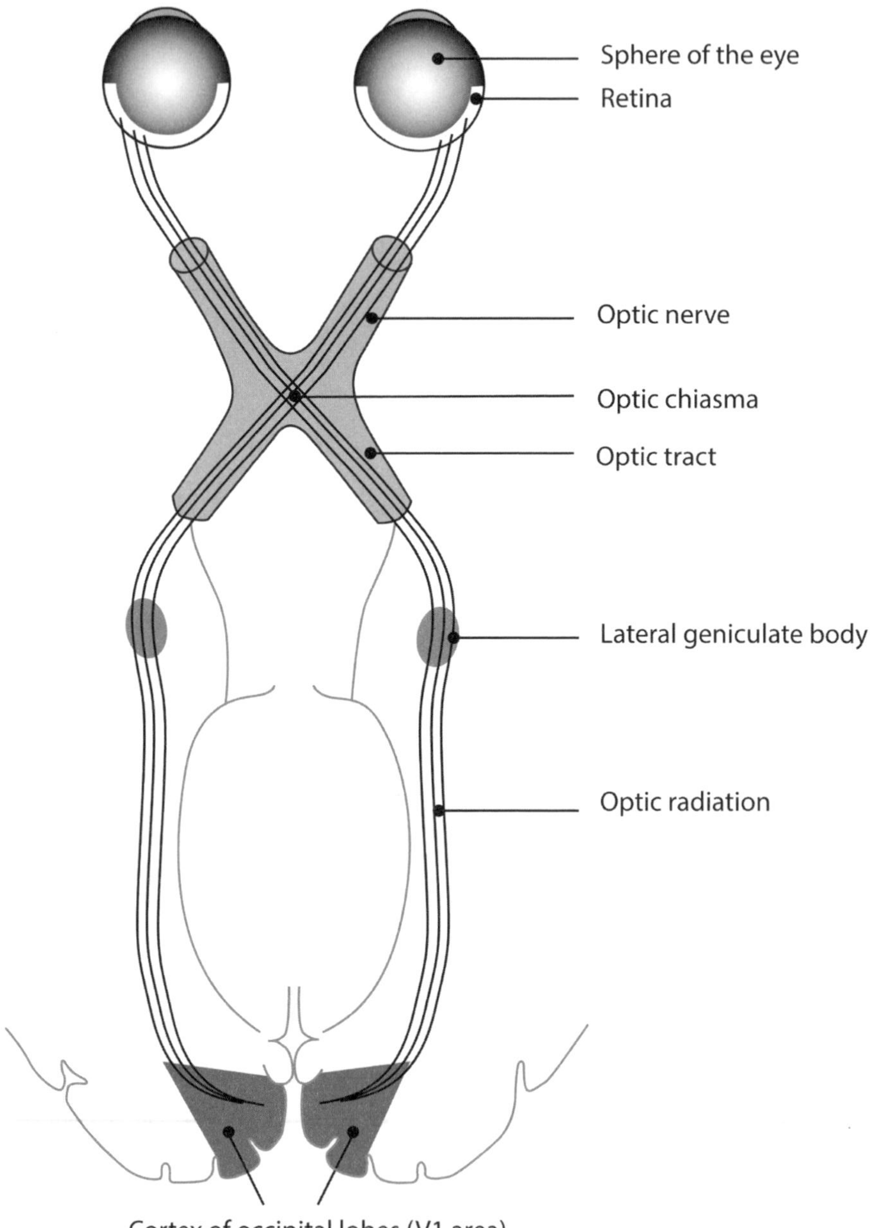

Figure 4.2 The visual system includes the eyes, with the main connecting pathway to the primary visual cortex V1 in the occipital lobe. In reality, only about half of the fibers cross over to the opposite side in the optic chiasma, the other half stays on the ipsilateral side. This partial crossing allows better stereoscopic vision. Throughout the visual pathway, there is a retinotopic organization whereby axons from specific regions of the retina project to a specific area of the lateral geniculate body and also the visual cortex V1.

visible manifestations of the different wave lengths of the light we perceive. Newton discovered that light can be split into different colors when going through a dispersive prism. Color perception is possible, because the retina possesses three types of color receptors, each type sensitive to a specific wavelength. These color receptors are called cones. Each class of cone has a different pigment and is receptive to either the short (blue), medium (green), or long (red) wavelength of the visible spectrum. Accordingly, our color vision is called trichromatic. The mapping between a given wavelength takes place in the retina, but our subjective experience of color will be defined by the visual cortex. By mixing these three colors, it has been calculated that we can perceive millions of different colors and shades.

Color is not a property of the electromagnetic waves, but a feature of visual perception by an observer. In other words, color perception is subjective, though we share the same perception. When looking at a red object, for example, a red tulip, we all see and perceive the same color. In physical terms the petals of the tulip absorb all the frequencies of visible light but reflect only the wavelength constituting the red. The cones in the retina—sensitive to the long wave frequency—will be excited and transmit this information to the brain, which will perceive it as red. But the visual brain is not like a picture book. There are no "red neurons" and there is no color center in the brain. The difficult question is to understand how the brain creates a representation which we register and "feel as red." Francis Crick (1916–2004), the British biologist and neuroscientist known for the discovery of the structure of the DNA molecule, has suggested that the information stored in the brain is a kind of symbol, standing for something, like the word dog signifies a particular animal, but is not the animal itself (Crick 1995). What is true for vision, is also the case for all perceptions of our surroundings. Information from auditory, olfactory, or touch sensors will reach the brain and be perceived as very specific feelings or representations. All perceptions from our senses are active processes, and vision is a particularly creative one. Given the complexity of visual representation and the importance of vision in understanding the world, the visual cortex is the largest sensory system in the human brain, and it is estimated that half of the sensory input going to the brain is visual. Let us discuss how visual information is processed in the cortex and gives us a coherent picture of our surroundings.

Organization of the visual cortex

The sensory information coming from the eye is not spread diffusely to the brain, but goes to a specific region, the visual cortex in the occipital lobe. This constitutes the only entering place. The visual circuitry in the cerebral cortex contains several dozen different functional maps. It is through the work of David Hubel and Torston Wiesel, two neuroscientists who received the Nobel Prize in 1981 for their work on the visual system, that our current understanding of how visual information is processed in the brain took shape.

The visual information flows from the retina in the optic nerve via the lateral geniculate nucleus and reaches the visual cortex. The primary visual cortex V1 corresponds to the striate cortex in the occipital lobe. Neurons in this part of the cortex are organized in cortical columns (Hubel and Wiesel 1968), not unlike the homunculus inscribed in the sensory-motor cortex. These columns display a very specific topical arrangement; there is a one-to-one topographic correspondence to the visual image on the retina.[11] For the purpose of accurate encoding, neurons in cortical columns have small receptive fields.

The primary visual cortex does not work like a camera that registers an image pixel by pixel. Instead neurons in a column respond to the orientation and contours of an object. They are sensitive to the edges of an object or the borders of light and dark areas. Contour analysis is the main function of the primary visual cortex (Hubel and Wiesel 1968). Understanding the subtle functional organization of neurons within these columns will require mathematical and computational models that are still being developed, although we do understand the general layout of the visual cortical system.

Cells from V1 collaborate with other areas to render the full high-resolution and three-dimensional quality of our visual world. It has been shown that cells in V1 connect to neurons in V2 and V3 areas that respond to virtual lines and are therefore able to complete contours. As Kandel (2012) reminds us: "The brain completes lines because nature often presents occluded contours that must be completed in order to perceive an image correctly" (263). This demonstrates one of our brain's fundamental abilities, the well-known "gestalt effect," that is, our ability to recognize whole figures instead of just a collection of disparate elements.

As discussed previously, an important cortical area outside the visual cortex V1 is V5, where neurons react to visual motion and are direction-selective and speed-selective; some neurons are responsive to fast-, others to slow-motion. These neurons, in order to analyze movements, register signals from wide regions of the visual field. This is unlike the situation in V1, where neurons are concerned with sharp vision and therefore are attuned to small regions of the visual field.

While V1 is concerned with the mapping of every region of the retina in the visual cortex, properties of visual objects, such as shape, motion, location, and color are processed in areas outside V1. Visual information arriving in V1 is reassigned into other areas and follows two major functional pathways (Fig. 4.3). One is the ventral stream, involved in the visual recognition of forms and objects and also their emotional content. This pathway projects to the medial temporal lobe, a region concerned with memory and the limbic system, a brain area involved in processing emotions. The part of the visual system that is specialized for facial recognition is also located in the ventral stream, as will be discussed below. The other is the dorsal stream that

[11] Cells with similar functions are organized into columns, tiny computational machines that relay information to a higher region of the brain, where a visual image is formed. The column is a unit of about 80–100 neurons that vertically traverse several lamina of the cortex.

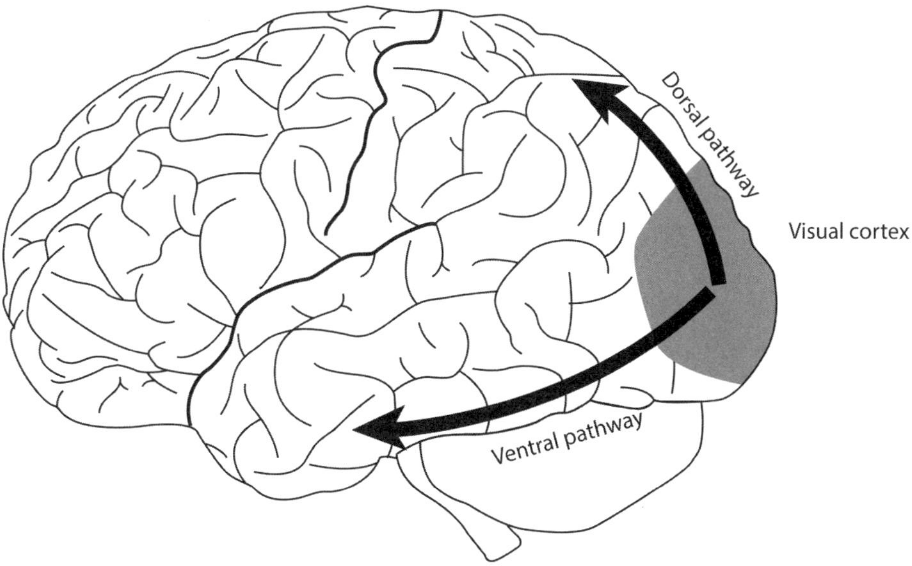

Figure 4.3 Schematic representation of two major pathways, each arising from the primary visual cortex V1. The first, known as the "where" pathway, spreads dorsally from V1 to the parietal lobe. The maps that together constitute this dorsal pathway process different aspects of spatial layout, such as location, distance, relative position, and motion. The second, the ventral route, known as the "what-pathway" allows us to recognize shape, size, color, face, and text. The visual information in the ventral stream terminates in the medial temporal lobe, hippocampus, and amygdala and is used for visual recognition, memory, and emotional content, while the dorsal route processes visual information for action and feeds into the motor cortex of the frontal lobe. (Adapted from De Haan and Cowey 2011).

projects to the parietal lobe, an area involved in localization of objects in space, and that feeds into the motor cortex and frontal lobe. This system is mainly concerned with analyzing and directing motor behavior of a subject in its environment and thus receives body-centered information. In contrast, the ventral system deals with the interface between visual input and cognition.

The idea of a division between a ventral and a dorsal visual stream goes back to experimental work in monkeys, but also in human subjects with lesions in either of these two streams (Goodale and Milner 1992; Ungerleider and Huxby 1994; Milner and Goodale 2008). According to Goodale and Milner, "the ventral stream of projections from the striate cortex to the infero-temporal cortex plays a major role in the perceptual identification of objects, while the dorsal stream projecting from the striate cortex to the posterior parietal region mediates the required sensorimotor transformations for visually guided actions directed at such objects" (20). The processing in the dorsal stream does not evoke a conscious perception in contrast to the ventral route, which does lead to conscious perception.

According to de Haan and Cowey (2011) these two main pathways do not work independently but should be viewed as a cross-model system. They argue that it is difficult to see how a strict division can be maintained in light of the fact that integration between these two networks is necessary for a full conscious visual experience. They propose a "patchwork" or network model, consisting of a conglomerate of roughly forty visual areas. Depending on the task at hand, different effector systems may draw information from different visual areas. This flexible model allows the effector systems to draw on all existing visual areas and not just on the endpoints of two pathways. Evidence for multiple subsystems arises from the observation that there is a temporal hierarchy in the perception of color, form, and movement (Moutoussis and Zeki 1997; Zeki 1999).

As we will discuss in chapter 9, a two-system framework has also been proposed in the auditory system (Hickok and Poeppel 2004). Here the dorsal stream maps sensory information into articular-motor representations, while the ventral steam is concerned with the transformation of auditory input into phonetic and eventually semantic words. While visual and auditory information is processed in parallel systems, these networks cannot function independently. In order to get a unified perception, information from these two systems must be merged. The brain arranges the visual and auditory information in such a way that we get a coherent picture of the outside world.

How the visual brain puts things together

As we have already described, visual information is subdivided into different sections of the cortex that are responsible for such things as color, form, depth, and movement. As this information is segregated in different areas of the cortex, it must eventually be put back together if we do not want to get a fragmented view of our surroundings. Barlow (1981) has shown that the visual cortex, when we look at an object, uses discernible properties of this object to organize the image into a representation by integrating or linking local properties. This "linking process" is based on the premise that neighboring points in an image are likely to belong to the same object. In doing so, the cortex integrates additional information such as luminescence, color, or texture. Our ability to discriminate the shape of an object is very much dependent on the capacity of the visual system to define its borders.

Gestalt psychologists have analyzed the conditions we use to analyze objects. In order to differentiate a figure from its background we depend on many cues. The case of ambiguous figures is interesting; if two competing images or objects are shown in a drawing, only one of the two possible percepts is seen at any instant. A classical illustration is the Rubin vase (Fig. 4.4). The perception is unstable so that one sees either the face or the vase, but not both at the same time. Brain mapping studies of subjects looking at this flipping figure have revealed transient changes in brain activity during perceptual reversals (Kleinschmidt et al. 1998). Activity in the brain shifts from the

Figure 4.4 Rubin's vase is a set of reversing two-dimensional forms developed around 1915 by the Danish psychologist Edgar Rubin.

face recognition area in the fusiform cortex to the object recognizing area in the parietal cortex. In addition, during flips there is a decrease in activity in the primary visual cortex. This rapid redistribution of neuronal activity between separate cortical areas is in keeping with a top-down processing, determining which precept is perceived, the face or the vase. In addition, there is an activation of the frontal eye fields emphasizing the link between attention and gaze orientation.

This example provides direct experimental evidence on how the brain engages spatially segregated and functionally different cortical areas in a smooth cooperative activity. In this case, the primary visual cortex functions as a convergence zone, engaging two specialized sensory areas involved in face and object recognition. In doing so there is a joint activation of multisensory units realizing a binding of sensory events. The ability to study brain cortical cellular networks and brain dynamics in the visual system, whether locally or at global brain-wide level, will help understand how visual perception—humans' most important sense—works (Marshel 2019).

Face recognition

The brain assigns more cortical space to face recognition than to the recognition of any other visual object. Faces are by far the most important category of physical entities our sight can perceive; it is how we recognize other people and make a representation of ourselves.

Figure 4.5 The "Face of Peace" by Pablo Picasso. His genius here is clear—with just one well thought-out line, he brought so much to this drawing.

We can recognize the drawing of a face from a minimal sketch consisting of a few lines for the eyes, the nose, and the mouth (Fig. 4.5). While this universal disposition is susceptible to infinite variations, each face is distinctive and unique. The mechanisms of face perception engage the "what pathway," that is, the system involved in the visual identification of objects (Tsao and Livingstone 2008) (Fig. 4.3). Faces are among the most informative stimuli we perceive. Even a split-second look at a person's face is sufficient to recognize somebody. Current psychological research demonstrates that human faces and also body parts are "gestalt percepts," that is, items perceived as a unified whole as soon as our senses detect them. Accordingly face processing is said to be "holistic," that is, faces are represented as a unified pattern rather than an assembly of separate parts. There is little object deconstruction and reconstruction. This explains why it is so difficult to recognize faces when they are upside down. Our brain is tuned to recognize faces when they are in the upright position and performs poorly when they are upside down.

The brain mechanisms underpinning face recognition emerge early in infancy. The brain regions that recognize faces have a unique cellular make-up (Weiner et al. 2017); it has been shown that structures within these regions change from childhood into adulthood over a timescale corresponding to improvements in people's ability to recognize faces. Improvements in face recognition depend on the interplay between structural and functional developmental changes in specific areas of the cortex (Gomez et al. 2017).

From birth onward, infants are much more likely to look at faces than any other object. Adults also respond preferentially to infants by smiling. As Conrad Lorenz suggested (Glocker et al. 2009), certain face characteristics of an infant such as large head, high forehead, wide eyes, chubby cheeks, and small nose are perceived as cute. This triggers a strong motivation for affection and caretaking in adults. Face recognition elicits not only an inborn caring response in parents but remains a lifelong fundamental function of social interactions (Glocker et al. 2009). The face recognition system contributes significantly to our everyday social life and well-being. How first impressions (such as a person's traits, interpreted as appealing or repulsive, or judgment about trustworthiness or dislike) can be made by just fleetingly looking at a face is a subject of considerable research dealing with interpersonal perception (Fiske et al. 2007; Vernon et al. 2014). Infants first see the contour of a face and are troubled if the contour changes, for example, if a mother changes her hairstyle or cuts her long hair very short (Dirks and Gibson 1977).

Perception as conscious and unconscious emotional experience

We not only look at people with our senses, but these encounters are emotionally felt. This is particularly true when we look at faces. A face with an angry expression immediately elicits fear and is accompanied by negative feelings. A friendly face evokes positive feelings such as sympathy or tenderness, and we simultaneously perceive a positive emotion. These emotionally charged perceptions can be processed consciously or unconsciously. While in conscious processing the emotional content can be readily reported by the subject, in unconscious processing an explicit report is not possible; conscious and unconscious perceptions are processed in different parts of the amygdala. According to Etkin et al. (2004), unconscious perception of fearful faces engages the basolateral part of the amygdala, while conscious perception triggers the dorsal part of the amygdala. It was found that anxiety prone subjects engage preferentially the part of the amygdala involved in unconscious processing, while this is not the case for less anxiety prone individuals. It is well known that unconscious stimuli may have a bigger emotional impact on our imagination than consciously perceived stimuli. The preferential involvement of the "unconscious amygdala loop" by anxious people may explain why these individuals repeatedly and predictably react with fear in situations that do not truly represent a threat. These studies provide a biological framework for understanding the basis of diverse forms of emotions and confirm a differential processing of conscious versus unconscious perceptions of images by the brain (Etkin et al. 2015). That these mechanisms may also be involved in other aspects of mental activities is obvious, underlining the importance of unconscious processes on our behavior in everyday life.

Faces transmit an abundance of social information. This would not be possible if there was not an extended face recognition system combining face processing centers with structures involved in emotion, memory, and cognition. Face recognition relies on a core system consisting of interconnected face selective areas in the occipital temporal region (Haxby et al. 2000). This system comprises three bilateral regions, the inferior occipital gyrus, the lateral fusiform gyrus, and the superior temporal gyrus. The early perception of facial figures is located in the inferior occipital gyrus. The recognition of identity, that is the invariant aspect of a face, is located in the lateral fusiform gyrus, while the changeable aspect of a face, that is the perception of eye gaze or lip movements, is located in the superior temporal gyrus. This model is thought to have both a hierarchical and a branching structure. The face perception system connects with other brain regions such as the frontal specialized attention system, brain areas processing emotion in the amygdala and insula, the auditory verbal system for speech-related lip movement, as well as mnesic areas in the anterior temporal lobe that serve to recall names and other information associated with a particular face. In essence the many face perception functions are accomplished by the coordinated participation of multiple regions of the brain. These regions can also participate in other functions by interacting with other systems.

We already discussed the biology of emotions when we explored perception, cognitive development, and emotions in chapter 2. None of the different aspects of mental functions we have described so far would be possible if we did not have the ability to remember. Memorizing is probably the most fundamental capacity of our brain. So, let us turn to the dynamics of memory.

Chapter 5

THE DYNAMICS OF MEMORY

Personal testimonies

Famous writers have highlighted the critical role of memory in life. One intriguing aspect of memory is that not all memories are distinct, just as not all moments of the present are clear. For Jean-Marie Gustave Le Clézio, there is a lot of imagination in memory. Memory is central not only for building our identity but also as a process by which our bodies encode emotions associated with losses or trauma, as Virginia Woolf's novels demonstrate. It is possible to remember with incredible clarity a moment that happened in early childhood, while the memory of more recent events seems lost in a kind of murkiness. We present excerpts from these two writers before we turn to the neurobiological aspects of how we form and retrieve memories.

Jean-Marie Gustave Le Clézio (1940) is a French writer who received the Nobel Prize in Literature in 2008. The Swedish Academy characterized him as an "author of new departures, poetic adventure and sensual ecstasy, explorer of a humanity beyond and below the reigning civilization." For Le Clézio, writing serves to find one's early child. Individual memory is the source of writing, something both conscious and unconscious: conscious because one writes it, unconscious because one does not know what prompted you to write it. The most beautiful novels according to Le Clézio are the initiatory ones, as he considers the period of adolescence as the most crucial for one's whole existence. In his Nobel lecture he said: "If I examine the circumstances that led me to write … I see that at the beginning of all this, for me, there is war." At the start of World War II, Le Clézio's father, a doctor in the British army, was in Nigeria and could not return to Nice, where Jean-Marie lived with his mother and brother. When the Germans entered and occupied Nice, they had to take refuge in the hinterland. Le Clézio writes: "For me war is what civilians experience, very young children first and foremost. Not once has war ever seemed to me to be an historical moment. We were hungry, we were frightened, we were cold … easy to understand the urge to escape … to dream and put those dreams in writing. So that in this third millennium, which has only just begun, no child on our shared planet, regardless of gender or language or religion, shall be abandoned to hunger or ignorance, or turned away from the feast. This child carries within him the future of our human race. In the words of the Greek philosopher Heraclitus, a very long time ago, the kingdom belongs to a child." In his autobiography *L'Africain—Traits et Portraits* (2004) he writes: "What is definitely missing from my childhood: having a father, growing up close to him, in the sweetness of the family home. I know I missed it".[12]

In his tale *L'enfant et la guerre* (2020, 106) he writes:

> War is the worst thing that can happen to a child. For the child I was in the war … it was a fear without a face, without a name, without history. Adults do not talk about the war, but the silence is no doubt more scary. This great void of my childhood in war, how am I going to fill it? More than the dangers, what fed me during my five years of solitude is the feeling of strangeness. This emptiness that has penetrated me carried far away everything that had preceded me. To have been hungry, to have felt fear and emptiness during the first years of my life did not harden me, but it made me violent. The explosion of the bomb marked the beginning of my violence.[13]

Le Clézio speaks in a television interview[14] about the child being secret and hidden; therefore, he does not write about his (inner) child, as he does not want to risk betraying him. "Memory," he says, "betrays us, there is a lot of imagination in memory. You must not betray yourself or others, you must write as closely as possible to the sense of your lived experience. Writing is a need to free yourself. I have a physical memory from the age of four years, when a blast threw me to the ground, a violent sensation from the explosion in the port of Nice. Children of war grow up with the feeling that there is no law outside, the child in war is a witness in spite of himself."[15]

Virginia Woolf (1882–1941) expresses in her novels so vividly and with great artistic talent and almost scientific insight how past memories profoundly shaped her life.[16]

"Life is a luminous halo, a semi-transparent envelope surrounding us from the beginning of consciousness to the end" (Woolf 1925, 212). "I now made the contribution of maturity to childhood's intuitions—satiety and doom; the sense of what is

12 Our translation.
13 Our translation.
14 *La grande librairie*, France 5, aired on March 11, 2020 (our translation).
15 Our translation.
16 See Briggs (2006).

inescapable in our lot; death; the knowledge of limitations; how life is more obdurate than one had thought it" (Woolf 1992, 492).

Virginia Woolf was born in London in 1882 and died in 1941 when she drowned herself. She is considered to be one of the most famous British novelists, essayists, publishers, and critics. Virginia was the second of four children to Julia and Leslie Stephen, having one sister and two brothers. As her mother had three children from her first marriage and her father one daughter from his first marriage, she lived in what she called a "crowded merry world which spun so gaily in the center of my childhood," with her mother representing an essential reference for her. With her brother Thoby she created the newspaper *Hyde Park Gate News* at the age of nine (Woolf 1976, 76–79).

In a letter to Robert Bridges,[17] Virginia Woolf (1940) writes:

> I very early became convinced that our emotions before works of art were of many kinds and that we failed as a rule to distinguish the nature of the mixture. … The most constant unchanging and therefore I suppose fundamental emotion … has to do with the contemplation of form. … I therefore assume that the contemplation of form is a peculiarly important spiritual exercise … it does not imply for me any connection with morals. … I should admit that the feelings we have to our kind are of a spiritual nature (love being a function of spiritual health and hate of spiritual disease) and that those feelings may issue in good or bad behavior. But in so far as they do not issue but remain "states of mind," they are spiritually good or bad but not morally (Woolf 1940, 229).

Her mother died of rheumatic fever when Virginia was thirteen years old, her loss leading to the Virginia's first psychic breakdown: "After that there was nothing left of it … everything had come to an end" (Woolf 1976, 84–91).

The second major breakdown occurred nine years later after her father's death from cancer. It was her father who had motivated and supported her writing. Two years later her brother Thoby died of typhoid fever. These losses aggravated her fragility and vulnerability, which she herself referred to: "Any break—like the house moving—causes me extreme distress." She describes her suffering as follows: "wearisome headache, jumping pulse, aching backs, frets, fidgets, lying awake, sleeping draught … all horrors of the dark cupboard of illness" (105).

Woolf's novel *To the Lighthouse* (1927) is generally regarded as her most autobiographical work, which she described as "easily the best of my books" and which her husband considered as a "masterpiece," "a psychological poem" (Bell and McNeillie 1980, 123). *To the Lighthouse* has been subject of multiple interpretations, one of which is Woolf's search: "What is the meaning of life? That was all a simple question; one that tended to close in on one with years" (1927, 153). She writes: "If life has a

17 January 24, 1924, as reported in her biography.

base that it stands upon, if it is a bowl that one fills and fills and fills—then my bowl without a doubt stands upon this memory" (Woolf 1976, 64).

She described her relationship with her mother as follows: "The presence of my mother obsessed me. I could hear her voice, see her, imagine what she would do or say as I went about my day's doings. She was one of the invisible presences who after all, play so important a part in every life. … If we cannot analyze these invisible presences, we know very little of the subject of the memoir; and again, how futile life-writing becomes. I see myself as a fish in a stream; deflected; held in place; but cannot describe the stream" (80). For her mother, "it was impossible to leave a very private and particular impression upon a child. … A general presence rather than a particular person to a child of seven or eight. Can I remember ever being alone with her for more than a few minutes? Someone was always interrupting" (83).

Woolf's continual longing for her mother, as well as her mourning the loss of her mother are of central significance in her novel *To the Lighthouse.* "The tragedy of her death was not that it made one, now and then and very intensely, unhappy. It was that it made her unreal; and us solemn, and self-conscious. We were made to act parts that we did not feel; to fumble for words that we did not know. It obscured, it dulled. It made one hypocritical and immeshed in the conventions of sorrow. Many foolish and sentimental ideas came into being. Yet there was a struggle, for soon we revived, and there was a conflict between what we ought to be and what we were" (95).

Having read Freud, she writes: "I did for myself what psychoanalysts do for their patients," working through the relationship with her mother in the person of Mrs. Ramsay (the central figure and the most important character in the novel): "She felt this thing that she called life terrible, hostile, and quick to pounce on you if you gave it a chance. There were eternal problems: suffering; death; the poor" (Woolf 1927, 91–92). "I expressed some very long felt and deeply felt emotion" (Woolf 1976, 81) and: "The things one does not remember are as important; perhaps they are more important" (69). For Woolf, intuition is "so instinctive that it seems given to me" (69).

About her breakdowns, she writes: "The best of these illnesses is that they loosen the earth about the roots" (Woolf 1919–1924, 166). "These curious intervals (due to illness) in life—I've had many—are the most fruitful artistically—one becomes fertilized" (220). "The shock-receiving capacity is what makes me a writer … followed by the desire to explain it. … A revelation. … It is only by putting it into words that I make it whole" (166).

"The whole world is a work of art; that we are parts of the work of art" (Woolf 1976, 72); "we are the words; we are the music; I had a feeling of transparency in words when they cease to be words and become so intensified that one sees to experience them; to foretell them as if they developed what one is already feeling" (93).

DeSalvo (1989) writes that Woolf—according to her own testimony—was sexually abused by her two older half-brothers George and Gerald Duckworth. The first abuse episode was initiated by Gerald Duckworth, when she was six or seven (her half-brother would have been eighteen or nineteen): "As I sat there, he began to explore my body. I can remember the feel of his hand going under my clothes; going firmly and steadily lower and lower, I remember how I hoped that he would stop; how I stiffened and wriggled as his hand approached my private parts. But it did not stop. His hand explored my private parts too" (Woolf 1976, 104).

The abuse of Woolf by her older brother (George Duckworth) began after their mother's death, Woolf being thirteen, and George around twenty-eight. DeSalvo writes: "She tells how, in a 'confused whirlpool of sensation' she undressed in her room in her adolescence, how she stretched out on her bed to fall asleep, and how George invaded her room: 'creaking stealthily, the door opened; treading gingerly, someone entered'. 'Who?' I cried. 'Don't be frightened', George whispered. 'And don't turn on the light, oh beloved. Beloved…' and he flung himself on my bed, and took me in his arms" (DeSalvo 1989, 121).

But Woolf criticizes her own memories in *Moments of Being* (1976), a collection of posthumously published autobiographical essays, as follows: "It is so difficult to give any account of the person to whom things happen. The person is evidently immensely complicated. … In certain favorable moods, memories—what one has forgotten—come to the top. Now if it is so, is it not possible—I often wonder—that things we have felt with great intensity have an existence independent of our minds; are in fact still in existence? And if so, will it not be possible, in time, that some device will be invented by which we can tap them? I see it—the past—as an avenue lying behind; a long ribbon of scenes, emotions. Why have I forgotten so many things that must have been, one would have thought, more memorable than what I do remember?" She writes: "Some of my first memories. But of course, as an account of my life they are misleading" (67–70).

Different types of memory

The study of how memory functions is at the center of the sciences of the mind. It is a topic of interest for neuroscientists trying to understand where memory is stored in the brain, for neurologists who study age- or disease-related memory loss in dementias, or psychiatrists studying the role of traumatic memories in the development of mental disorders.

An important distinction among memory processes concerns the division between short- and long-term memories. Short-term memory, also described as working memory, refers to a neuro-cognitive system with a limited capacity that is responsible for temporarily holding information. Working memory is involved in everyday tasks, from remembering a telephone number—while entering it in the phone—to understanding a sentence. It is also called immediate memory and represents facts or events that are currently present in one's mind. Long-term memory by opposition is a long-lasting memory ranging from just a few days to many years. It is commonly divided into the explicit or declarative memory type and the implicit or nondeclarative memory type (Fig. 5.1). Explicit or declarative memory refers to the conscious, intentional retrieval of past information or events. Clinical studies have shown that the hippocampus and the temporal lobe are essential for declarative or explicit memory because damage to these areas leads to severe memory deficits as observed in patients following surgery for epilepsy (Scoville and Milner 1957) or suffering from Alzheimer's disease (Ball et al. 1985). Explicit memory does not reflect a unitary function, but can be further divided into memory for facts, also called semantic memory, and memory for events, called episodic memory (Tulving 1983). Semantic memories are impersonal and devoid of autobiographical context, whereas episodic memories are personal. These categories demonstrate that the brain processes different kind of memories in different ways and in various regions of the brain as further exemplified below. Implicit memory refers to the faculty of remembering motor or perceptual skills as well as emotional experiences.

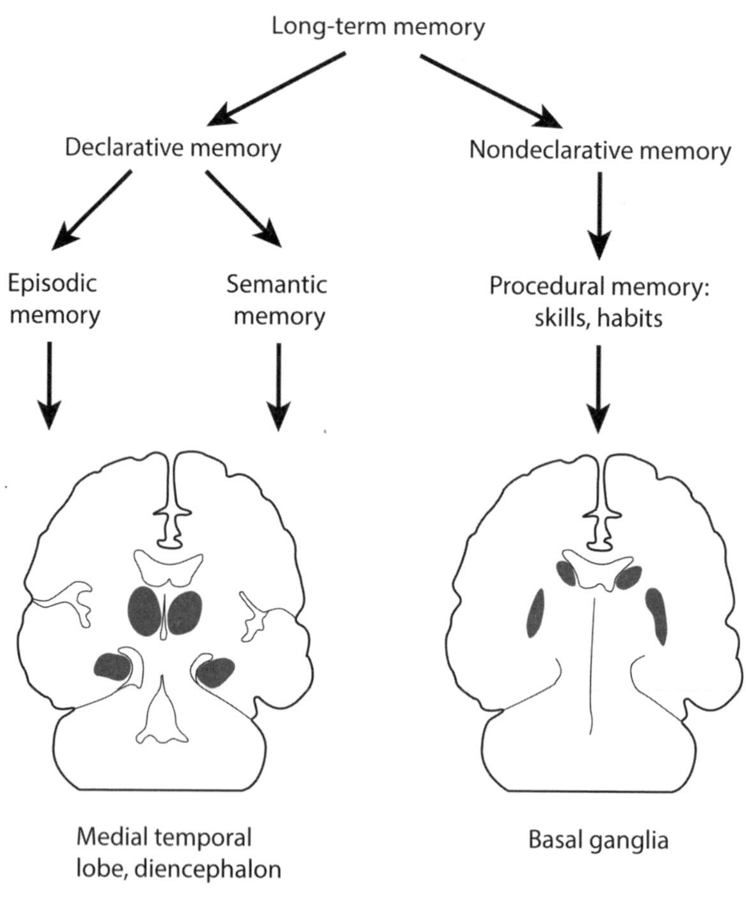

Figure 5.1 Model of memory systems processing. Long-term memory is divided into two broad classes: declarative or explicit memory and non-declarative or implicit memory. Declarative memory relies on hippocampal structures (medial temporal lobe) and diencephalon, while non-declarative memory depends on basal ganglia structures. (Adapted from Henke 2010).

Short-term memory can only remember seven digits (e.g., numbers), which is why as much as possible has to be put in long-term memory. Long-term implicit memory, also called procedural memory, helps us perform many tasks and utilize our skills without conscious awareness: it is automatized. There are, however, more than just skills in implicit memory. Implicit memory also reflects the operations of different memory systems, in particular the emotional memory network. Declarative memory contains facts and events; they can be recovered, consciously recalled, and worked on, for example, in order to find a solution and eventually be stored in implicit memory and automatized.

The biology of memory

Memory is a highly dynamic phenomenon, from the moment of encoding to the time of retrieval. After encoding, labile memories undergo consolidation and are stabilized over time. This process depends on interactions between circuits located in several brain areas. The hippocampus plays a crucial role in the initial encoding and storage of labile memories, storing them in engrams, the basic units of memory (Josselyn and Tonegawa 2020). Memory formation involves the transfer of the encoded information from the hippocampus to long-term storage sites in multiple and widespread areas of the cortex. How this transfer occurs is not known in detail, but it is thought that the hippocampus guides gradual changes in the cortex, making a sort of coupling. Interestingly this coupling is increased during sleep (Vaz et al. 2019), supporting the well-known notion that sleep benefits the retention of memory. Recent research also demonstrates that new memory traces can be formed directly in the cortex. For example, visual areas can process memory content, suggesting that memory storage can take place at this level, bypassing the hippocampus (Brodt et al. 2019), though a constant dialog between the cortex and the hippocampus is essential for memory recall (Norman et al. 2019).

While the hippocampus plays an essential role in the formation of recollections, memories are stored in networks of neurons across several circuits in the brain. How stable over time the memory information remains, seems to be proportional to the number of neurons that are synchronously active for a given memory trace or representation (Gonzalez et al. 2019). Information stored in individual neurons is relatively labile, therefore it needs to be stored in larger networks of synchronously active neurons in order to become stable.

Memory representations should be viewed as global features of the brain and not of single structures. Memories are arranged into many domains of the brain, as depicted in Figure 5.2. The corresponding cortical regions also contain the receptive maps, where the five sensory systems such as taste, olfaction, touch, hearing, and vision converge in the brain. In this sense, we should regard perception and memory not as faculties of different systems but as being localized within the same neural circuits.

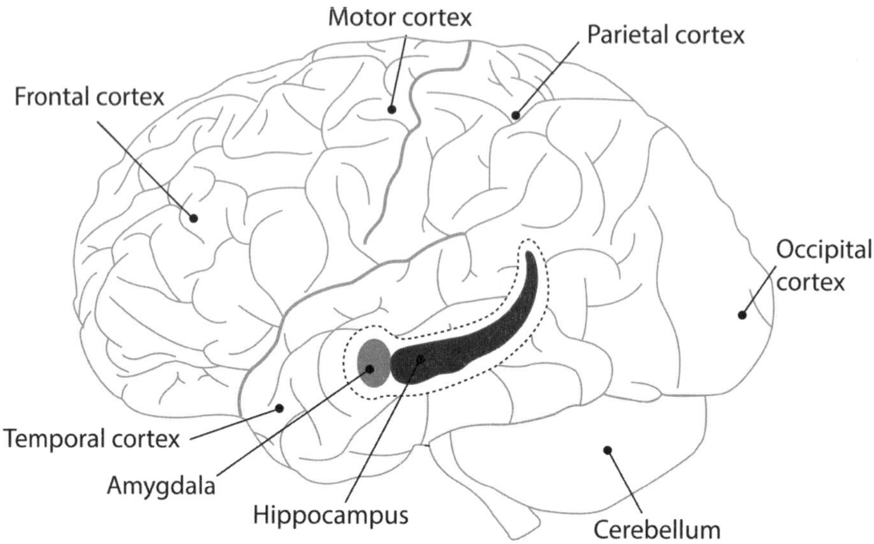

Figure 5.2 Memories are arranged into vastly distributed domains. The hippocampus serves to encode memories, and the amygdala is vital for storage of emotional memories (dotted lines signify embedded structures in the brain). Other large areas include frontal cortex for episodic and semantic memories, motor cortex for procedural memories, parietal cortex for learned skills, occipital cortex for visual memories, temporal cortex for verbal memories, and cerebellum for procedural memories.

Amazing memorizing capacities

Eidetic memory refers to the ability of an individual to accurately recall a large number of images, sounds, and objects in a seemingly unlimited fashion. Eidetic memory means to have an extraordinarily detailed and vivid recall of visual images. It is controlled primarily by the posterior part of the brain, through which visual stimuli are processed and images retained. These images are usually retrievable for a short time, though some people have impressive memories (also called photographic memories) that allow them to recollect past events in great detail for extremely long periods. Eidetic memory may be an early form of memory, since this ability seems strongest with young subjects, but declines later. While the terms eidetic or photographic memory have been criticized, they are applied to people with exceptional memory capacities, as illustrated in the following examples.

Theodore Roosevelt (1858–1919) is one of the most famous American presidents. He redefined America's place in the world. Roosevelt suffered from asthma as a child, experiencing severe nighttime asthma attacks, which terrified him and his parents. He overcame his physical disability by adopting a demanding lifestyle. Homeschooled first before going to Harvard college, he was a curious and brilliant student. He was endowed with a photographic memory, being able to recall not just articles, but entire newspaper pages long after he first read them. He used this capacity to its full extent: as a child he was already a speed-reader, typically reading one to three books a day. He read in many different languages, including German, French, Italian, and Latin. He was always learning and looking for actionable knowledge, becoming a prolific author, writing many books and about 150,000 letters in his lifetime. His phenomenal memory served him well, allowing him to develop wide interests and enabling his prodigious career. Roosevelt had a special admiration for his father, a man of great courage and tenderness, who was a prominent leader in New York's cultural and political scene. His father's sudden death, when Roosevelt was nineteen, affected him profoundly and led him to intensify his activities. He began studying law, but eventually dropped out of law school to follow in his father's steps and enter politics. At age forty-two, he became the youngest American president.

Sergei Rachmaninoff (1873–1943) was a Russian composer, virtuoso pianist, and conductor, whose works are among the most popular in the Romantic repertoire. He was born into a musical family and was a musical prodigy. He began piano lessons at age four with his mother. She noticed his ability to reproduce passages from memory without a wrong note. He graduated from the Moscow Conservatory at age nineteen having already composed several pieces of music. While successful as a musician and composer at a young age, Rachmaninoff was not spared from profound disappointments. He suffered severe depressive episodes, caused by the poor reception of his Symphony No. 1, or when his marriage plans were opposed by his parents and the church. After receiving hypnotherapy and psychotherapy sessions he started composing music again, to renewed success. He also was able to marry his first cousin, sidestepping the church's opposition. He left Russia following the Russian revolution and embarked on a highly successful career as a composer, conductor, and concert pianist. Rachmaninoff possessed a "photographic" memory. He could hear a piece of music, even a symphony, then play it back the next day, the next year, or a decade later. Apparently, he was able to remember any composition, classical or contemporary, and play it as if it were a work he had recently thoroughly studied. When we think about the memory performance of a musician, we wonder how a pianist can remember the 30,000 notes of Rachmaninoff's Piano Concerto no. 3. Considering it has to be performed on stage in a perfect sequence, with rhythmical and dynamic variability in order to create an emotional and narrative performance, such an achievement reveals an exact encoding specificity and a truly phenomenal organization of the information in brain memory systems.

As these two examples show (but there are indeed many more), all sorts of people have been reported to be endowed with amazing memorizing capacities, allowing them to perform the most complex tasks. In general terms, we can not only store and retrieve a prodigious amount of information, but our brain is able to generate new information by construction and association. To some degree, every act of memory is an act of imagination and creation. Human memory is unique because it possesses an inherent representational capacity that enables many symbolic activities characterizing our mental lives, also giving us the ability to develop countless skills.

PART II

Chapter 6

AESTHETIC EXPERIENCE AND ARTISTIC CREATION

There are universal characteristics in artistic production throughout history. One essential element is the search for harmony, meaning the coherence of parts within a whole. This often requires from the artist an extensive trial and error approach to reach the desired harmony, or in case of music the most pleasing melody or arrangement. Another is the principle of parsimony that leads us to find a simple, elegant pattern in the middle of an apparently complex and chaotic field. The aesthetic aspect of parsimony may be found in Italian renaissance painting, sculpture, or architecture, with its emphasis on symmetry and regularity, discarding what is superfluous. In the scientific world the principle of parsimony can be observed in many areas—the "beauty" of solving a mathematical or scientific problem lies in the fact that it explains much from little. In economic terms, parsimony is the quality of being careful with money or resources.

Aesthetics in ancient Greece

Throughout history, creative genius was thought to arise from insanity. Plato called creativity a "divine madness … a gift from the gods," while Aristotle wrote that "no great genius was without a mixture of insanity" (Neihart 1998).

The ancient Greeks believed in the ideal of an alliance between the beautiful and the good. The Greek *aisthesis* has the meaning of perception of all senses: feeling, hearing, seeing and their impact on the body. Ancient Greek art expresses this ideal of somatic perfection and mental beauty, known as *kalos kagathos*: *kalos* for beautiful, *agathos* for good and virtuous, *kai* for and. The ideal of kalos kagathos originates in the epic poems of Homer. The term is also used by Herodotus, Socrates, and Plato and discussed in Aristotle's *Nicomachean Ethics*. Socrates sought the ideal of kalos kagathos in the pursuit of precise knowledge. Plato believed that improved intelligence would enable people to attain the ideal of kalos kagathos, while according to Aristotle, a stable equilibrium of the soul enables the individual to achieve the ideal of kalos kagathos within himself.

The Greeks have left us poetic and dramatic texts, where people and heroes struggle with unpredictable gods. The myth in the Greek tragedies is reinterpreted again and again in manifold versions. Classical tragedy is founded on the unity of time, place, and action. In his work *Poetics*, Aristotle describes tragedy as being characterized by seriousness and involving an outstanding person who experiences a reversal of fortune, which is caused by the tragic hero's error. In tragedy, the transgression of the faith-based collective human order and its restitution is shown. Transgression is felt by the hero and the audience as an error, *hamartia*; the rules and orders, consecrated by the gods, are expressed in symbols and reflected in laws and prohibitions. Commandments and prohibitions determine human generations and sexual relationships. The tragic hero, who transgresses these regulations, is a man whose misfortune is brought about not by vice or depravity, but by some error or frailty. He eventually gains revelation or awareness about human fate, destiny, and the will of the gods.

The Socratic *gnothi seauton*, "know thyself" is the theme of Plato's *Symposium*, a philosophical text. The banquet in the *Symposium* is attended by Socrates, Alcibiades, and Aristophanes. In the dialog between Alcibiades and Socrates, Alcibiades expresses his love and admiration for Socrates. He sees images of gods in Socrates (*agalmata theon*) and images of virtues (*agalmata aretes*). Socrates reveals to Alcibiades that what he loves are the treasures within himself and gives Alcibiades the task of submitting his desire to the search and discovery of his own treasures (his fantasized agalmata). The aim of Socrates was the pursuit of reason, but at the same time he believed that an inner voice, which he called his *daimonion*, guided him in his decisions and represented his ethical source.

It is Socrates who first used the word psyche and described the human soul or mind as consisting of three elements: "impulses and desire," "reason and thought," and in between the two, "restraint and containment," similar to Freud's model of the psyche: the id contains uncoordinated instinctual impulses, the super-ego plays the critical and moralizing role, and the ego acts according to the reality principle and mediates between the desires of the id and the inner critic of the super-ego.

The ancient Greeks valued male, youthful, and athletic beauty, whose sculpted representations have survived in representations of Apollo (Fig. 6.1) and statues of Olympian winners. Juvenile feminine beauty is represented naked, for instance, in the theme of Aphrodite coming out of the bath, but otherwise covered. Beauty signaled its relation to good nature, a gift of the gods, by the right physical proportion of the human body. If the impression of beauty was subjective and perhaps incommunicable, a Greek sculpture represented the classical ideal in terms of female or male psychophysical human beauty as an abstraction, harmonizing soul and body.

Figure 6.1 *The Apollo of the Belvedere* is a well-known marble sculpture from the classical Greek period showing the ideal male beauty. Rediscovered in Italy in the late fifteenth century, it belongs to the Vatican Museum.

Aesthetic concepts and art production

Ideals of beauty have been modified over time, based on changing cultural and aesthetic norms. Historically, the visual arts showed a wide range of different models for beauty. Concerning physical attractiveness, young men and women with well-proportioned figures and regular features have been judged the most beautiful. The Enlightenment took up Plato's belief that truth, beauty, and goodness relate to the understanding that truth and beauty, disseminated widely, will sooner or later lead to goodness (Neiman 2008, 117).

What is beauty? How do we distinguish beauty from the ordinary or the ugly? The term beauty or beautiful is no longer placed at the center of reflection on art—where it stood for centuries. What the greatest Greek philosophers and poets described as criteria for beauty are now disputed by representatives of the artistic and social scene and by proponents of the psychological and neurobiological sciences. One of the reasons for this paradigmatic change is the realization that beauty cannot be considered in isolation; it is intimately linked to the values and beliefs of the society we live in. A definition of beauty can only be given within the context of a given cultural and historical epoch, in other words it requires an all-encompassing worldview, a *Weltanschaung*.

That beauty is in the eye of the beholder and can be difficult to endure is expressed by **Rainer Maria Rilke** (1875–1926) in *Duino's Elegies*: "Beauty is nothing but the beginning of terror, which we are still just able to endure, and it amazes us so, because it serenely disdains to destroy us" (Rilke 1992, 132–3). Segal (1986) in her psychoanalytic approach to aesthetics writes of Rilke: "Every work of beauty still embodies the terrifying expression of depression and death" (203).

François Cheng (1929–), a Chinese-born French academic, writer, and poet, said in his reception speech at the French Academy in 2003: "I became a Frenchman in law, mind and heart more than thirty years ago … especially from that moment when I resolutely went over to the French language, making it the weapon or the soul of my creative work. This language, how can I say everything that I owe to it? It is so intimately bound up with the way I live and my inner life that it has proved to be the emblem of my destiny."

In his book *Five Meditations on Beauty* (2008), François Cheng writes:

"Objective beauty exists … as long as it is not seen, it is in vain" (102). Beauty is "virtually there, always there, a desire that springs from the inside of beings, or from being, like an inexhaustible fountain … radiant and connecting presence," inciting us "to acquiescence, to interaction, to transfiguration" (37). "The more intense the experience of beauty, the more the poignant character of its brevity engenders the desire to renew the experience" (51). The "gaze of a subject, who in the moment captures the scene of beauty, leads to a new encounter, situated on another plane … of memory" (106). "The beauty of the face comes from a light that rises up from the depth of being" or "from the outside … illuminating it" (136). "Not everyone is an artist, but everyone can have his own being transformed, transfigured by the encounter with beauty; as it is true that beauty arouses beauty, increases beauty, elevates beauty" (98). "When the authenticity of beauty is guaranteed by goodness, it is the supreme state of truth" (75).

In an interview,[18] Cheng spoke of his own life experience:

[18] *La grande Librairie*, France 5, aired on January 29, 2020.

To live real joy—for him—one has to go through suffering, to cross the bottom of the abyss. I am not seeking wisdom, or serenity, I am a man in constant transformation. From the age of fifteen, I suffered from existential anxiety; writing is for me a rescue, a reason to live. Beauty is an encounter; it is a sign that life has meaning; beauty introduces the idea of the value of a moral and spiritual artistic creation. Among body, soul and spirit, the soul is the most intimate and the most sensitive and leads to artistic creation and connects us to a form of transcendence. It is our gaze that gives meaning to the splendors of the universe.

Modern art and society

Gustav Klimt (1862–1918) was one of the founding members of the Vienna Secessionist movement in 1897. This movement initiated modern art, emphasizing the sociohistorical context out of which art emerged and generated entirely new aesthetic inspiration (Fig. 6.2). According to its members, art had to be all-embracing, leading to the inscription above the Secession Building in Vienna: *To the age its art, to the art its freedom*. In 1901, Klimt painted the Beethoven Frieze for the 14th Vienna Secessionist exhibition in celebration of the composer. The frieze was painted directly onto the walls and illustrates human longing for happiness in a distressing world. Klimt was criticized for an overly sexual and crude display of human passions, challenging the accepted norms of social and moral principles. Analyzing this modernist movement, Kandel writes that artists in every age educate the public to look at art anew to find novel forms of expression (2012).

Since then, the twentieth and twenty-first centuries have seen an increasing rejection of "classical" beauty by philosophers and artists, culminating in an "anti-aesthetic" movement (Foster 1983). Post-modern movements, starting after World War II, such as outsider art, pop art, and video art have emerged as reactions against established forms of art displayed in museums. In this respect the emergence of the movement called *art brut,* conceived by Jean Dubuffet (1901–1985) in 1945, is an example of an art form arising outside the established art scene. He was interested in art created by mentally ill patients, but also by artists living at the margins of society and with no formal artistic training. On can easily draw similarities to early twentieth-century artists, such as Marcel Duchamp (1887–1968) or Pablo Picasso (1881–1973), who rejected established values to create new art forms such as Dada and cubism.

Jameson (in Foster 1983), an analyst of contemporary cultural trends, notes that an important factor in this revolution was the erosion of the older distinction between so-called elite culture and mass or popular culture. He emphasizes the strong relationships between art production and cultural and social life. What we call classical modernism, such as expressionism and cubism, are movements that were originally a form of oppositional art. They emerged within the industrial society of the Victorian era in Britain and the Belle Epoque in France and were viewed as scandalous and offensive by the middle class and widely condemned by the bourgeois establishment as ugly, bohemian, and sexually shocking. This modernism did not suit Victorian moral taboos. Our current conception of modern art has completely changed. There is little that we find outrageous or shocking in works from Henri Matisse (1869–1954) or Picasso, which are now referred to as belonging to the classical period of modern art.

According to Jameson, we witness in the current day's post-modern art a movement marked by the emergence of consumerism, media development, market globalization, and unprecedented technological changes, especially characterized by the proliferation of new communication tools. In trying to understand the development of post-modern art, we have to consider the impact of virtual images, which often distort representations of everyday reality. This is exemplified by works of Francis Bacon (1909–1992) or Lucian Freud (1922–2011), where one feels a voluntary form of protest, deforming human bodies in such a way that may make the viewer feel nauseated (Fig. 6.3). There is a search for sensation in this form of art, imposing and confronting the viewer with a disturbed, menacing, and strange world. Looking at such paintings may evoke feelings of distress and anguish.

Figure 6.2 *The Kiss* (1908) is one of Klimt's most famous paintings, depicting a couple embracing one another, their bodies entwined in elaborate robes decorated in the typical new art style of the Viennese secessionist movement.

Figure 6.3 Francis Bacon. Study for portrait of Lucian Freud, sideways (1971). Oil on canvas.

As Baudrillard (in Foster 1983) states: "This is the time of miniaturization, telecommand and the microprocession of time, bodies and pleasures. There is no longer any ideal principle for objects at a higher level or on a human scale" (129). This change, away from a human scale to a system of molecular patterns is exemplified in the human body, which "often appears simply superfluous, basically useless in its extension, in the multiplicity and complexity of its organs, its tissues and functions, since today everything is concentrated in the brain and in genetic codes, which alone sum up the operational definition of being" (129). He points to a new phenomenon resulting in a fragmentation of time where we find ourselves in a "perpetual present." Living in a permanent present means that we are carried along in a continuously moving world, eliminating the traditions upon which social forms were established. Art will always be a mirror of our society. At the same time, an essential function of artistic creation is its critical role, in how we perceive the world we live in, and in providing us with cues to better understand our surroundings and give them sense and meaning.

Art has a social function; the artist always attempts to share with the viewer his conception of the world. This is true not only of religious but also of secular art. Thus, art may introduce order and meaning to a world perceived as vain and senseless with the aim of offering a mutually shared aesthetic perception. Artistic creation tends to express and communicate the constant need for renewal in an extreme and rapidly changing world. The concept of an ideal beauty, as exemplified by the Greeks, is, however, often viewed by contemporary artists as an outdated notion. A work of art is a product of the human brain, it is an artifact, a manmade object, and something that is not naturally present. The artist as a creator constantly searches for novelty and the unanticipated. The brain, as is well known, is especially stimulated by what is surprising and unexpected, and artists extensively utilize this property. Modern art makes widespread use of the unusual, shocking, and startling in its objects or installations. The American painter Barnett Newman (1905–1970) characterized his paintings as "action painting," because of the fundamental importance of gestures, the paint being splashed or smeared onto the canvas. He stated: "I believe that here in America some of us, free from the weight of European culture, are finding the answer by completely denying that art has any concern with the problem of beauty and where to find it."[19]

In the aftermath of postmodernism's rejection of beauty, the philosopher Elaine Scarry (1999) has returned to the classical idea that beauty incites us toward a greater concern for justice. She remarks that beauty and justice have a common synonym, which is "fairness": we speak about fair faces, fair skies, or fair arrangements. She emphasizes the importance of symmetry, which is true for a beautiful face, but equally important in "every one's relations to each other" in a just world. Scarry points out that in our response to beauty we often reach a state of sudden happiness, in what she calls acute pleasure. We receive a stimulus and enter into an "opiated" state: beauty may put us on the sideline, but we are almost happy to be marginalized.

Finally, in the aftermath of the perception of a beautiful sight, object, or face, we may come into a creative mood. Exposure to beauty leads to a desire to create. At a more common level we often take a picture of something beautiful, an encounter, a landscape, to perpetuate the moment. Beauty, with its strong appeal to our senses, captivates and fascinates us, shifting our preoccupation with ourselves to centering our attention to others, to more empathy, and as a corollary, ethical fairness. The British novelist Iris Murdoch (1919–1999) wrote extensively on the relationship between art and morality, offering a reinterpretation of Plato's views on art and beauty. Looking at beautiful objects represents a spiritual experience leading to a transformative process, where the viewer achieves a state of unselfishness by redirecting psychic energy away from the self towards others.

[19] Citation in the exhibition *Être moderne: Le MoMA à Paris*, Fondation Louis Vuitton, Paris, October 11, 2017 to March 5, 2018.

Neuroscientific perspective

Exploring the neural elements corresponding to mental representations such as thoughts, feelings, and behavior and, by extension, analyzing the neurobiological basis of artistic creativity is a field in constant expansion. At any one moment the number of representations provided by our brain is so enormous that an artist has to make a choice. There must be rules that control and restrict this combinatorial experience ultimately giving rise to what is known as a given artistic style. For Changeux (1997), the neural correlates of these rules are an acquired pattern of connections, stored in the frontal cortex and part of the long-term autobiographical memory system, that ultimately contribute to a given form of artistic creation and to the personal style of an artist. The human brain is an exploratory and self-organizing system, operating in a top-down and bottom-up projective style and engaged in social communication. We have described in previous chapters how the neurophysiological bases of perception, exploration, cognition, sensation, language, and memory provide us with representations of the world that are both reliable and truthful. Cultural marks such as beauty, truth, and goodness are laid down as "cultural circuits" in the brain. Forms and colors from artworks stimulate the recall of stored autobiographical memories, acquired symbolic systems, and social and cultural references, tainted with strong emotional significance.

We should, however, be careful not to fall prey to an ill-advised neurodeterminism that could imply a loss of self-determination, as if the wiring and interconnections in our brain would eventually determine us. Such a thesis amounts to nothing other than the self-imposed destruction of our free will. For if the traditional self-attribution of freedom and responsibility is to be abandoned, then the belief of artistic creation and the concepts of human dignity, not least of personal morality, become irrelevant. The brain is neither a passive repository of external inputs nor an innately wired genetic organ, but a place of autonomous activity.

The brain is the seat of anticipatory activities for all kind of actions at different time scales (Zirnsak 2011). According to Berthoz and Debru (2015) the brain is a "mental projector" that propels our perceptions onto the world. Our actions in everyday life—parts of our autobiographical experience and our imagination—are constantly accompanied by anticipation. Expectations and predictions are at the heart of our lives and the heart of each of our actions. We do not stick to an external reality, but we constantly analyze and compare different scenarios for the future. When Picasso painted a portrait of several views simultaneously, it reflects the possibility that our brain gives us different reference points for our surroundings, allowing us to "manipulate" external reality and create different perspectives of the shapes we perceive. For Zeki (1999) artists are, through their works, unique explorers of our brain and its functions. They escape dominant cultural norms to reveal to us modes of apprehension of the world that are at variance with established standards, making use of the immense capacity of our brain to create new combinations.

Changeux's thesis (1997) on the neurobiological basis of beauty is derived from the concept that the brain's cultural circuits give us representations of the world allowing us to make judgments, so that we can undertake planning and decision-making. In following this argument, he adopts the classical theory of biological naturalism stating that all mental phenomena, including social behavior, are correlates of neurobiological processes. In this naturalistic conception, only objectifying methods are recognized as legitimate, and neurobiological explanatory principles are proposed in an attempt to develop a scientific understanding of how we behave.

In his book *Du vrai, du beau, du bien* (2008), Changeux returns to the concept of beauty, giving it new importance. For him beauty is also related to truth and goodness, a view that is similar to the perception of beauty in classical Greece. Aesthetic pleasure calls into play neuronal networks that are involved in the making of the most synthetic mental representations in the frontal lobe together with the activation of the limbic system at the origin of emotions. The make-up of aesthetic contemplation consists of two aspects, a cognitive rational and an emotional pleasurable. When contemplating a work of art, the unfolding of a sequence of representations of affective points of reference takes place in the frontal cortex, leading to an awakening faculty, both at a symbolic and emotional level. This allows viewers to put themselves in the place of the characters represented in a painting and to feel and express empathy. According to Changeux (1994), aesthetic pleasure results from a concerted mobilization of sets of neurons located at several organizational levels of the brain, from the limbic system to the frontal cortex, realizing a magnified and enlarged mental object of "harmony of sensuality and of reason" (46).

Neuroaesthetics

Neuroscientists, following Changeux and Zeki, have suggested we study art with the aim of understanding the neural bases of the creation of an artwork and examine how we look or listen (more broadly how we contemplate an artistic production), leading to a new discipline called neuroaesthetics.[20] While science is devoted to the search for objective truth, art is a cultural activity carrying prominently subjective aspects such as emotions and feelings. This dichotomy between objectivity and subjectivity is immediately apparent when one is trying to define beauty or what is considered as beautiful. Beauty, with its implications of aesthetic judgment and how it can be achieved, has been discussed ever since art came into existence. Can beauty be defined by objective parameters or does it depend mostly on subjective factors? In any case, it seems difficult to propose a general definition of the beautiful, without any exceptions, mainly because there are several levels of categorization of beauty.

[20] In 2002 neuroaesthetics received the formal definition of the scientific study of the neural bases for the contemplation and creation of a work of art (Nalbantian 2008).

There could be an equivalence between beautifulness and goodness, as expressed in the Greek idiomatic word *kaloskagathos*. Beauty also means attractiveness and—considering the major role of beauty in a romantic relationship—a sexual reference is an important aspect in the definition of the beautiful. On a more practical level an object can be regarded as beautiful when it fulfills its function, realizing the principle of simplicity and economy. What is particularly advantageous should be preserved, an idea that is at the basis of Darwinian evolution theory, giving scientific support to the definition of beauty, in keeping with the idea that nature knows best what is beautiful.

Ishizu and Zeki (2011)—in an experimental setting—observed what happens in the brain when we look at persons, objects, or productions that are classified as beautiful. They asked subjects to contemplate works of visual art and music. The visual stimuli included paintings of portraits, landscapes or still lifes, and the auditory stimuli included classical and modern excerpts of music. Imaging of the subjects' brains when they looked at something they found beautiful revealed an activation of the medial orbito-frontal cortex (mOFC). The extent of activity in the mOFC was directly proportional to the declared intensity of beauty. Both modalities, visual and musical shared and activated the same cortical region. The mOFC is connected with all sensory modalities and acts as a kind of polymodal convergence zone. In the case of the visual experience there was a coactivation of the visual cortex, while in the case of the musical experience there was a coactivation of the auditory cortex. Activity in the mOFC correlates with the experience of pleasure and reward, whether real or imagined (Bray et al. 2010). The finding that the experience of beauty is processed in the brain pleasure circuits is not unexpected, since aesthetic feelings are gratifying and moving and are known to increase creative thinking, imagination, and inspiration. On the other hand, when subjects look at something aesthetically displeasing, something they find ugly or fearful, no activation of the mOFC takes place, but activity is confined to the amygdala, a region of the limbic system, which is active when we look at frightening stimuli. This suggests that there is a functional specialization within the brain for these two different kinds of aesthetic judgment, those related to positive rewarding experiences and those related to negative ones. What is really encoded or processed in those brain areas remains unknown. While it is appealing to consider that the brain functions in a modular way—this probably holds true in the context of rather simple experimental paradigms—we should, however, consider the whole brain in terms of connectivity and temporal dynamics, when interpreting mental processes such as aesthetic judgment. Neuroscience provides an interesting framework for understanding the control of affective states when contemplating artworks, but cannot yet capture the breadth of the reflective states associated with aesthetic experiences, which mobilize, beyond our perceptual senses, a range of conscious and unconscious memories at the base of our cultural identity.

In his book *Consilience*: *The Unity of Knowledge* (1998), Edward Wilson makes the point that "arts and science, despite the similarities in their creative spirit, have radically different goals and methods" (211). Neuroscience has an important role in explaining artistic creation, trying to define and understand its mechanisms. However, an artistic production is above all a unique human experience, where the artist transcends an aesthetic and emotional response in his work. Wilson states: "In this defining quality the arts are the antithesis of science" (218). While scientists try to know and want to explain everything, artists recreate their own inner world and avoid a direct explanation of their productions. It is the task of the viewer to find an interpretation.

For the Swiss author and playwright Friedrich Dürrenmatt (1921–1990) "Science and art are not the same but equal human creations. In both there is progress; in science there is a continual search for new interpretations, in art, technology constantly provides it with new possibilities: there is a reason why the Greeks used the same word for art and technology" (1998, 94).

Bioaesthetics

Art, as proposed by the German philosopher Peter Sloterdijk (2012), reexamines the basic bioaesthetic division of the world into attractions and aversions, or into eye-catchers and inconspicuous things. Actors in the field of beauty who can afford so much vanity (as, for example, the peacock when he opens his train, or in another category, the famous owner of an art collection) incarnate a particularly high fitness. The showcasing of fashion or art can reach the point where applause for excellence may be sufficient, without the need for a sexual acting out. The peacock train has long been considered as a symbol of human vanity. For Sloterdijk the "human ego" is metaphorically a psychic peacock train. In this case the "ego" would not be a useless exaggeration, but a much-needed evolutionary concept.

Ornaments do not necessarily signal a particular fitness benefit. For Prum (2017) natural selection will reach standards of beauty that do not necessarily confer an adaptation benefit. The classical Darwinian theory of evolution, proposing that the goal of natural selection is to stimulate the survival of the fittest, may be one-sided as in particular it neglects the important aspect of mate choice. To argue that females choose males with traits enhancing survival is an oversimplification. In fact, female sexual choices may favor ornaments in males that are not necessarily good for fitness but are selected for their aesthetic value. In this sense we should view evolution not only from the standpoint of the survival of the fittest, but also of the survival of the prettiest.

Collecting and displaying art

In all societies, humans not only place their energy in making works of art, but also manifest a wish to keep and save them for posterity. An artwork appeals to our senses and leads to self-reflection. Works of art are testimonies of an era, a style, or a fashion. The need to collect them is driven by the compulsion for possession and responds to a desire for curiosity and exploration. Such a desire can go overboard and become an obsession, as John Fowles in his novel *The Collector* (1963) narrates. This is the story of a lonely young man who collects butterflies, catches them, breeds them, pins them in display cases, and pores over their beauty in his spare time. Then he "catches" a more exciting "specimen," a beautiful young woman, to add to his "collection." The theme of this novel brilliantly recounts and explores the dividing lines that run through all of us: on one side the more intellectual and aesthetic aspects arousing our curiosity and, on the other side, the strong emotional and sexual forces driving our exploratory needs. For Freud, collectors are individuals sublimating their libidos by acquiring objects: he wrote that collecting is a "redirection of surplus libido onto an inanimate object" (in Ehrenfeld 1993). Freud's proposition still stands today and can be understood in modern terms as involving the motivational drive system. In analyzing how these driving forces are expressed, we should consider the multiple unconscious and conscious processes that motivate people to collect and gather almost every imaginable object.

Changeux (2008), himself an art collector, states that art collectors look for works that they regard as beautiful and attractive. In so doing they bring into play knowledge acquired by the frequentation of museums and the reading of specialized works. The art-lover who becomes a collector is a connoisseur and may eventually become an authority on one particular aspect and identify with a stylistic movement, but the knowledge acquired will not remain only academic. The contemplation of a work of art, and all the perceptual activity associated with it, are part of an eminently subjective domain and introspective process. The exploration of a piece of art, beyond all the intellectual reasoning, provokes very strong emotional reactions. This subjective fascination may not be easily communicable. The craze for a given artist appeals as much to feelings as to aesthetic values. This combination of unconscious and conscious activities allows us to eventually grasp the "beauty" of an artwork. The collector is an explorer, the field of collection has no limit. From the collector of butterflies to the collector of artworks, the scope is infinite. As illustrated by Fowles (1963), the pleasure of assembling a collection and admiring it when it is established can develop into an immoderate need for possession. But a collection of art objects, often a testimony of a bygone era, remains one of the highest forms of culture. It is an instrument of knowledge and a showcase, and when a collection is public, we become spectators to a dream, a shared idea, in which each painting is linked with the other, completing each other, so that a new reality emerges. This evocative power tears us out of our daily lives, elevating our spirits.

While in ancient times art collections were private and belonged mostly to wealthy people, in the seventeenth century the advent of public galleries allowed the open display of art collections. Since then, museums, private or public, have flourished all over the world and are increasingly popular, contributing significantly to public education and the enrichment of social life. Museums not only bring art to a large public, but by hosting exhibitions and events, they also bring narratives, chronicles, and history to life. Museums have amassed huge collections of art for society's benefit, protecting and conserving them, but just a tiny fraction of that art is actually open for people to view and enjoy, the rest being stored away. In the future, new ways of presenting art, by using virtual reality or displaying collections on the web, may allow unlimited access to pieces of art. The ability to put entire collections online not only provides more access to stored works but allows the listing of all the known works of an artist in the form of a *catalogue raisonné*. Such comprehensive, annotated listings, often compiled after the death of a master, are now available, often online, for all major artists.[21]

Quantifying reputation and success in art is a difficult endeavor. Quality cannot be easily defined, as art will always inspire in each viewer different feelings and emotions. Recognition of an artist depends on many variables that are external to the work itself but depend on its provenance, display venue, time, context, and its relationship to the art world as a whole. Ultimately recognition and artistic value is defined by the judgment of experts, curators, and collectors. Their opinion will be a determining factor in opening access to museums, galleries, and auction houses.

Great artists are innovators and often revolutionary spirits. There are multiple examples when—in defense of cultural norms and academic orthodoxy—important artists were refused recognition or entry to exhibitions. Notable was the *Salon des Refusés,* first held in 1863 in Paris, an art exhibition of rejected painters. Artists such as Gustave Courbet, Édouard Manet, and Camille Pissarro—whose works were refused by the jury of the official Paris Salon, a showcase of the best academic art—exposed their work in the *Salon des Refusés*, which eventually, after repeated exhibitions, gained more popularity than the Paris Salon.

A study has pinpointed the role of art institutions in shaping the recognition of artists by mapping out the network that captures the movement of art between institutions (Fraiberger et al. 2018). Not surprisingly, this survey showed that early entry of an artist to famous institutions offered the best chance for a long access to high-prestige venues. By contrast, artists starting in lesser known institutions had only limited access to prestigious institutions. Obviously, various barriers will always exist and sometimes only time will help under-represented artists gain recognition or allow neglected artworks to be discovered.

[21] In Switzerland, SIK-ISEA archives include online catalogs and digital artist holdings.

Chapter 7

CREATIVITY AND PSYCHOPATHOLOGY

Introduction

Greek philosophers, as already described, wrote about the creative process and recognized the fact that creativity often involves a return to more primitive mental processes, requiring a predisposition to navigate the lines between rational and irrational thoughts. Plato put it in these words: "Creativity is a divine madness, a gift from gods." Ever since, there has been a strong debate over the possibility of co-occurrence of outstanding creativity and psychopathological traits.

Rybakowski et al. (2008) conducted a review on the relationship between mental disorders and creativity. Looking at family research in affective disorders, they point out that an evaluation of the frequency of occurrence of mental disorders in the biography of prominent people and their families reveals that affective disorders are frequently observed in creative people. Several studies showed that a history of affective disorders was more common in families of famous scientists and artists such as writers, poets, or painters. It appears that a bipolar illness, particularly a hypomanic state, is advantageous to creativity. The American poet Emily Dickenson (1830–1886) wrote a large number of poems in her upswing mood states. Similar observations were made for Robert Schumann, who composed in a hypomanic state, and Virginia Wolff, who was particularly productive when she experienced mood upswings. Among painters who suffered from depression, Paul Gauguin, Henry Matisse, Jackson Pollok, and Georgia O'Keefe are often mentioned. A predisposition to psychotic states may be observed in creative people, though an overt psychosis is a factor limiting artistic creativity. It has been reported that children of famous creative people are not infrequently diagnosed with schizophrenia; while this association may be anecdotic, Nancy Andreasen (2005), an American neuropsychiatrist, states that there is good evidence suggesting a correlation between artistic creativity and affective disorders. Also "psychotic thinking," resulting in the reduction of cognitive or affective inhibition, can promote creativity. Biographical data showing that scientific inventiveness and creativity is often found in relatives of people suffering from schizophrenia support this idea. However, the development of creativity involves numerous other determinants such as the influence of the family, parents and siblings, and the impact of society, including peers, teachers, and mentors. While creativity may sometimes be linked to mental disorders and thus due to psychopathological familial factors, this is neither a requisite nor a necessary precondition for creativity to develop. One should not underestimate the negative impact of mental disorders. They are devastating conditions that can lead to severe cognitive, emotional, and social disturbances, and result in great suffering. But there is no question that patients with psychiatric disorders may possess exceptional or unusual abilities. Their creativity cannot be separated from their physical and psychological condition.

From the art of the insane to psychopathological art

Ceasare Lombroso (1835–1909), an Italian professor of psychiatry, was one of the first to analyze in psychiatric terms creative works by people with mental illness in his book *Genius and Madness* (1894). He collected a quantity of all of kinds of works in asylums, constituting a collection of curiosities. Lombroso's approach was very much influenced by the theory of phrenology, developed by the German physician Franz Joseph Gall (1758–1828). For both these men, character traits could be gathered from an analysis of the skull and the physiognomy of a person. Lombroso was criticized for his biological determinism; nevertheless, phrenological thinking remained influential into the nineteenth century.

Later on, other psychiatrists, or alienists as they were called, such as Hans Prinzhorn in Germany, Walter Morgenthaler and Hans Steck in Switzerland, Leo Navratil in Austria, Jean Delay and André Vollmat in France, built up collections of works produced by patients during their internment, later analyzing them in psychopathological terms as artworks of the mentally ill. In his book *Artistry of the Mentally Ill: A Contribution to the Psychology and Psychopathology of Gestaltung* (1972[22]), Hans Prinzhorn (1886–1933) in Germany laid the groundwork for what would be later called "psychopathological art." His book has not lost its relevance because of its remarkable modernity. Prinzhorn spent his youth in Vienna and was strongly influenced by Freud. He witnessed the considerable evolution of psychoanalysis and observed the development of new trends in literature, music, and painting. At that time, the limits of the naturalistic conception of figurative art, drawn by classical aesthetic canons, were definitively shattered. The different currents of nonfigurative painting broke down the conventional

[22] Original in German 1922, English translation 1972.

image of reality by substituting a subjective inner reality. This allowed surrealism and cubism to express the unfathomable. The reconciliation of art and psychopathology was therefore inevitable, especially since the stylistic affinity of the graphic expression of the mentally ill with many works of modern art became undeniable.

The increasing interactions and contacts between art, psychology, sociology, and psychiatry during the twentieth century led to many important developments and publications. An overview of this evolution can be found in the book *L'art psychopathologique* (1956) by Robert Volmat. Prinzhorn was the first to consider the drawings of mentally ill patients as an expression of their whole personality. Under the influence of phenomenology and structuralism, proposed by anthropologists such as James Frazer and Lucien Levy-Brühl, the artworks of psychiatric patients were analyzed with the aim of identifying a certain number of phenomena that would allow the mental structures of the artist-patient to be understood. They described characteristic features which, although not pathognomonic for schizophrenia, are nevertheless found with a particular frequency, emphasizing the notion of "otherness" in the painting practice of mentally ill patients. One characteristic aspect is stereotypes: the drawing is tirelessly repeated, sometimes in an identical way or with infinite variations. The phenomenon of stuffing is another structural element: the patient fills the surface to be painted by juxtaposed or superimposed patterns by constantly adding new patterns. Other features are fragmentation, the scattering of patterns, and the distortion of the representations. The tendency to stylization is often dependent on a repetition of forms.

According to Delay and Volmat (1956), the intrapsychic dissociation observed in schizophrenia is found in patients' works under different aspects: change of style or technique, violent contrast of colors, distortion of perspective, bizarreness of subjects, heterogeneous assemblages. The symbolic richness of the works of the mentally ill has been the subject of detailed analyses. Every object can become a symbol— a tree, mountain, road, house, mask, hand: the list is inexhaustible. Themes encountered outside the nonexplicitly psychopathological area such as landscape, portraits, or scenes of life are topics relating to sex, realistic or obscene, but especially symbolic, such as weddings or births. Mystical and religious themes are common. There is a propensity for dehumanization, metamorphosis, and depersonalization. The body is transformed and modified, resulting in representations of humans in an animal, plant, machine, or mineral form, or as a pure abstraction. These various phenomena are found in myths and tales. In this sense psychopathological art is akin to dreams and inspired by mythology.

Freud and other psychoanalysts used the discoveries of anthropologists concerning magical-archaic thoughts and experiences of "primitive peoples" to better understand the abnormal psychic phenomena and the functions of the "deep psychic layers." A schizophrenic patient is not a primitive being, but nevertheless pathological art is often a fantastic art inspired by myths, religions, and dreams. Carl Jung (1875–1961), a Swiss psychiatrist and psychoanalyst, contributed to the understanding of pathological art by his work on archetypes, considered as universal archaic patterns and images derived from the collective unconscious. Freud insisted that plastic works, like dreams and fantasies, were an expression of desires, often remaining hidden and obeying the laws of displacement, disguise, and condensation.

On a more general level, there is a kinship between psychopathological art and certain other forms of art, such as primitive art, children's art, and modern art with its fantastic painting, surrealism, or cubism. As modern psychiatry has moved from the asylum era to community centers, today we no longer talk about psychopathological art when referring to the artistic production of mentally ill patients. We present some instructive examples of artists—analyzed from psychiatric and neurological viewpoints—to illustrate the many aspects and roots of creativity.

Neurological and psychiatric disorders

We know that psychiatric diseases (as do neurological disorders) arise from abnormal functions in the brain. However, there are major differences between psychiatric and neurological disorders. Mental disorders are characterized by behavioral and mood changes as well as disturbed thoughts. Mental health and wellness are not easily defined: for example, mood swings leading to euphoria or depression are normal experiences. However, in a mental disorder, mood changes and feelings are overwhelming, leading to anxiety and interfering with everyday life, as well as creating difficulties in social interactions and causing significant distress for the subject.

Psychiatric disorders are by and large not related to permanent biochemical or anatomical changes in the brain and are therefore considered to be functional disorders. There are, however, exceptions: in schizophrenia, morphological changes are observed in the brain, with a thinning of the cortex and atrophy of the hippocampus, abnormalities that are correlated with a cognitive decline in the patient (Ho et al. 2003). This is why, based on neuroimaging research, the authors make an argument for a neurological basis of schizophrenia. The same is true for autism spectrum disorders, where neurological comorbidities, in particular motor impairment, sleep disorders, and epilepsy are associated with more severe phenotypes (Jeste 2011).

Neurological disorders tend to produce a specific impairment in a given function, such as sensory or motor difficulties, or problems with language or memory. We now know more about the underlying brain circuits affected in neurological diseases, for instance, in the control of movement, speech, and memory. On the contrary we have a poor mechanism-based understanding of the underlying brain circuits involved in disorders of thoughts and behaviors in schizophrenia, or mood changes in bipolar disorder.

The complex combination of sensory, cognitive, emotional, and motor activities involved in any mental task emphasizes the holistic functioning of the brain in creative processes. Any artistic creation is contextual and influenced by familial, social, and cultural traits. The emotional state of the artist will have a considerable impact on production, ranging from a lack of emotion in autistic patients, to stereotypes in schizophrenic patients or the urge to create in the manic phase of bipolar disorder.

There has been considerable interest in the study of how creativity is influenced by neurological or psychiatric disorders. While it would be naïve to find and attribute simple links between psychiatric or neurological disorders and creativity, there are nevertheless many examples of great artists who suffered from a neurological or psychiatric condition, such as epilepsy for Dostoevsky, stroke for Caspar David Friedrich, and a neurodegenerative disorder for Ravel.

In his biography of **Fyodor Dostoevsky** (1821–1881), Carr (2016) cites the doctor's notes documenting Dostoevsky's epileptic seizures as a young man, especially during his student years. One of these episodes included a rather serious, generalized tonic-clonic (or grand mal) seizure, which was observed by several of Dostoevsky's friends. Dostoevsky made journal descriptions of his seizures. He also narrated how certain triggers, such as a lack of sleep, alcohol consumption, or overwork, induced his seizures. Epilepsy continued to affect his work and literary production throughout his whole life. Dostoevsky wrote about his own experiences, and many of his characters suffered from epileptic seizures. He described the various symptoms of seizures, such as the sensory auras, the sense of déjà vu, and the fatigue felt after a seizure. According to historian Howard Markel,[23] Dostoevsky wrote that he was grateful for his seizure disorder because of the "abnormal tension" the episodes created in his brain, which allowed him to experience "unbounded joy and rapture, ecstatic devotion and completest life." At other times, the author regretted the disability because it had wreaked havoc with his memory. What remains so exceptional about Dostoevsky is that he was able to create such great art out of his illness rather than allow his affliction to determine or defeat him.

Vincent Van Gogh (1853–1890) is one of the most gifted creative artists of all time. There have been various medical theories about the mental state of this tormented artist. A particularly dramatic event in his life was his breakdown in 1888 in Arles, southern France, when van Gogh argued with his friend, Paul Gauguin, and cut off his own ear in an episode of self-mutilation. This was the first of several breakdowns, and he continued to be in and out of hospital until dying of a gunshot wound in 1890 in an apparent suicide. The last two years of his life were characterized by repeated psychotic episodes for which he was hospitalized but recovered in between. There are numerous debates as to the nature of Van Gogh's illness, and it has been suggested that Van Gogh suffered from a bipolar disorder (Carota et al. 2005). Triggering events for these episodes may have been alcohol intoxications, work stress, and the termination of his friendship with Gauguin, which represented a significant personal loss for van Gogh. During his several hospitals stays, he kept painting, receiving support

[23] "For Dostoevsky, Epilepsy Was a Matter of Both Life and Literature," *PBS News*, PBS, November 10, 2017.

from his physicians, Drs Rey and Gachet, and his brother Theo. He created some of his most celebrated paintings such as *Starry Night* (Fig. 1.3) while in the hospital in Saint-Remy. After he left the hospital, moving to Auvers-sur-Oise, close to his brother Theo and to Dr. Gachet, van Gogh was again most productive and created one of his greatest and probably one of his last works, *Wheatfield with Crows*.

Caspar David Friedrich (1774–1840), a German Romantic artist, was the sixth of ten children; he lost his mother at the age of seven and one year later a sister to childhood illness. At the age of thirteen he was traumatized by witnessing his brother Johann's death by drowning in a frozen lake. Years later, he lost another sister to typhus. These cumulative traumatic life experiences may have been the origin of his depressive episodes or contributed to his melancholic and manic mood states. He was known as the "taciturn man from the North." Of the oil-painting *Woman before the Rising Sun and Woman before the Setting Sun* (1818–20) Friedrich quotes: "All authentic art is conceived at a sacred moment and nourished in a blessed hour; an inner impulse creates it, often without the artist being aware of it."[24]

He believed in the beauty of nature, considering that the majesty of the natural world could only reflect the magnificence of God. He portrayed sunlit vistas and foggy expanses to convey the beautiful power of the divine.

In the magnificent painting *Two Men Contemplating the Moon* (1825–1830) (Fig. 7.1), human figures and nature are symbolized together. Interpretations of the paintings are manifold: do the two persons represent the painter and his wife Caroline? Or is Friedrich himself painted on the right with his younger friend and disciple, August Heinrich? Is the uprooted tree—an oak, which goes through many changes in its life cycle and can reach an age of 1,000 years—confronted with death? Yet the tree is painted in front of a bright sky, illuminated by the moon.

When in 1837 he stood before the paintings *Two Men Contemplating the Moon* and *A Man and Woman Contemplating the Moon* Samuel Beckett was visually inspired for the writing of his play *Waiting for Godot*. "This was the source of waiting for Godot, you know," Beckett said (Knowlson 1996, 378). Allusions to the influence the painting had on the play can be observed in the setting of the opening scene: *A country road. A tree. Evening.* And at the end of Act 1: *the moon standing still, shedding a pale light.*

Friedrich's repeated depressive episodes were associated with diminished or altered creativity. In 1835, at the age of sixty, he suffered his first stroke, which led to a right-sided paralysis and greatly reduced his ability to paint. His last oil painting *Seashore by Moonlight* (1835–36) was described as the "darkest of all his shorelines, in which richness of tonality compensates for the lack of his former finesse" (Vaughan 2004). Friedrich was forced to return to watercolors and small formats. He probably suffered from a poststroke depression resulting in an accumulation of death symbols in his late work. He became lonely and lived his last years in poverty (Siegel 1978).

[24] "Caspar David Friedrich," Artnet, accessed December 13, 2020, http://www.artnet.com/artists/caspar-david-friedrich/.

Figure 7.1 Caspar Friedrich. *Two Men Contemplating the Moon* (ca.1825–1830). Oil on canvas.

The famous composer **Maurice Ravel** (1875–1937) is thought to have suffered from primary progressive aphasia, a rare neurological syndrome that affects the ability to communicate, express thoughts, and understand or find words. His final compositions, such as *Bolero*, one of his most played works, has an extraordinary rhythmic complexity. The *Piano Concerto for the Left Hand* (1929–1930), written for Paul Wittgenstein who had lost his right arm during World War I, has a striking irregular style and is technically very demanding to play. While these works were written when Ravel may have already showed subtle signs of cognitive decline, they are still among the most interesting of his compositions. He eventually lost his wonderful creativity and ability to compose when his aphasia became evident. In September 1933, at age fifty-eight, four years before his death, he spoke of his planned opera *Jeanne d'Arc* to one of his friends: "I will never write my Jeanne d'Arc; this opera is here, in my head, I hear it, but I will never write it. It's over, I can no longer write my music" (Amaducci et al. 2002).

The mechanisms leading to creativity are poorly understood and the capacity for creativity is ubiquitous. In trying to decompose the different elements leading to creativity, one of the primary competences is the ability or the skill required to solve a specific problem or achieve a particular goal. In the case of a neurological disorder, where a given function is impaired (such as movements in Friedrich's stroke or speech with resulting aphasia in Ravel's neurodegenerative disorder), the artist is incapacitated, and his production becomes severely compromised. Another main factor for creative expression is the ability to let one's mind wander and freely associate. Thus, access to hidden resources or unconscious thoughts or feelings seems to be an essential feature of any creative process. Whether people with mental disorders have different associative capacities and better access to unconscious thoughts or feelings is an idea that is often suggested but remains questionable. Surrealist artists have for their part tried to escape aesthetic norms by refusing social constraints and—by this move—believed they reached a liberated state that allowed them to be better aware of unconscious feelings.

Many artists, as we show in subsequent chapters, are tormented subjects and we believe that another important motivation of the creative process is the unraveling of unresolved conflicts often as part of a grieving process after a loss, going back to early life events, or following recent traumatic experiences. Thus, artistic creation tends to seek a way out and may be part of a healing process.

Chapter 8

PSYCHOPATHOLOGICAL ART AND MODERN ART

Introduction

At the beginning of the twentieth century, when psychiatrists became interested in the artworks of patients interned in psychiatric hospitals, they used the term "psychopathological art." We have described how Hans Prinzhorn in Germany and Robert Vollmat in France established art collections of patients' works and through their publications proposed a detailed analysis on the links between mental illness and artistic creation (Prinzhorn 1972, Volmat 1956).

As psychiatric hospitals opened themselves to the outside world and works by mental patients were shown to the public, departments of psychopathological art were established within these institutions. While at the beginning discussions focused on psychopathological aspects, artistic values and aesthetic emotions were also taken into consideration. These departments—originally focused on the conservation function of the works of patients (or patient-artists)—opened themselves to a therapeutic function and theoretical research; eventually art studios and art workshops were established in psychiatric hospitals.

Works produced by patients in the context of art therapy reinforce creative processes in the patient and stimulate exchanges between a patient and his therapist. Most of the works created in art therapy do not have a priori an artistic interest but should be considered as projections of psychic states. The interest of psychiatrists in the artworks of mentally ill patients helped ascribe true artistic value to certain works. It must, however, be remembered that true artists are just as rare among patients as they are in the general population.

Previously developed psychoanalytic and aesthetic theories had already demonstrated that plastic art and paintings could be considered as a means to approach the hidden or the unconscious. Following Freud and Jung, who through their teaching on symbolization and the exploration of the unconscious brought new insights to the understanding of the links between our inner mental life and our compulsion to create, the surrealist movement that began in the 1920s explored painting techniques that allowed the expression of unconscious feelings.

The surrealists challenged the tradition of academic art and were looking for new creative avenues. They found inspiration in the works of Freud and Prinzhorn. Prinzhorn's richly illustrated book showing the artworks of patients was a particular source of inspiration for surrealist painters such as Max Ernst, Giorgio de Chirico, Joan Miro, René Magritte, and Salvador Dali. The naïve scenery and the often-strange composition depicted in patients' artwork, full of symbolism and fantastic and ambiguous visual images, made a strong impression on the surrealist painters. Surrealist artists were interested in the world of legends, myths, dreams, and symbols.

The similarities between the works of mental patients and modern art were reemphasized by Dubuffet in the 1940s (see below). He was also inspired by Prinzhorn's book when he founded the art brut movement and included hundreds of compositions of patients and artists in his collection. Comparisons with works of Chagall, Matisse, and Picasso can be made, but often the naïve character of the paintings of art brut artists are reminiscent of primitive art found in the artifacts of tribes in Africa, Asia, or South America. Structuralism and structural anthropology, as pioneered by French anthropologist Claude Lévi-Strauss (1908–2009), proposed that there are universal laws governing myths in all societies. The similarities between cultural characteristics in different societies, primitive or advanced, find support in modern ideas on the biological roots of culture. Common behavioral strategies, as well as similar cultural instruments and practices are thought to play an important homeostatic, almost therapeutic role in helping individuals in all societies to navigate an often uncertain and menacing world. This is particularly relevant for psychotic patients living in isolation and suffering from fears, delusions, and hallucinations. Their art is inspired by their own fantasized and frightening world. By expressing disturbing feelings and strangeness in their artwork, they are able to discharge themselves of their distress and terror. As they are untrained as artists, their work is often naïve, showing similarities to that of children and artists from primitive societies. Similarly, modern artists, like surrealists or cubists, draw inspiration for their creativity from their unconscious fantasies.

We follow here the opinion of Eric Kandel (2018), who when writing about creativity and mental illness states:

> By viewing psychotic states as totally foreign to normal behavior, we fail to recognize that such states are often dramatic representations of character types or temperaments found in the general population—and often

found to a greater degree in the minds of creative thinkers, scientists and artists. That said, people with a brain disorder may very well have readier access to certain aspects of their unconscious than people who are not mentally ill. That difference is particularly critical in terms of creativity. Equally important, the ready accessibility of a mentally ill person to the creativity of his or her unconscious world can be emulated, as surrealist artists have attempted to show (148).

Art brut and outsider art

The term "art brut" was coined by the French painter Jean Dubuffet (1901–1985) for art created by people living in institutions such as psychiatric hospitals and prisons (Thévoz 1975). He was influenced by the German psychiatrist Hans Prinzhorn, who has already been mentioned for his influential book published in Germany in 1922. He worked at the psychiatric hospital at the University of Heidelberg and was also an art historian. He dedicated much of his efforts to expanding an earlier collection of art created by the mentally ill and started by the famous German psychiatrist Emil Kraepelin (1856–1926). Prinzhorn's book was lavishly illustrated and was concerned with the borders between psychiatry and art. It represents one of the first attempts to analyze the work of the mentally ill from a psychopathological point of view. It did not draw much attention outside the psychiatric community when it was published, until Jean Dubuffet, an art visionary (Picon 1973), who as an artist experimented with all kinds of art forms and materials (Fig. 8.1) and gave his works unusual forms and surfaces, discovered Prinzhorn's book. Together with other artists and writers, notably Jean Paulhan, André Breton, and Michel Tapié, he established the *Compagnie de l'Art Brut* in Paris in 1948. This association was devoted to the discovery, documentation, and exhibition of art produced outside the mainstream of artistic culture by artists avoiding traditional conventions. In the beginning, the art brut movement was only known to a small group of interested people and had difficulties in establishing itself. Not well accepted in France, Dubuffet moved his collection to the United States in 1951. The Filipino American abstract painter Alfonso Ossorio (1916–1990) agreed to house the collection in his residence in East Hampton, near New York, where it remained for ten years. Thereafter the works were repatriated and exhibited in a townhouse in Paris. The collection developed extensively: Dubuffet traveled to Switzerland and brought back paintings by artists such as Aloïse Corbaz and Adolf Wölfli (to be discussed later), who produced stunning artworks while they were hospitalized in mental institutions. In 1971 Dubuffet donated his art brut collection comprising some 5,000 pieces to the City of Lausanne, and his collection was housed in the Château de Beaulieu in Lausanne. The *Collection de l'Art Brut* opened to the public in 1976. Dubuffet did not want a museum in the classical sense and his art collection is often referred to

Figure 8.1 Jean Dubuffet. *La vision Tisserande* (1976). Acrylic and assembly of papers pasted on canvas.

as a "museum without walls." According to Kent Minturn (2004), "such a collection transcended national and ethnic boundaries and broke down barriers between nationalities and cultures" (255). What Dubuffet did by creating the art brut movement was to take the artworks of mentally ill patients out of the psychiatric archives, where they had been kept as part of a psychopathological art form, and into an aesthetic and cultural field of their own, away from their former psychiatric frame where they had previously been held. The *Collection de l'Art Brut* in Lausanne was the first public exhibition of its kind and encouraged the spread of this art movement in Europe (Peiri 2012).

By art brut, Dubuffet originally meant an art movement represented by artists untouched by mainstream cultural actors. This distinction was often arbitrary, as artists

Figure 8.2 Louis Soutter. *Volagie* (1937). Black ink on paper.

like Louis Soutter[25] (Fig. 8.2), who maintained relationships with traditional artists, was considered by Dubuffet to belong to the art brut movement. In 1952 the American abstract expressionist Alfonso Ossorio (1916–1990) exhibited art brut artists alongside works of such unconventional artists as Jackson Pollock (1912–1956), famous for his drip paintings, and Willem De Koonig (1904–1997), who created sculptures so extravagantly crude that they seem to come from an art brut artist. Dubuffet's original view that art brut did not belong in museums and should have no part in the art market turned out to be untenable. Influenced by Dubuffet but seeking a less restrictive definition, the British art critic Roger Cardinal coined the term "outsider art" in 1972. This expression encountered a tremendous success and is now used very broadly to characterize art created by people who are outside the mainstream of the "art world" or "art gallery system." Outsider art became a label for very successful exhibitions, literary and artistic productions, and a growing art market not only in English-speaking countries but worldwide. As Tansella (2007) remarked, "Outsider Art understood

[25] *Louis Soutter* (1871–1942) was a Swiss painter and graphic artist. He produced most of his work while under care in a hospice in Ballaigues, Vaud. His famous cousin Le Corbusier recognized his skills and helped him in his artistic endeavors.

as artistic category, became after the seventies a convenient and popular label for the classification of any artwork born far from the fine arts, and—from the moment it was exported in the United States—started losing its original meaning as intended by Dubuffet" (134). Tansella makes the point that although Dubuffet's contribution in recognizing a novel art form is indisputable, a strict definition of art brut as proposed by Dubuffet was no longer defensible. The obvious explanation is to be found in the profound changes that have occurred in our society and especially in psychiatry. Dubuffet was interested in artistic productions of self-taught artists untouched by culture, and he found them in particular in psychiatric hospitals, where patients were kept in social isolation. Since Dubuffet's time, psychiatry has witnessed marked changes: today patients are hospitalized for shorter periods, and the aim of community health services is to reinsert them rapidly into their neighborhood, fostering contacts with the outside world.

Art brut and outsider art today

The idea of art brut was based on certain social characteristics, such as artworks produced in ateliers in psychiatric institutions and on particular concepts and styles. The art brut movement, as defined by Dubuffet, can no longer be found in its original form, but its essence and spirit remain. Today there are still artists living on the margins of society and working outside the mainstream artistic scene, who are less dependent on artistic norms. Outsider art has become the common denominator for all artists working outside the system of fine art and comprises categories such as art brut, folk art, marginal art, and visionary art. In 1989 John Maizels founded the magazine *Raw Vision*[26] as a forum for the work of self-taught artists. According to Maizels, the term "raw vision" denotes particular attributes such as the intensity and purity of the vision of artists working outside accepted cultural norms, bringing a unique freshness to their work.

Outsider art is very fashionable today: there are large collections of works by art brut/outsider artists in museums and galleries throughout the world, and there are many museums that showcase extensive art brut collections. The *Museum Gugging* in Vienna, originally founded in 1981 by the Austrian psychiatrist Leo Navratil as a place for art therapy, called the Center for Art and Psychotherapy, is now a cultural center with a museum. The Lille Métropole Museum of Modern, Contemporary and Outsider Art (LAM), in Lille, France, which opened in 1983 has a rich collection of outsider art. An exhibition *Danser brut*[27] explored the relationships between the field of dance and motion with the art brut movement. The American Folk-Art Museum in New York presents works by self-taught artists through exhibitions, publications, and educational programs. A recent exhibition featured outsider artists as storytellers (Rousseau 2018).

[26] *Raw Vision* is a British magazine devoted to outsider art and an important international platform.
[27] Exhibition catalogue, LAM, Villeneuve-D'ascq, France, 2018.

Outsider art fairs are regularly held in cities like Paris and New York, and auction houses frequently organize public sales of outsider art. Outsider art has entered the trade system, and one has to recognize that the art brut movement, created by Dubuffet, which for a long time remained outside the realms of profit, is now part of the art market and of the same commercial system as modern art, though its prices are still far below those of works of contemporary art.

After World War II had ended, Dubuffet began collecting works from untrained, socially marginalized, often institutionalized and emotionally disturbed artists. While critics maintained that the works produced by these psychiatric patients were not fully "art," but belonged to a category called psychopathological art, Dubuffet recognized the true artistic value of these works. Between 1966 and 1978, Sandoz, a Swiss pharmaceutical company that produced anti-psychotic medication, published a series of twenty-three folders entitled *Psychopathology and Pictorial Expression.* Each folder contained high-quality, color reproductions of art brut works, along with commentaries by leading psychiatrists. The illustrations made some of the most fascinating treasures of the Prinzhorn and art brut collections accessible. We would like to illustrate, by making use of this international iconographical collection, the extraordinary life and exceptional richness of the artistic production of two art brut artists, Adolf Wölfli and Aloïse Corbaz, affected with mental illness and diagnosed with schizophrenia, who spent their entire adult life in psychiatric institutions in Switzerland.

Adolf Wölfli (1864–1930)

Walter Morgenthaler (1882–1965) was a Swiss psychiatrist and psychotherapist. His publication in 1921 of the medical history of the schizophrenic artist Adolf Wölfli, hospitalized in a psychiatric clinic in Waldau near Bern, produced quite a sensation (Morgenthaler 1921). In his monograph, Morgenthaler described in great detail the artistic output of his patient, for whom he had cared while he was hospitalized. He was also familiar with the research of Hans Prinzhorn, who in 1919 was mandated to organize and enlarge the collection of psychotic art at the Psychiatric Clinic in Heidelberg. Prinzhorn's book was published in 1922, one year after Morgenthaler's book. In his book Prinzhorn lists Wölfli, including a color reproduction of a drawing he had received from Morgenthaler.

Morgenthaler's monograph raised a great deal of interest in artistic and intellectual circles: a number of avant-garde artists began collecting similar works, setting the stage for Jean Dubuffet's later movement. The German poet Rainer Maria Rilke bought Morgenthaler's book and sent it to Lou Andreas-Salomé in Göttingen, together with a long letter which is often quoted: "Apparently, the impulse to order, the most relentless among the creative forces, is elicited most forcefully by two kinds of inner states: by a feeling of inner superabundance and by a person's total inner collapse, which in turn also generates a superabundance. … The Wölfli case will help us some day to gain new insights about the origins of creativity and it also makes contributions to the strange, apparently growing realization how many of the symptoms of the illness (as Morgenthaler suspects) ought to be supported because they bring to the open the rhythm through which nature is striving to reclaim that which has been alienated from it and to bring into a new melodious congruence." Andreas-Salomé replied: "What must have moved you vehemently is, I imagine, the remarkable fact that the compulsive productive urge of the creative artist clearly reappears in the schizophrenic. The book I immediately recommended highly to Freud" (Baumann 1997).

Biography

Adolf Wölfli was born in Bowil, a village in the Bernese Emmental, Switzerland, in 1864, the youngest of seven children. The same year, the family moved to Bern. The father was a stonecutter and was known to be a heavy drinker. In about 1870, Wölfli's father abandoned the family. The mother earned her livelihood as a washerwoman, and Wölfli grew up in dire poverty. In 1872, together with his ailing mother, Wölfli was resettled by the authorities in the family's community of origin Schangnau, in Emmental, where the community took over their financial support. After the death of his mother in 1873, he was placed in foster families where he was often physically and emotionally abused. Wölfli had very little schooling, was shy and withdrawn, and became an itinerant farm worker.

According to the autobiography he wrote at the beginning of his hospitalization in Waldau, in daydreams he would long for tenderness: "Often on Sunday I cried for hours in a corner thinking about my dead mother." He wrote that he suffered from a serious illness, apparently scarlet fever. As a result of this disease his mood became unstable: at times as gay as a finch and at others feeling numb and sinking in a deep torpor, "according to weather changes" (Spoerri 1964, np).

At age eighteen, while working on a farm, he fell in love with the daughter of a neighbor, but her parents forbid this relationship. Wölfli wrote about his profound disappointment: "I felt sad and even melancholy; I did not know what to do. That same evening, I was rolling in the snow in prey to a burning heartache, crying over the happiness that was so brutally ripped away" (Morgenthaler 1964, np). In 1890 Wölfli was arrested for attempted sexual assault on two young girls and sentenced to two years in prison. Following his release, he worked as a laborer in Bern and surrounding areas, in increasing social isolation and hardship. In 1895 Wölfli was again arrested for attempting to molest a very young girl. In order to examine his mental state, he was committed to the Waldau Mental Asylum, near Bern, for evaluation. There he was diagnosed as schizophrenic and remained a patient until his death in 1930. Profoundly psychotic, suffering from severe visual and auditory hallucinations and often violent, he was held in solitary confinement for several years. Toward the end of 1899 he started to draw, compose, and write poems, activities which calmed him. In 1904, when his acute psychosis had to some degree subsided, he regularly made drawings, initially in pencil and later in colored pencils. His drawings quickly engaged the attention of the hospital staff, particularly of his psychiatrist, Walter Morgenthaler, who encouraged and supplied him with materials, and purchased a number of his works. When Morgenthaler's book was published in 1921, the works of Wölfli were for the first time publicly exhibited and eventually his art became known to a wide European audience. Jean Dubuffet discovered the work of Adolf Wölfli in 1945 and called him "le grand Wölfli." The surrealist artist André Breton considered Wölfli's oeuvre one of the three or four most important works of the twentieth century.

Artistic production

The artistic production of Wölfli comprises writings, poems, and drawings. His art is difficult to follow and to understand; suffering from delusions of grandeur he often signed his works "St. Adolf II." Driven by an irresistible impulse, he executed hundreds of drawings. He wrote a gigantic autobiography; his accumulated notebooks make up a pile more than two meters high. He described in words and pictures the fantastic journeys he undertook in his imaginary world, leading him on a fantasized peregrination, going to Africa and meeting heroic and famous figures like queens and kings.

Wölfli's works are composed of richly colored drawings, usually backed by lengthy, grandiose, and often incomprehensible pseudo-autobiographical texts; they often include musical passages scored in a notation of his own devising. He made with his own hands a trumpet to play the arias he had composed himself. His drawings are characterized by features such as complete filling of available space, flat design without perspective, additions of writings, and the stereotyped repetition of ornaments. The form and content of his work borrow from the contributions of folk art and of primitive or archaic paintings. His scenic compositions include small figures, human or animal beings. Inspired by his own life and fantasized inner world, he turned to social or religious themes, sexual or aggressive subjects, together with magical objects or symbols. He also drew landscapes or complex architectural constructions.

The Sessions of the Swiss Plateau 1904 is a black and white drawing belonging to his first period (Fig. 8.3). The theme is the condemnation of Wölfli himself for a sexual offense, to which the scenes distributed in the corners of the drawing relate. Multiple figures appear as miniatures, interwoven by garlands carrying enigmatic inscriptions, and the title of the painting is written on the frame of the picture *Assiisen des Mittellandes 1904*. Among these figures one can recognize (at the top-right) a female figure, no doubt the victim (under the raised skirt, we can distinguish her genitals). Wölfli himself appears at the bottom-left as a devil, wearing a kind of bonnet with bells and with an erect penis. Typical is the complete use of the available space. There is a solid framing with black and dotted ribbons, in which stellar ornaments are arranged.

In 1916 Wölfli drew a series of images dedicated to his hometown of Bern with colored pencils, which he would use from that point on for all his works. The cathedral (Fig. 8.4), the houses, and the hotels all receive the name of Saint Adolphe, as Wölfli named himself. Every human head in this drawing is wearing an eye mask.

Figure 8.3 Adolf Wölfli. *Assiisen des Mittel Landes* (1904). Pencil on paper.

Figure 8.4 Adolf Wölfli. *West Frontt des Zehntheiligen Skt. Adolf Kathedral Schiffes* (1916). Pencil and colored pencil.

There are strange shapes like stretched ovals, representing snails with a black eye and ear. These motifs could, according to Spoerri (1964), represent the visual and auditory hallucinations from which Wölfli suffered.

Holirod 1927 refers to Holyrood Palace, the official residence of the British monarch in Scotland, where Maria Stuart lived and was executed (Fig. 8.5). The central medallion shows Wölfli surrounded by a circle. Toward the periphery of the drawing are four oval medallions each depicting two faces. In addition, there are four cup-shaped medallions containing a confederate cross and a violin. The geometric construction of successive circles and ovals is reminiscent of the mandala, which in Hindu and Buddhist symbolism is a circular figure that represents the universe. The circle leads back into itself and is thus a symbol of unity and, according to Jung, a protective symbol, a kind of antidote for chaotic mental states. Rilke spoke of Wölfli as the "insane one" who through his work finds a new "harmony."

Wölfli stayed at Waldau until his death in 1930. His fertile imagination pushed him to compose, write, and draw up until the end of his life. His final drawings are entitled *X-rays,* performed after radiographs were taken for his gastric carcinoma; they represent Wölfli himself on the operating table, surrounded by doctors at the surgical clinic.

Figure 8.5 Adolf Wölfli. *Holirod* (1927). Colored pencil on paper.

In the years after his death, his drawings were carefully studied and exhibited in museums and galleries worldwide (Spoerri and Glaesemer 1976; Esman 2004). Much of his work, together with his vast handwritten autobiography and other writings, is preserved by the Adolf Wölfli Foundation in the Museum of Fine Arts in Bern, Switzerland.

Aloïse Corbaz (1886–1964)

Hans Steck (1891–1980), a Swiss professor of psychiatry at the University of Lausanne, took great interest in the creations produced by his patients, especially by those in the Cery psychiatric hospital near Lausanne, where he began working in 1920 and was later appointed director. He played a major role, together with Jacqueline Porret-Forel (1916–2014), a young doctor working under his supervision, in the discovery of the works by Aloïse Corbaz, a patient hospitalized in Cery and later confined to La Rosière, an establishment for chronic mentally ill patients, in Gimel, a village in the canton of Vaud (Steck 1975). It was the exceptional visual quality of Aloïse's work, as well as its aesthetic impact, that Hans Steck came to appreciate in her production. He encouraged Jacqueline Porret-Forel to devote her medical thesis to the artist, which was published with the title *Aloyse or the Magical Painting of a Schizophrenic* (Forel 1953). She visited Aloïse regularly when she was confined in La Rosière, bringing her drawing material, and accompanied her until her death. Porret-Forel devoted herself to the study of every aspects of Aloïse's work and in 1947 brought it to the attention of Dubuffet. She published several scholarly works (Forel and Mac Gregor 2014) and lectured extensively. Her account of the life and work of Aloïse, as well as of her personal relationship with the artist, became the subject of a documentary film (Edelstein 2000).

Biography

Aloïse Corbaz, born in 1886 in Lausanne, died in 1964 after having been confined for forty-six years in a psychiatric institution. She was raised in a family of seven children. Her father was a post-office employee, who was said to be a drinker. Aloïse was twelve years old when her mother died, and an older sister took over the role of the mother. Aloïse attended a senior girl's school. She developed artistic gifts, loved music, sang in the church choir, took private music and singing lessons, and dreamt of becoming a singer. But instead she went on to look after children in a family. Described as being reserved and with mystical tendencies, she spread religious propaganda. According to some sources, she fell in love with a theology student, a relationship not accepted by her family. In 1911, at the age of twenty-five, she went to Germany as an au pair, working first in a family in Leipzig, before eventually moving to Potsdam, where she lived with the family of the chaplain of Emperor William II at Sans-Souci Castle. On Sunday she sung works by Handel for the Emperor in the castle's chapel. The outbreak of World War I took her by surprise, and she had to return to Switzerland under difficult conditions.

On her return home, her family was alarmed by Aloïse's poor physical condition and her disturbed mental state. She started to write religious tracts and pretended she could preach like a clergyman and had the power to heal people. She claimed to be engaged to a well-known professor of theology and was convinced she was pregnant. Her behavior became erratic: she cried aloud in the streets and fantasized that she, her husband, and children had been stolen and that people wanted to kill her. She also started to write profusely, addressed letters to famous people such as Emperor Wilhelm II, and distributed propaganda against the military. Her behavior became more and more unpredictable and aggressive, including toward her family, who asked for her admission to the psychiatric hospital of Cery. She entered the institution in 1918.

In the hospital she was at first quiet, but—in recounting her experiences—she rapidly expressed delusional ideas with a mystic content and ideas of grandeur, presenting herself as the "Emperor of Peace." She presented with delirious ideas, dissociation of language, neologisms, and maniform flight of ideas. She was diagnosed as suffering from schizophrenia. The Swiss psychoanalyst Raymond de Saussure, who underwent an analysis with Sigmund Freud and also took care of Aloïse, noticed her intense sensitivity and strong emotional feelings, which were hidden behind a frozen mask. She remained in the Cery psychiatric hospital for two years. She never received electroshocks, which came into use in the late 1930s, nor anti-psychotic drugs, which only became available in the 1950s.

In October 1920, she was transferred to La Rosière, a newly opened clinic that cares for chronic psychiatric patients. In the following years, her mental state worsened, and her dissociative thoughts increased. She was agitated, seized by states of erotic excitement involving obscene speech, aggressiveness, and physical violence, which were directed mainly at the medical personnel. She developed a graphomania in a handwriting that was difficult to read, and her speech became at times an incomprehensible mumble.

From 1925 on, her aggressive behavior decreased, and she eventually adjusted to the hospital's daily routine. She led a withdrawn life and, in an autistic fashion, started drawing and writing poetic reminiscences with stereotyped words on scraps of paper. Gradually she was given regular work, such as sewing and ironing, and in parallel her creative activity developed and became a regular occupation, which was sustained by a formidable inner compulsion.

Pictorial production

Aloïse's lifetime production is prodigious; she painted close to two thousand pictures.[28] She was very generous, often giving her paintings as soon as she produced them. It was as if she wanted to free herself in order to create something new.

[28] An electronic catalog of Aloïse's works is available in the SIK-ISEA website.

Her first drawings, done in black pencil and dating back to 1919, one year after her hospitalization, were rigid and static, but of high calligraphic quality. Her meticulous and accomplished realization already indicated great skill and drawing talent—Figure 8.6 portrays a woman, the wife of a medical director at the Cery clinic.

Figure 8.6 Aloïse. *Lulu Mater dolorosa*. Pencil drawing (ca.1917–1924).

Aloïse catches the likeness of her subject, a woman of statuesque beauty. The inscription "mater dolorosa" is probably an allusion to the death of the woman's son, who was killed in the war. In this portrait the eyes are still uncovered, that is, without the mask-like appearance which characterized her subsequent work. The curly hair and the small heads below are the first intimations of the rich ornamentation typical of her later art.

When she was given color crayons and paper, she plunged herself into an artistic fervor. She worked quickly, often mixing the color of her crayon with saliva. While working she was quiet and appeared less anxious. At first, she used drawing blocks, but then changed over to larger formats, using wrapping papers, until she was given new sheets of a larger size. However, they were still not big enough for her, so she sewed them together into rolls reaching up to fourteen meters in length. They were painted in lush colors on both sides with pictures featuring grandiose theatrical themes.

Taking her work as a whole, it is clear that one of the main themes of her artistic creation, and the focus of her thoughts and feelings, is love, particularly erotic love. The world of Aloïse is feminized with exaggerated sexuality, as can be found in the pictures of Klimt. The eroticism is intimately woven together with mysticism. In the style of medieval pictures, she often placed enigmatic inscriptions on her paintings. The basic subject of her pictures remains the pair of lovers. The woman is usually featured as a voluptuous character (Fig. 8.7), whereas the man, unless he is a famous figure such as Napoleon (Fig. 8.8) or the Pope, is depicted as a singular small figure, an auxiliary, sometimes confined to a medallion or necklace, clearly revealing Aloïse's sense of irony. The inscriptions on her pictures show that she identified herself with the characters of famous and tragic women: Cleopatra, Mary Queen of Scots, Marie-Antoinette, Josephine, Lucrezia Borgia, Ophelia, Manon Lescaut, and many others. Among the male figures are Francois I, de Gaulle, Mozart, the Swiss General Henry Guisan, different popes, William II of Germany, and of course Napoleon. Her rendering does not aim at historical similitude, with exceptions, such as Napoleon.

The way Aloïse portrays women is particularly striking, presenting them as the great lady, the seductress. The richly ornamented deep-cut dresses, revealing prominent breasts, which turn into red roses; the genitalia, which are drawn as camelias; and the womb, depicted as a fruit basket or a bird's nest containing eggs, are testimony to her unbridled imagination. The woman is at the same time the sphinx, the unapproachable one. She is also the mother goddess or great Venus in the form of a monumental nude, richly ornamented, revealing three breasts such as are seen in the statuettes of Hindu deities.

The eyes are a particularly striking feature of the faces drawn by Aloïse. They are usually hidden behind a blue cover, giving a mask-like theatrical illusion. This is in line with the dramatic representativeness of the beautifully dressed up and idealized couples, but in fact, they are something other than masks; although the eyes are visible, they do not show the brilliance of the pupil. The gaze is dissociated from sight: these eyes, uniformly tinged with blue, do not see. They are hidden eyes, which the viewer cannot observe, thus giving the characters a sense and feeling of strangeness. It

Figure 8.7 Aloïse. *Enleve le manteau royal de la sirène*. An imposing picture dominated by the majestic lady. The man, looking small, is in the back (ca. 1941–1951). Colored pencil, paper in notebook.

Figure 8.8 Aloïse. *Le fiancé à la rose Schwilge sur son cœur*. A picture of Napoleon in a long blue coat. Kneeling by him is his favorite love offering him a rose (ca. 1941–1951). Colored pencil on paper.

suggests that Aloïse is projecting into her characters a detachment from the real world (Boissière 2018). It contributes effectively to the feeling of bizarreness that seizes us in front of these large drawings worked with colored pencils or chalks that constitute the paintings of Aloïse. Angels and princesses, students and mermaids, queens and kings, which she likes to present in a multicolored parade, all have one thing in common: a blue cover blinds the eyes, leaving a mysterious look. The environment in which she puts her characters is full of anachronisms, giving her the liberty to manage her figures according to her imagination.

Aloïse had an exceptional memory, and her creative work did not appear ex nihilo but had multiple sources, for instance, famous paintings that she could only have seen as reproductions as she never left Switzerland apart from her stay in Germany. The consecration of the emperor Napoleon by David, held in the Louvre museum, inspired her (Porret-Forel and Muzelle 2012). Aloïse made numerous drawings on the theme of the Adoration of the Magi, and there are clear analogies to the eponymous religious work of the Spanish painter Francisco de Zurbarán.

Thematically Aloïse continually developed new ideas. This is particularly evident in all the small details present in her pictures. The way she represents vehicles is particularly interesting: coaches, in which her figures are sitting or standing, are drawn by horses, depicted in a curiously flat perspective. There are splendid carriages, two-wheeled carts, boats, gondolas, steamers, railway coaches, in which her romantic, amorous scenes are set. Her pictures are also full of small accessory figures, an entire bestiary of horses, birds, peacocks, butterflies, elephants, sphinxes, or sirens, giving a surprising metamorphic flux.

Aloïse knew the symbolic and emotional value of colors: red, the most commonly used color certainly has an erotic significance. Blue is restful, green is, as she herself says, "spiritual." For example, when drawing the holy family, the dominant colors are green and pale yellow.

Another major theme of Aloïse's paintings are God and Eros. This potent love drive is sometimes spiritualized in pictures, for instance, in *The Holy Family,* where Mary and the Christ Child occupy the center with the inscription *Gloria in excelsis Deo* (Fig. 8.9). In this picture, the links between erotic delusion and religious aspiration come to light very clearly as Mary and another female figure reveal ornamented breasts.

An exceptional and monumental work, considered by many as her masterpiece, is the *Cloisonné du theatre* (the compartmentalized theater). This remarkable scrolled work is unique for its heroic proportions; it measures fourteen meters and is the only work signed by Aloïse. The major divisions are determined either by the stitched connections between pieces of paper or by clearly drawn partitions. When viewed sequentially from top to bottom, the scroll portrays a theatrical performance, which features scenes of Aloïse's typical primordial couple involving a central female figure in various interrelationships with less imposing male figures. It culminates in an immortal Eros and Psyche. Porret-Forel interprets the overall progression of images as a visual narrative of Aloïse's own inner life, leading from the first flowering of love,

Figure 8.9 Aloïse. Drawing depicting Mary in blue and the Christ child surrounded by enigmatic scenery typical of her work, entitled *Gloria in excelsis Deo – Singer Bornod* (ca. 1960–1963). Colored chalk on cardboard.

through stages of passion and separation, eventually leading to a more static couple, to the final ambiguous imagery as a kind of spiritual resurrection (Porret-Forel 2006).

Aloïse was fortunate in her misfortune to have been protected and supported in her artistic endeavor, allowing her to live a peaceful life. Unlike Camille Claudel (see chapter 11), who was confined in a psychiatric hospital and died without taking up her work as a sculptor, for Aloïse the asylum was beneficial and salutary. Particularly gratifying was the recognition of Aloïse in her own canton of Vaud; in 1963 the Cantonal Museum of Fine Arts organized an exhibition honoring her among Swiss women painters and sculptors. Her fame grew steadily, heightened by the praise, texts, and prefaces written about her by poets, art dealers, critics, and artists such as Jean Dubuffet and André Breton. She is now considered as one of the most famous art brut painters. Her work—spanning more than forty years—has been exhibited all over the world, and she has been the subject of multiple essays, books, and analyses.

When we approach the works of art brut artists and those of Aloïse in particular, we cannot avoid the question of the extent to which her art is shaped by her mental disorder. For a long time, the approach, mainly by psychiatrists, was to search in patients' artistic productions for what is specifically schizophrenic. In this context, the status of the work itself, but also the relationship the viewer established with it, was prejudiced. However, even at that time, the exceptional artistic quality of Aloïse's production was recognized. Hans Steck saw similarities in the prolific and expanding surroundings in Aloïse's works with Chagall's magical universe. There is in Aloïse an animation of space that takes on an almost cosmic dimension. Aloïse drew and painted with an immense talent. She put her personal imaginary world down on paper, driven by her creative forces. Her work appeals to us because her artistic formulation succeeds in transcending a personal message, valid for us all (Porret-Forel 1993).

Wölfli's and Aloïse's legacy

The virtually simultaneous publication of Morgenthaler's *Madness and Art* (1921) and Prinzhorn's *Artistry of the Mentally Ill* (1922) touched a large audience and was particularly appealing to avant-garde artists of the period such as Max Ernst, Paul Klee, and later André Breton, Jean Dubuffet, Henri Michaux, and Joan Miro. As modern art movements, such as expressionism and surrealism, aligned their aesthetic positions with "madness" and "psychosis," it rendered the works of patients—kept in psychiatric archives—intelligible as a form of experimental art. Some critics, however, maintained that the works produced by psychiatric patients were not art at all, but only technical productions. Psychoanalyst Ernst Kris believed that the artworks of psychiatric patients were mere artisanal productions, characterized by crowded and repetitive images, psychotic symbols, delusional visions, and primitive technique (Esman 2004b). It is true that Adolf Wölfli crammed his pictures with figures, but so did Pieter Breughel and Hieronymus Bosch. Kris's criticisms appear to be based on his aesthetic views that were strongly influenced by classical and Renaissance models. Similarly, the great art historian Ernst Gombrich had little understanding of abstract or nonfigurative art, which would play a dominant role in the art movements of the twentieth century. Dubuffet on the contrary argued that the artwork of such artists as Wölfli and Aloïse spoke for itself and was as fully Art as any work produced by trained artists, and especially notable, because it was unaffected by the traditions of Western art, the influence of society, or any commercial interest.

Wölfli and Aloïse and many other artists with a disturbed mind teach us that certain forms of creativity arise in association with mental disorders, though creative capability is obviously not dependent on a psychiatric condition, as creativity is universal. We still do not know much about the neurobiological mechanisms of creative processes. What is particularly striking in inventive and original artists with mental disorders, such as Wölfli or Aloïse, is the preservation of particular areas of incredibly imaginative functioning in spite of the presence of severe psychotic states. They appear to be able to wander more freely in unknown territories and seek new connections. Such ability to communicate with the unconscious is shared by all creative people but is particularly striking in artists with mental disorders.

Finally, there are restitutive and healing functions in the creative work of Wölfli and Aloïse. Their productions are clearly autobiographic in their themes and are obviously motivated by their need to deal with conflictual feelings about their family, by concerns about their illness, and by losses they encountered. A knowledge of the context of the work's creation helps us understand their intentions and gives additional meaning. However, they are true artists, and we cannot help but be struck by the unquestionable aesthetic value of their works and admire their artistic skills, even if we are unaware of the details of their personal history.

Today's psychiatric world is far different from that experienced by Wölfli, Aloïse and other artists, all long-term hospitalized psychotic patients and each remarkably creative. The conditions that in the past favored the rare emergence of the spontaneous artistic productions of the mentally ill are no longer available. Brief hospital stays and the now systematic use of anti-psychotic drugs have profoundly changed the way in which mental patients are treated. There is a strong body of evidence that for many patients, drug treatment reduces the risk of relapse and harmful behavior and enables them to live better lives. Others may improve without medication, and the value of psychotherapy to treat mental illness has been increasingly recognized in recent years.

Whatever the circumstances in which an artist lives and works, it is always helpful to consider their intentions and apprehend their aims. We should not forget that even in modern minimalist art, where the purpose appears to reduce the message to the bare minimum, there is always a statement and an attempt to communicate an inner meaning to the viewer.

PART III

Chapter 9

MUSIC

Music expresses ... that which cannot be said and on which it is impossible to be silent.
Victor Hugo (1802–1885)[29]

Music is the art which is most nigh to tears and memory.
Oscar Wilde (1854–1900)[30]

I know that the most joy in my life has come to me from my violin
—I often think in music—I live my daydreams in music.
Albert Einstein (1879–1955)[31]

The origin of musicality

Music is omnipresent in human culture. It has similarities with language in that it is recognized throughout the world. Music perception, like language perception, is an innate capacity that appears early in development. There is an inner "knowledge" of music just as there is an inner "knowledge" of language (Chomsky 2000). The function of music is unique in the sense that unlike language, which allows us to communicate our thoughts or share information, music is concerned with sharing experiences and feelings. Music is a preeminent social media.

[29] Hugo (1886).
[30] Oscar Wilde (2007).
[31] Waldrop (2017).

Music lacks a direct referential meaning such as an idea or concept—so important in language—allowing "listeners of all ages to engage in some form of social or pretend play, projecting imaginative fantasies onto the musical forms that they hear, and forging interpersonal bonds in the process" (Trehub 2003, 672). From a neurohormonal perspective it is thought that the effect of music in creating and strengthening social bonds depends on oxytocin mediated processes, as well as the release of endorphins, both of which are triggered by rhythmic activities (Tarr 2014).

Neuroscientific aspects

Studies in infants show that musical communication exists between babies and their mother before the emergence of propositional speech. With maturation, the diverse emotional-musical communications of the infant separate into two streams—propositional speech flows toward the left hemisphere, while the prosodic-emotional stream flows more forcefully into the right hemisphere. The same rhythmic phrases and affective tones, melodies, and prosody of intentional activity are shared in music and language from their earliest stages through the most complex elaborations. The brain that learns language is not only focused on cognitive tasks but is an organ of intersubjective collaboration and to this end has systems of emotional regulation that are fundamentally musical (Panksepp and Trevarthen 2009).

From a neurophysiological point of view, music has strong links with speech. Neuroimaging studies show that music and speech engage similar overlapping brain regions such as the temporal, parietal, and inferior-frontal areas, including the speech center in the inferior part of the motor cortex and the auditory cortex in the superior temporal gyrus (Fig. 9.1). Music and language are communication systems that utilize similar acoustic cues such as tone, pitch, and rhythm and are perceived as a temporal sequence. Speech and especially music cannot, however, be reduced to a simple sensorimotor processing system. In language, the musical contribution is important, especially in children, for whom speech melody and intonation play such an essential role. Music relates more strongly to emotion than speech. According to Panksepp and Bernatzky (2002), music has particularly strong influences on subcortical emotional systems. The effect of music on our mind results from the interplay of many brain areas.

The connection between music and movement is thought to derive from subcortical areas such as the basal ganglia and the cerebellum. Music is much more suited to inducing synchronous movements than speech and fosters a tight coupling between sound and movement. It can act as a coordinating force at a group level, thus promoting social bonding (Dalla Bella et al. 2013). Importantly, vocal dialects indicate the cultural context of a person.

Music has great emotional power; it is an emotional language that evokes bodily movements and incites us to move or to be moved, helping forge bonds that have similarities to the love that people feel for each other (Panksepp and Bernatzky 2002).

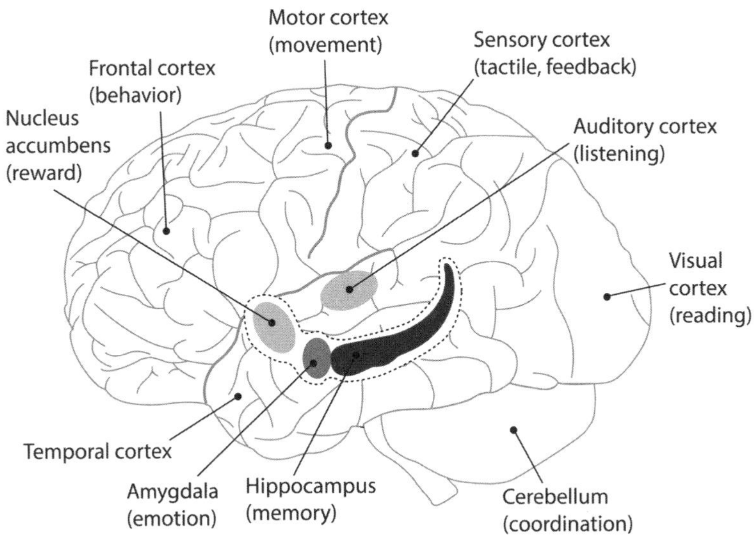

Figure 9.1 The many cortical brain regions engaged in music. In addition, subcortical structures such as the nucleus accumbens, the amygdala, and the hipoccampus are involved (dotted lines signify embedded structures in the brain).

The high affective impact of music stems from the strong interaction between the auditory system and the dopaminergic reward system. Music initiates profound resonance and has a great influence on mood.

Individual appreciation of music is a key factor for the capacity of music-hearing to evoke positive emotions and diminish stress. If music is disapproved of, negative emotions can be aroused. Neuroscientific investigations demonstrate that hearing one's favorite music is related to dopamine activity in the mesolimbic reward system (Jiang et al. 2016; Ferreri et al. 2018).

The neurophysiological study of music lies at the heart of auditory processing by the brain and involves the language system, as well as, most importantly, social, and emotional aspects (Peretz and Coltheart 2003; Sacks 2007). Current research exploring the interrelations between music and language pinpoint both similarities and differences. While processing music and language involves separate brain mechanisms, music and language also share important neural connections (Patel 2008). There is a clear overlap in the brain networks processing acoustic features, but music places a higher demand on the auditory system than ordinary speech. Patel (2014) stresses two aspects that are particularly important for music perception. The first is that music is much more demanding in terms of precision, timing, and temporal processing. Music, for example, requires a much higher precision in tone or pitch perception and in timing than speech. On the other hand, speech communication is not so dependent on subtle acoustic constraints, because it relies on semantic and syntactic content. The second feature of music is its very close connections to emotional systems, such as the mesolimbic circuit and in particular the nucleus accumbens (Blood and Zatorre 2001). The strong interaction between the auditory system and the dopaminergic mesolimbic circuitry is at the root of the rewarding aspect and gratifying sensation when listening to music (Salimpoor et al. 2013).

The impact of sound waves on the basilar membrane within the cochlea of the inner ear makes this membrane resonate in a tonotopic way, and sounds are represented topographically in terms of their frequency.[32] The motion of the basilar membrane causes a depolarization of auditory receptor cells producing an action potential that travels along the auditory nerve. This signal is transmitted through fibers in the brainstem to the auditory cortex. As with all sensations, auditory signals gain perception only when they are processed in cortical areas. The human auditory cortex consists of core areas within the superior part of the temporal lobe. The auditory information coming from the ear is processed, similarly to the visual system, into two main streams, a ventral and a dorsal stream (Fig. 9.2). The ventral stream projects to the ventrolateral prefrontal cortex and is involved in the identification and recognition of complex sounds, in other words, phonemes and words, so-called auditory "objects." The dorsal pathway, projecting to the parietal, premotor, and dorsolateral frontal cortex, is involved in sensory motor perception of sounds and concerned with actions and movements in music and speech. The connection of the dorsal pathway with motor-related areas provides an explanation for why time-related structures in music induce movement in people listening to music. The fact that these two pathways represent bidirectional functional loops targeting several regions of the frontal cortex allows for the integration of auditory information with brain areas involved in planning and organization of motor action, as well as in areas involved in mnesic performances.

In analyzing a melody, the brain extracts the individual tones and pitches that compose it. Sound patterns are extracted and evaluated in different cortical areas involving both the ventral and dorsal streams. The computational algorithms used by the brain allow a perfect music perception, including tonal discrimination, rhythm, resonance, timber, and melodic recognition. This analysis allows a fully expressive and stylistic musical rendering.

We also have a well-developed musical capacity for differentiating musical pieces, which would not be possible if the auditory cortex could not contain memory traces of past musical events. This faculty of retrieving past melodies plays an important role in the pleasure we take in listening to music. When listening to a piece of music, we often compare it to previous musical experiences. We simultaneously can hear what is in our "mind's ear" and what we momentarily perceive with our ears. This interplay between stored musical information and the actual musical piece being heard is an important ingredient in the pleasure we derive from listening to music and depends on a set of reward mechanisms that are explained below.

[32] The frequency range of human hearing includes sounds from about 20 to about 20,000 cycles/second.

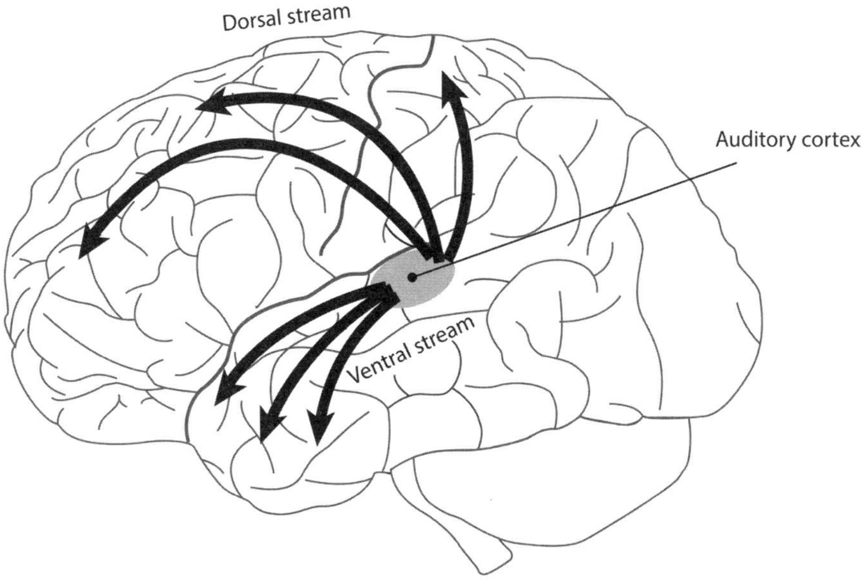

Figure 9.2 The auditory information coming from the ear is processed into a ventral and a dorsal stream. The ventral stream projects to the temporal lobe, the dorsal pathway projects to the parietal areas and frontal cortex. (Adapted from Zatorre 2013).

A faculty for music is not a quality a person either has or does not have. There is no musical center. Rather musical ability is made up of different processing modules, each having the potential to be specialized for music. This functional architecture for music processing allows for the many different musical expressions that exist, as well as for diverse individual musical faculties.

Why do we love music or why is listening to music so rewarding (to use a term very much in vogue in behavioral neuroscience)? For a long time, the subjective experience of listening to music made it difficult to understand the nature of what makes music so likeable. Advances in our understanding of the emotional circuits of the brain, such as the reward system, have brought new insight into what sustains our interest and pleasure in music: the strong interactions between the auditory cortex and subcortical systems responsible for releasing dopamine are central features in explaining the pleasure we derive from listening to music (Zatorre 2015). Music is thus a most important part of our affective experience.

The mesolimbic reward system was originally designed to support biologically significant behaviors such as eating, promoting sexual activity, and caring for offspring. Fulfilling these basic needs is rewarding; in the pursuit of these objectives we derive a subjective feeling of pleasure contributing to positive emotional experiences, which act as reinforcers, leading to the repetition of a given behavior. There are, however, beside these basic needs, numerous other situations where similar reward functions play an important role; for example, learning is very much dependent on the reward system that provides the necessary motivational drive. Dopaminergic neurons are activated when the answer to a task is correct and the activation is even more pronounced when the correct answer is unexpected or better than predicted (Schultz 2013). These findings can be extrapolated to music. Music is essentially a sequence of sounds organized through time. As we listen to music, our expectations and anticipations with respect to the temporally unfolding pattern of a melody stimulate dopaminergic neurons, exerting a powerful affective impact.

The pleasure of listening to music cannot be reduced to the role of one neurohormone such as dopamine. Music is a system for emotional communication and many other neurochemical changes beyond the reward motivational system are involved. Parallel domains such as social bonding, where oxytocin is a key player, or arousal systems including serotonin, cortisol, and ACTH should be considered, demonstrating how far-ranging the effects of music on brain functions are. There is good evidence for the beneficial effects of music; music therapy has been used in a wide range of clinical settings associated with a dysregulation of the reward system. In these conditions, music therapy helps reduce stress or pain and aids in improving mood (Chanda and Levitin 2013). Obtaining insight into how music is perceived and how it affects so many brain areas will improve our understanding of the impact of music therapy.

Music, a universal art

Every disease is a musical problem; every cure is a musical solution.
Novalis (1772–1801)[33]

My soul is a hidden orchestra; I know not what instruments, what fiddlestrings and harps, drums and tamboura I sound and clash inside myself. All I hear is the symphony.
Fernando Pessoa (1888–1935)[34]

A sound one wishes to be and unite into a heavenly song.[35]
Friedrich Hölderlin (1770–1843)

Music, a universal language, is understood in all cultures and throughout the world. Art may be considered as one form of human communication, transferring information, conveying emotions, and even evoking resonance in the receiver. All forms of art—literature, music, paintings, and so forth—tell us a kind of story, which through identification arouses our imaginations, emotions, and above all significance related

33 Novalis (1798/1799).
34 Pessoa (1998).
35 Original text: Zum Tone möchte man werden und sich vereinen in *Einen* Himmelsgesang (Hyperion to Bellarmin). Hölderlin (1979).

to human experiences. Music is the art of sounds, not ideas, and sounds affect our feelings more than our cognition and intelligence. Music is neither speech nor language. Unlike linguistic signs, music is universal, affects our body and mind and moves us by the emotion it expresses. It lets us perceive a more humane and harmonious world than the one we ordinarily inhabit.

In Greek mythology the power of music is represented by Orpheus, who, thanks to his singing voice and playing the lyre, was able to charm wild animals, uproot trees, and convince Hades to return his wife Eurydice. The ancient Greek chorus accompanied and commentated the drama of the hero in epic poetry.

Aristotle described catharsis as the effect of music and tragic drama on the audience, as a "purging of the spirit of morbid … ideas or emotions by witnessing the playing out of such emotions or ideas on stage" (Aristotle 2001, 1458). Through pity and fear the spectators of the ancient tragedies experienced a purification of their affects. "All experience a certain purge (catharsis) and pleasant relief … cathartic melodies give innocent joy to men" (Aristotle 2001, 1131). Aristotle was of the opinion that music should be used for education and relaxation. For Socrates, too, the task of philosophy consisted in the purification of the soul. For Hippocrates, catharsis was a medical treatment of purification and as such had a healing effect.

During the Renaissance, Vincenzo Galilei, a member of the Florentine Camerata, wrote: "Music exists primarily to express the passions with greater effectiveness and to communicate these passions with equal force to the minds of mortal for their benefit and advantage" (1581, 306).

For Arthur Schopenhauer (1788–1860), "music is by no means like the other arts … the effect of music is so very much more powerful and penetrating than is that of the other arts, for these others speak only of the shadow, but music of the essence" (1819).

Philosopher Michel Serres (1930–2019) states: "There is no noise-proof wall. There are impervious walls for the look or the light, there are cases of shadow, no one has found silent places" (1982, 107). Hearing seems constantly in touch with the ambient world, as Freud noted about sleep: a sound can reach sleepers and stimulate dream formations without their knowledge, without them even waking up (Freud 1900). Everything happens as if the noise could still be heard, even during the deepest sleep. Hearing thus embodies a particular openness to the world; Michel Serres describes it as: "It is still active and rich when the eye either gets lost or goes to sleep. Hearing is continuous where the other senses are intermittent" (1982, 23).

Music is an essential way to express emotions and can serve as a coping mechanism. It may influence perception of time, appear in dreams, attribute meaning to emotional states, contribute to conscious awareness, and is helpful in mourning. Music is also an act of memory highlighting our autobiography. In a social way music allows migrant peoples to maintain their identity. Music links generations from the nursery rhyme to the senior choir.

Music in early human development

The origin of music is rooted in social experiences. It goes back to early interactions between mother and child, where musical aspects of speech such as rhythm and melody are the first means of communication. The fetus can hear sounds in the external environment by the third trimester of pregnancy (Partanen 2013). For infants, the power of music derives from its social nature and links to positive emotions and feelings. Mothers provide musical guidance to their prelinguistic infants and speak in melodious forms to infants who cannot yet understand the content of a mother's words. Children are sensitive to music from a very young age: they dance and sing to music and are able to distinguish happy from sad feelings in music (Peretz 2006). Music is at the center of social adjustment and not only for infants and young adults—musical experiences remain important during one's whole lifetime (Trehub 2003).

Musical memories are particularly long-lasting. What children hear at an early age seems to be "engraved" for the rest of their lives (Sacks 2007). Music reaches the earliest emotional experiences encoded in memories. Human fetuses can detect "pseudowords" in the last trimester of pregnancy and remember them in the days after birth, demonstrating that memory traces are already formed before birth. Prenatal experiences enable newborns to generate specific language behavior and eventually also language acquisition during infancy (Partanen et al. 2013).

"What so attracts the infant are not the parents' words, but their musical qualities: rhythm, variations in intonation and tonal ranges at a particular pitch. … Across cultures parents, intuitively sensing this, automatically exaggerate the musical features of speech, speaking or sing-songing to the infant in a higher and more variable pitch than in adult conversation. Before linguistic exchanges are established, the earliest communication system is then primarily an affective one" (Rose in Sabbadini 2002, 265). The voice highlights the nonverbal and enacted features of lived experiences. The embodied nonverbal dimension of interactive encounters occurs at an early stage in development and remains a fundamental component of communication throughout life. Nonverbal internalizations of encoded affective memories are evoked by music. Emotional belonging is felt in the earliest relatedness of the baby with its mother, in their shared nonverbal musical-emotional stories, and are stored as corresponding relationship representations. Human communication is an ongoing arrangement and integration between the senses and their perception, emotion, cognition, interpretation (Ogden 1995).

Tactile and auditory perceptions are the fetus' main sensory modes in the interaction with its mother. Thanks to its motility, the fetus is able to come into contact with the uterine wall. Hearing, on the contrary, is a question of passively receiving sounds. The fetus has no means to influence its mother's voice but is probably able to recognize or differentiate the emotional state of its mother. Does her voice express joy or sorrow? The question arises of how the infant perceives the voice of, for example, a depressed mother. Only at and after birth is the infant capable of crying and creating and evoking sounds (Maiello 2001).

The listening fetus is embedded in an internal sonorous continuum created by its mother's heart sounds and her voice. The steady rhythm of the heart sounds represents an existential beat, whereas the mother's prosody imprints the fetal ear with her melodic dialect. At the moment of birth, the infant discovers that mother's heartbeat and familiar voice are silenced. The sounds of this first continuous intimacy will be missed, and the infant will try through music to rediscover the mother's sonorous presence. According to Sloterdijk (2014), the road to music is inseparable from the retrieval of individual and intimate hearing.

The fetus and then the infant recognize the maternal voice, its prosodic features, and the mother's response to the infant's emotional condition. This happens well before the understanding of cognitive and semantic meaning of speech. Rizutto (cited in Etchegoyen 2004, 1479) considers that the mother's voice mirroring the infant's internal affective state is as important as the mother's mirroring of the baby's face, one of Winnicott's well-known concepts (1971). Mother's face is a face in motion and in emotion, with her sounds and "singing." Anzieu (1976) described the "sound envelope of the self," a kind of "sound mirror" between the voices of the baby and its mother. The baby is held in its mother's arms; tight against the mother's body, so that it can feel her warmth, smell, and movements; carried; handled; rubbed; washed; and caressed, all usually accompanied by a bath of words and humming (Anzieu 1974). The "sound mirror" is particular in the sense that it introduces dissimilarity: the mother who speaks to the child brings a qualitative difference in her answers by expressing herself with verbal communication (Anzieu 1976). Her response contains the ability to think and verbalize what the child experiences, feels, needs, or desires. The mother interprets the sounds of the baby. If the mother herself responds abruptly, violently, or impersonally, the "sound mirror" no longer plays its symbolic function for the development of the child (Anzieu 1976).[36] According to Bollas (1987) the voice, with its components such as melody, pitch, timbre, rhythm, tempo, and loudness, underlies verbal communication and is influenced by the different interacting elements of body, emotions, language, music, culture, self, and other. Vocal styles are related to specific idioms and a specific "aesthetics of being," revealing individual features of a subject's identity. Vocal dialects indicate the cultural context of a person.

36 According to Anzieu (1979), the legend in Greek mythology of Echo and Narcissus "illustrates the precedence of the sound-mirror over the visual-mirror, as well as the primary feminine character of the voice, and the link that exists between the emission of sound and the request for love" (32).

Music and psychoanalysis

Music is considered as the language of emotions, that is, "music sounds the way emotions feel" (Pratt 1952, 26), and both emotions and music are dynamic processes. The Latin *ex movere* demonstrates the essence of movement in the experience of emotions, as the German word *Gemütsbewegung* illustrates. Affects are a matrix of pleasurable or unpleasurable feelings. Attributing meaning to life events relies more on emotions than on words. According to Rose (2004, 97), "music is a representation of the emotional quality of subjective, lived time made audible—an auditory apparition of felt-time. ... Music can foster a reintegration of feelingful experience with perception, and psychoanalysis aims at a similar reintegration with memory. Thus, both contribute to an enhanced sense of wholeness in a person's experience" (Rose 1999, 3).

The relationship between psychoanalysis and music is as old as the history of psychoanalysis itself. Psychoanalysts have extensively explored musical phenomena and analyzed musical creativity in their work. Psychoanalytically oriented interpretation of art always refers to mostly unconscious emotions that need to be felt, expressed, and bound into a meaningful narrative. Music seems to be the preferred artistic media for expressing emotions and arousing feelings in the listener, while at the same time it tells a narrative without relying on verbal means. It is above all a transmission of affects through nonverbal communications, their variations being expressed by tone, pitch, intensity, rhythm, or timbre. Music may awaken feelings of early lived experiences, stored as preverbal implicit memories, symbolizing bodily expressions of affects and imitate expressions of emotions of weeping or laughing (Noy 1991).

Freud (1936) considered himself as totally unmusical yet he recognized "being moved by a thing without knowing why I am thus affected and what it is that affects me" (Freud 1914). "If a few bars of music are played and someone comments that it is from Mozart's *Figaro* (as happens in Don Giovanni) a number of recollections are roused in me all at once, none of which can enter my consciousness. The key-phrase serves as a port of entry through which the whole network is simultaneously put in a state of excitation" (Freud 1900–1901, 249).

Freud (1985)—in a letter to Wilhelm Fliess (1887–1904)—described the analyst as a musician playing on the patient's psyche, creating a harmonious composition on the hidden resources of his or her "instrument" (the patient) (432). Psychoanalytic therapy was called "the talking cure" and could also be considered as a "listening cure," but Freud apparently was more interested in visual dimensions, contrary to music, which does not use words but sounds, and occupies acoustic spheres. Freud mentions music in his work *Interpretations of Dreams* (1900–1901).[37]

[37] For a review of Freud and music, see Baralea and Minazzi (2008).

Artistic creativity has its roots in the unconscious; of course, artists may be fully aware of their working processes and describe their techniques, similar to the dreamer recounting his dream. "Music has become a symbolic language of the unconscious mind" (Ehrenzweig 1953, 164–165). "Because music *is* feeling, not sound, it is pure emotion, and presents a way of hearing and listening which can (and perhaps should) be a model of psychoanalytic intersubjectivity" (Stein 1999, 412). "Music can serve compound defensive or coping functions in transforming our perceptual and sensory experience of time to evoke temporally distant events or reminiscences, provoke a heightened or accelerated anticipation of a future moment, induce or relax states of tension, or seeming to altogether suspend time's ineluctable forward movement. Music's discursive narrativism engenders a sense of time's passage, of a beginning traveling toward an end" (Stein 2004, 763).

Present time "lived stories" or shared nonverbal lived narratives are characterized by Stern (2004) as short emotional episodes or emotionally charged intersubjective states, which are not cognitively and verbally constructed. The musicality of voice and body captures the listeners' attention, who then is able to participate and share the emotions of the moment. The learning of language is linked with some losses in rich, authentic, individual nonverbal expressions, which easily can be observed during the developmental processes of children. Part of these nonverbal manifestations are then silenced but might be—for instance in psychoanalytic therapy—relevant for a patient's felt, but unnamed experiences.

The question "who is speaking to us" in art and in therapy is formulated by Bollas (1987) as "who is speaking to whom and why now" and is equally relevant for the therapist. But the voice may also serve to hide—in its expression—feelings perceived as treacherous, threatening, or prohibited.

For Stein (2004b) music evokes affects related to grief and is therefore distinct from other arts. In mourning, music may console in reducing or relieving feelings of pain and despair and provide the bereaved person with an illusionary hope of the wish to reunite with a lost loved one, similar to the latent wish underlying a dream. He considers music-listening as a creative internalization of the properly attuned and regulated self-other interaction, an imaginative resurrection of an internalized other (not only the dead or absent other). Music can be perceived as a "pre-verbal, essentially pre-representational registration of the mother's presence" (Bollas 1987, 39), facilitating a restitutive transformation of the internal affective experience of being held, understood, and consoled.

"Our relationship with music fosters a restructuring of emotional experience, especially during periods in which trauma and sorrow have created a world experienced as fragmented, disorganized, isolating, distemperate" (Stein 2004b, 807). "Music can function as a surrogate or auxiliary cry or wail, an externalization of an intolerably … incomprehensible, or crushing internal state. It can give voice to feelings otherwise inexpressible, to the vast zone of overwhelming affect for which spoken and written language may be inadequate, in essence speaking for the self-obliterated or muted by despair, or symbolizing experiences and affects otherwise too intense … to express directly" (808). Music has the power to create an intrapsychic link to the lost one and at the same time induce a feeling of relatedness with others.

Theodor Reik (1888–1969), a psychoanalyst, provides an example of a different music-related response to trauma. In *The Unknown Self Sings*,[38] Reik (1953) describes his feelings after being informed of the death of Karl Abraham, his friend, mentor, and former analyst. Reik recalls a reaction of intense shock, which is soon overtaken by numbness, but admits feeling no immediate grief. Walking alone through a snowy wood, he tries to focus his thoughts on composing a speech Freud had asked him to deliver in Abraham's memory at the next meeting of the Vienna Psychoanalytic Society, but he is too absorbed by his mood and unable to concentrate. He notes that the trees have suddenly become "menacingly" high, and that the landscape itself has been transformed into something "solemn and sinister"; he is aware of a "heavy and oppressive silence" (221). Amid this somber reflection, he becomes aware of humming a melody to himself. At first he does not recognize it, but eventually the refrain reveals itself to be the first measures of the chorale from the last movement of Mahler's Second Symphony, the *Resurrection*. Later, he recalls the text that the chorus sings to the accompaniment of the particular melody he keeps hearing in his mind's ear: "You will rise again, my dust, after a short rest; immortal life, will He who called you grant you." Reik realizes that this strain of music and its accompanying text has become the leitmotif of his mourning. But far from consoling him, it begins to recur with such intrusive insistence and becomes a disturbance. He wonders what his unconscious is communicating by way of this motif. The experience, he writes, was that he could hear its message but could not understand its meaning; it was as if "it had been expressed in a foreign language," one he did not speak. The text and music of Mahler's *Resurrection Symphony* can be understood as the unconscious expression of Reik's wish for his beloved mentor's return—his resurrection—and to thereby reverse the reality of the loss: "You will rise again, my dust, after a short rest." That Reik reports his conscious experience of the musical hallucination as "intrusive" and of little initial solace does not contradict this understanding. Rather, it speaks to the presence of an inner conflict between the recognition of the reality of loss and the unconscious wish fantasy, which is symbolically ensconced within a framework of rhythm, sound, and text.

Feelings related to stressful or traumatic events are multiple, intense, confusing and vary over time. Stupefaction, rage, despair, bewilderment, helplessness, and hopelessness are highly subjective in their expressions associated with adverse experiences and lead to loss of confidence, self-worth, and bodily and mental integration.

[38] A chapter in his book *The Haunting Melody: Psychoanalytic Experiences in Life and Music* (Reik 1953).

Music and dreams

While images are more frequent in dreams than the hearing of music, musicians create musical themes in their dreams and play or listen to music. It is therefore not astonishing that music is more frequent in dreams of professional musicians, especially those who were instructed in music at a very early age (Uga et al. 2006). According to Walker (1979) "the background level of musical structure is truly unconscious" (1643). Many composers recount that music first appeared to them in a dream, initiating the creation of their musical composition. Music, like other arts, has its roots in unconscious motivation. There is not necessarily a direct correspondence between the content of a dream and the musical partition that may arise from it, but it emphasizes the importance of unconscious processes leading to creative activities such as musical composition.

For Carta (2009), music is "the most fundamental human symbolic experience" (85). He considers music in dreams as "the most direct representation of the emerging self" (85), the core affect, previous to visual pictures or verbal meaning. Music contains an expression of sense and time and holds the subject in an emotional sphere. Images and words arise afterward, from the source of music.

In his book *Musicophilia*, Sacks (2007) tells of his own musical dreams, which continued into the waking state. "I found something deeply disturbing and unpleasant about the music and longed for it to stop" (280). His attempts to drive out the music failed as he continued to hear hallucinatory German music. Finally, after the interpretation of a friend who revealed to him "your mind is playing Mahler's *Kindertotenlieder* (Songs on the Death of Children) (280), the music disappeared and never recurred. The dream symbolically expressed an event from the previous day: Oliver Sacks had resigned his position at the Children's Unit at the hospital where he had been working and had burnt a book of essays he had written. In the intermediate states between waking and sleep, "free-floating reverie and dreamlike or hallucinatory apparitions are particularly common" (281).

According to Vogelsang et al. (2016), musical activities during the day are related to the frequency of musical dreams, thus demonstrating a kind of continuity between daily activities and themes in the following night's dreams.

Ludwig van Beethoven (1770–1827), a German composer and musician, dedicated in a letter to Tobias Haslinger[39] a canon he had heard while dreaming, entitled "O Tobias," which he later transformed into three voices. Beethoven lived a succession of critical life events: his father's seemingly violent teaching, the loss of his mother at the age of seventeen, the burden of supporting his family, and finally his lifelong struggle with deafness. His unchallenged desire to compose music, to

[39] Tobias Haslinger (1787–1842), Austrian music publisher and composer.

express himself emotionally through music was, as he said, a way of living "through suffering to joy." Beethoven could not *hear* the ovation given at the premiere on May 7, 1824 of his *Ninth Symphony*—with Friedrich Schiller's poem *Ode to Joy* in the final movement—but only *see* it, when one of the singers turned him toward the public.

In a dream, **Paul McCartney** (1942–) of the Beatles once heard a tune; at first he doubted whether it was his song. Only after the death of his father did he name it *Yesterday* (Barrett 2001).

> Yesterday all my troubles seemed so far away
> Now it looks as though they're here to stay
> Oh I believe in yesterday
> Suddenly I'm not half the man I used to be
> There's a shadow hanging over me
> Oh yesterday came suddenly
> Why she had to go I don't know
> She wouldn't say
> I said something wrong, now I long for yesterday
> Yesterday, love was such an easy game to play
> Now I need a place to hide away
> Yesterday all my troubles seemed so far away
> Now it looks as though they're here to stay
> Oh I believe in yesterday

Beatles legend has it that Paul McCartney composed the melody for *Yesterday* in his dream one night in 1964. It is one of the most popular songs in music history. McCartney described the process of composing the song in *The Beatles Anthology*: "I was living in a little flat at the top of a house and I had a piano by my bed. I woke up one morning with a tune in my head and I thought, 'Hey, I don't know this tune—or do I?' It was like a jazz melody. … I went to the piano and found the chords to it, made sure I remembered it and then hawked it round to all my friends, asking what it was: 'Do you know this? It's a good little tune, but I couldn't have written it because I dreamt it'" (The Beatles 2012).

Music and narrative

In his ballet works, **Youri Vámos** (1946–) explores human relationships on an emotional level and in a narrative form. His choreographies tell the dramatic stories of literature-based themes such as *Romeo and Juliet* and *A Midsummer Night's Dream*, as well as the classical ballets scenes of *Cinderella*. Youri Vámos's choreographies of

The Nutcracker[40] and *Swan Lake* are representations of psychoanalytically interpreted narratives. He has been called the best choreographic storyteller of the present.[41]

Swan Lake tells the tragic story of Prince Siegfried, who falls in love with a young swan princess, but is manipulated by the magician Rothbart into betraying her and finally dying with her. For Youri Vámos, the essence of the story is not the working of sinister mythical forces; he is interested in the Prince's mind, the reason why he strayed into a fantasy world on his way to adulthood, tracing the psychological motivation of the young hero. Sensitive by nature, the Prince experiences the relationship between his mother and her lover Rothbart as an agonizing trauma. He flees into the world of fantasy where he meets the young swan Odette. In her he finds his ideal object of love, and yet at the same time recognizes aspects of his mother. He is finally forced to see that there is no place in reality for his vision of love.

Vámos's *Swan Lake* can be considered not only as one of the choreographer's best achievements, but also as one of the best readings of *Swan Lake* in the entire history of ballet. Vámos integrates the classic ballet scenes into a narrative, which is drawn from the depths of human psychology.

Songs written in a timeless and universal language have the infinite ability to enchant entire communities, as their lyrics expresses essentials truths in a most humble way. To this category belongs *Bridge Over Troubled Water*. The words and music were written in 1969 by **Paul Simon** who later called it his best song, and was sung by **Art Garfunkel**, accompanied by the piano. At the time of the Vietnam War it became one of the defining songs of the 1970s.

> When you're weary, feeling small,
> When tears are in your eyes
> I will dry them all
> I'm on your side
> When times get rough
> And friends just can't be found
> Like a bridge over troubled water
> I will lay me down
> Like a bridge over troubled water
> I will lay me down
>
> When you're down and out
> When you're on the street
> When evening falls so hard

[40] *The Nutcracker* is a narration of two stories: Charles Dickens's *A Christmas Carol* and E. T. A. Hoffmann's *The Nutcracker and the Mouse King*.

[41] In the recent arte-edition book *Tanzgeschichte des 20. Jahrhunderts in einem Band*, by Jochen Schmidt, Henschel Verlag, Berlin, 2002.

I will comfort you
I'll take your part
When darkness comes
And pain is all around
Like a bridge over troubled water
I will lay me down
Like a bridge over troubled water
I will lay me down

Sail on, silver girl
Sail on by
Your time has come to shine
All your dreams are on their way
See how they shine
If you need a friend
I'm sailing right behind
Like a bridge over troubled water
I will ease your mind
Like a bridge over troubled water
I will ease your mind

Musicians

"What I enjoy best is playing music … I am a musician, who happens to be blind … I have been blessed with a God-given gift and my prayer is that I can continue to be a blessing and inspiration to others."[42] **Matthew Whitaker** (2001–) is an American jazz pianist, organist, drummer, and composer. He has been blind since birth due to premature retinopathy.

The selection of a few musicians presented here aims to illustrate the existential significance music had in their lives. They mastered experiences of adverse or traumatic life events and expressed in their musical compositions or performances their lived emotions and feelings.

Music evokes sorrow and mourning and simultaneously offers compassion and relief. Music may lead to movements of regression with a temporal standstill and therefore restoring feelings of being held, of repose and peacefulness.

Music helps express the inexpressible—"Everything, in a manner of speaking, is in the music … serving most significantly as a musical hallucinatory coping mechanism" (Stein 2004, 755–756)—and represents the human capacity for finding the

[42] "The Matthew Whitaker Trio," LA Phil, accessed December 10, 2020, https://www.laphil.com/musicdb/artists/6135/the-matthew-whitaker-trio.

means to overcome silence, associated with the horror of isolation, suffering, and loss, through a nonverbal medium. "Analogous to the latent wish underlying the dream-work, music in mourning proposes a creative solution to an intolerable reality. One way, then, in which music consoles—and with such satisfaction—is in temporarily relieving or diminishing feelings of pain by providing an illusory response ensconced in rhythm and sound to the dominant wish of the bereaved-reunion with the lost object" (Stein 2004b, 807).

Music has the "unique and remarkable capacity both to convey grief and to provide solace in its wake" (809).

Friedrich Hölderlin (1770–1843)

At the age of two, Hölderlin lost his father and seven years later his stepfather. In a letter to his mother he wrote: "When my second father died, whose love for me I shall never forget, when I felt, with an incomprehensible pain, my orphaned state and saw, each day, your grief and tears, it was then that my soul took on, for the first time, this heaviness that has never left and that could only grow more severe with the years" (Henrich and Förster 1997, 6).

In his famous poem "Song of Fate," Hölderlin describes an idealized state of the sleeping infant; it may represent his nostalgic wish to retrieve this past time.

> Like sleeping infants the gods
> breathe without any plan;
> the spirit flourishes continually
> in them, chastely kept,
> as in a small bud,
> and their holy eyes
> look out in still
> eternal clearness.

Hölderlin's "Song of Fate," which appears in the second volume of *Hyperion*[43] was set as a choral work by Johannes Brahms (Op. 54).

Franz Schubert (1797–1828)

In 1817 Schubert composed *An die Musik,* one of the most brilliant lieder from the six hundred songs he wrote.

[43] A novel in two volumes, 1797 and 1799.

To Music[44]

Beloved art, in how many a bleak hour,
when I am enmeshed in life's tumultuous round,
have you kindled my heart to the warmth of love,
and borne me away to a better world!
Often a sigh, escaping from your harp,
a sweet, celestial chord
has revealed to me a heaven of happier times.
Beloved art, for this I thank you!

Music is an essential mean for expressing unverbalized but felt emotions in adverse life experiences. It is an attempt to overcome silence, one of the most characteristic aspects of lived traumatic events. It is as if music expresses what a subject feels: somatic, kinesthetic, or aesthetic sensations.

Pyotr Ilyich Tchaikovsky (1840–1893)

"To regret the past, to hope in the future, and never to be satisfied with the present: that is what I spend my whole life doing" (letter to his brother Anatoly on 3–15 August 1878). "Music is heaven's best gift to humanity. It alone clarifies, reconciles and consoles" (letter to Nadezhda von Meck, 1879). When Tchaikovsky was recovering from a depressive episode, he composed the Violin Concerto in D major op. 35, one of his most emotionally moving concertos. "I have found nothing—neither religion nor philosophy—to ease my troubled soul. But I would go mad were it not for music" (1879).

In a letter to Nadezhda von Meck (on March 5–17, 1878), who supported him financially, Tchaikovsky wrote:

> Only that music can stir, touch, shake, move, embrace, and grasp what flows from the depths of the artist's soul excited through inspiration. … In writing an opera the author must constantly keep the stage in mind, that is, remember that the theatre requires not just melodies and harmonies but also action; that one must not abuse the patience of the opera audience, which has come not only to listen but also to look; and, finally, that the style of theatrical music must correspond to that of the set-painting, which means it must be simple, clear and colorful.

His last composition was the Symphony no. 6 in B Minor, named by Tchaikovsky the Passionate Symphony, but at the suggestion of his brother Modest changed to *Pathétique*, in Russian *pateticheskoy*. "Without exaggeration, I have put my whole soul into this work," Tchaikovsky commented. He led its premiere in Saint Petersburg, nine days before his death.

[44] English translation by Richard Wigmore.

Välimäki (2005) in *A Psychoanalytic Approach to Musical Signification* analyzes and interprets Tchaikovsky's *Pathétique* with Freud's concept of the Uncanny, describing the musical themes, and their instrumental and imaginary representations, and writes: "An uncanny experience almost overcame me … at moments when the work corresponded almost too well with Freud's theory of the uncanny" (299). One might only approve such a comparison, if by uncanny, marvelous, miraculous, magical, enchanting, charismatic, or entrancing feelings are meant.

Boris Asafyev, one of the founders of Soviet musicology, wrote the following regarding Pyotr Ilyich Tchaikovsky: "He was the first composer of a new Russian type. … In a deeply original, personal and national style he united the symphonic thought of Beethoven and Schumann with the work of Glinka,[45] and transformed Liszt's and Berlioz's achievements in depictive-programmatic music into matters of Shakespearian elevation and psychological import" (2008).

Gustav Mahler (1860–1911)

During his childhood, Gustav Mahler, an Austrian composer, witnessed the death of six of his eleven siblings, two in infancy. He was the second child—the first had already died before his birth. Mahler wrote his first composition *A Funeral March with an Introductory Polka* at the age of five. In 1889 Mahler lost his mother, his father, and one sister; his brother Otto shot himself in 1895 at the age of twenty-two. Mourning became "a fixture in Mahler's inner life and would find expression and representation repeatedly in his music" (Feder 2004, 34). "Mahler was in a state of endless mourning" (142–43).

Between 1901 and 1904, Mahler composed five *Songs on the Death of Children* (*Kindertotenlieder* in German) based on poems by Friedrich Rückert (1788–1866), who wrote 428 children's poems shortly after the death of two of his ten children.

One of the song cycles is the following:

> I often think: they have only just gone out,
> and now they will be coming back home.
> The day is fine, don't be dismayed,
> They have just gone for a long walk.
>
> Yes indeed, they have just gone out,
> and now they are making their way home.
> Don't be dismayed, the day is fine,
> they have simply made a journey to yonder heights.
>
> They have just gone out ahead of us,
> and will not be thinking of coming home.

[45] Mikhail Ivanovich Glinka, Russian composer, regarded as the father of Russian classical music.

> We go to meet them on yonder heights
> In the sunlight, the day is fine
> On yonder heights.

Then in 1907, Mahler's eldest daughter, Maria-Anna, died suddenly at the age of five of scarlet fever and diphtheria. Mahler's creations *The Song of the Earth*, which ends with *Farewell,* the *Songs on the Death of Children*, and the *Sixth Tragic Symphony*, whose hero—in Mahler's words—suffered "three blows of fate, the last of which fells him as a tree is felled" (Feder 2004, 124), have been interpreted as reflecting his constant preoccupation with death (a repetitive theme also in his dreams) and as representing his process of mourning. Mahler himself said: "My whole life is contained in my two symphonies. … To anyone who knows how to listen my whole life will become clear" (De La Grange 1973, 272).

"There is no doubt that our music involves everything human, including the intellect. When we make music, we do not paint or tell stories. Music represents the whole human being—feeling, thinking, breathing, suffering" (Mahler 1982, 239). "I am thrice homeless. … As a native of Bohemia in Austria, as an Austrian among Germans, and as a Jew throughout all the world; everywhere an intruder, never welcomed," said Mahler of himself (Mahler 1946, 98).

The psychoanalytic interest in Mahler's biography may partly be attributed to the fact that in 1910, Mahler—in a state of acute crisis after discovering the relationship between his wife Alma and Walter Gropius—sought help from Freud, with whom he had one long consultation. Max Graf[46] (1942) recalled: "When Gustav Mahler became director of the Viennese Opera, Freud was an admirer of the energy and greatness of the man. Freud was a man of great artistic sensibilities, but to his great regret he was quite unmusical. It was the spiritual and personal energy of Gustav Mahler that he admired" (473–74).[47]

Freud met Mahler only once on August 26, 1910, in Leiden, Netherlands. The two spent four hours strolling through the town and conducting a sort of psychoanalysis (Jones 1955, 88). Freud told Mahler that his wife Alma had fallen in love with him as a fatherly figure, as Mahler was twenty years older than Alma, and directed his attention to the fact that Alma's father, who died when she was thirteen, had been "ein Maler," that is, a painter (Feder 2004).[48] Freud also suggested that the name of Mahler's wife had to be Marie, just like his mother's (Mahler's mother's name was Marie Herrmann.) In fact, Mahler's wife was called Alma Maria. During their conversation on the features of Mahler's music, Mahler exclaimed: "Now I understand

[46] Max Graf (1873–1958) (see chapter 19) suggested that music "functioned for the listener as a way to gain access to the unconscious and as a way to develop increasing psychic balance between the unconscious, preconscious, and conscious levels of the psyche" (Abrams 1993, 301).

[47] According to Mächtlinger (2002), Mahler was the godfather of Graf's son Herbert.

[48] Feder (2004): *Gustav Mahler: A Life in Crisis,* a comprehensive historical-psychoanalytic study of the encounter between Freud and Mahler.

something about my music. I have often been criticized for crude changes from the noblest melody to one that is banal" and he told the following story:

> One day, while he was sitting in his room, he heard his father in the next room engaged in a violent scene with his mother. He eavesdropped by the door until he could bear it no longer, and then ran out into the street. There was a barrel organ playing a well-known tune: *Oh, my dear Augustine, Augustine,* an old Viennese melody. … The boy Mahler heard this and for the rest of his life he reproduced in his music the strange contrast of a common hurdy-gurdy tune alongside one reminiscent of the violence of his father (Feder 2004, 229–230).

"Although Mahler emerged strengthened from his visit with Freud, with his considerable resources mobilized for strenuous undertakings ahead, he never recovered fully and remained vulnerable to physical illness. Within a year he was dead" (Feder 2004, opening chapter).

Mahler's biographer Donald Mitchell (1958) writes that Mahler's compositions frequently re-enacted his traumatic childhood experiences, how the vivid contrast between high tragedy and low farce, sublimated, disguised, and transfigured as it often was, emerged as a leading artistic principle in his music, a principle almost always ironic in intent and execution (11).

The American composers Leonard Bernstein and Robert Greenberg have suggested that Mahler's heart disease directly influenced his musical compositions. Bernstein said: "The opening bars [of Mahler's Ninth Symphony] are an imitation of the arrhythmia of his failing heartbeat. … That Mahler opened his symphonic message of farewell with the representation of his soon-to-be-fatal heart condition should only add an element of poignancy rather than seem an intrusion of stark reality into the aesthetic world of music, especially in a work like the Ninth Symphony" (Amenta 2005, 17–18). Gustav Mahler died of endocarditis.

In 1894, inspired by Stéphane Mallarme's poem, **Claude Debussy** (1862–1918) composed *Prelude to an Afternoon of a Faun*, considered his most famous composition and one that represents Debussy's ingenuity. Around this time, he wrote: "Music is not something that can flow inside a rigorous form. It consists of colors and of rhythmicized time."[49] Debussy believed that instead of a musician, he should have been a painter. He considered music to be an enigmatic harmony connecting nature and imagination and not a precise representation of nature. In his view, only musicians are able to apprehend an enchanting landscape or a captivating sunset and

[49] David Dubal, "The Piano as Paintbrush: The Wondrous Colors of Debussy," The Wall Street Journal, December 18, 2012, https://www.wsj.com/articles/SB10001424127887324355904578159631080

interpret it in music for the listener (Reich 1965, 207). In 1911 he wrote: "I want to write my musical dream … I want to sing my inner landscape with the naive candor of childhood" (Tadié 2008, 23). "I used … silence as a means of expression! … Maybe the only way to make the emotion of a sentence stand out …. Silence is a beautiful thing …. Music for the inexpressible. Music must come out of the shadows. Be discreet" (226–227).

For Debussy, an artist is a man accustomed to dreaming and living among ghosts "There is no greater pleasure than to go down in oneself, to set one's whole being in motion, to seek new and hidden treasures" (np). Debussy felt that he was not able to live in a real word consisting of people and objects and was sure that those around him would never understand. "I live in remembrance and regret … to be relieved of anxiety by successful work" (34–35). Melancholy for Debussy was "the fact of not being able to think. … The sea continues to perform its coming and going sound, which rocks the melancholy" (42).

His wife Emma Debussy said in 1924: "Twice a day, with a car, I drove him in the morning on the beach, and in the evening on the cliffs that he adored." As Tadié (2008) writes in his biography of Debussy: "Writers teach us to read the world and painters to watch it, Debussy teaches us to listen to the sea" (202). Debussy died of rectal cancer in 1918. His daughter, called Chouchou, whom Debussy loved with all his heart, died a year later, at the age of thirteen.

According to Ogden (1996), "Debussy felt that music is the space between the notes. Something similar might be said of psychoanalysis. Between the notes of the spoken words constituting the analytic dialog are the reveries of the analyst and analysand. It is in this space occupied by the interplay of reveries that one finds the music of psychoanalysis" (883). For Ogden, "use of language must be equal to the task of capturing and conveying in words a sense of what it is 'that's going on here' in the intrapsychic and intersubjective life of the analysis, the 'music of what happens' in the analytic relationship" (Ogden 1999, 978–979).

Wladysław Szpilman (1911–2009), a pianist, composer, and writer, survived the Holocaust. He was able to narrate his traumatic experience of the Nazi occupation of Poland. The memoir he wrote in 1946 was finally published in English in the late 1990s—thanks to his son Andrzej—with the title *The Pianist: The Extraordinary Story of One Man's Survival in Warsaw, 1939–1945.* Andrzej Szpilman wrote in the foreword: "Until a few years ago, my father never spoke of his wartime experiences" (Szpilman 1999, 7). He suggests that his father wrote this story "for himself rather than humanity in general … to enable him to work through his shattering wartime experiences and free his mind and emotions to continue with his life" (8).

Roman Polanski, also a survivor of the 1939 German occupation of Poland (his parents were interned in a Nazi concentration camp, where his mother died), directed the adapted version of the book for the film *The Pianist*, which was released in 2002.

The music of Chopin's Scherzo in B minor and Nocturne in C# minor, played by Szpilman,[50] serve as a "narrative" of his traumatic experience in the film.

Yehudi Menuhin (1916–1999), an American-born violinist and conductor, believed that if you really want to record a sound in its entire dimensions, you must have experienced silence. Silence as a real substance, not as just an absence of noise. This true silence is clarity but is never a lack of color. It is rhythm, the foundation of all thinking, on which all worthy creativity grows. Everything that lives and lasts arises out of silence: those who carry this silence in themselves can meet with serenity the loud demands from the outside.

In an interview, Menuhin recounted the following incident about his name Yehudi, which means "Jew" in Hebrew:[51] "Obliged to find an apartment of their own, my parents searched the neighborhood and chose one within walking distance of the park. Showing them out after they had viewed it, the landlady said: 'And you'll be glad to know I don't take Jews.' Her mistake made clear to her (my mother), the anti-Semitic landlady was renounced, and another apartment found. But her blunder left its mark. Back on the street my mother made a vow. Her unborn baby would have a label proclaiming his race to the world. He would be called 'the Jew.'"

[50] Wladyslaw Szpilman played F. Chopin's Nocturne no. 20 in C sharp-minor at his home in Warsaw in 1997, recorded by cameraman Jaroslaw Mazur. He had also played this piece in the last live broadcast for the Polish Radio on September 23, 1939. An hour later German bombs destroyed its power supply and the Warsaw Radio closed for long six years.

[51] New Internationalist, Judeophobia, Issue 372, October 2004: 3.

PART IV

Chapter 10

GRIEF

The violence and impression of an excessive grief must of necessity astonish the soul, and wholly deprive it of its ordinary functions: as it happens to every one of us, who, upon any sudden alarm of very ill news, find ourselves surprised, stupefied, and in a manner deprived of all power of motion, so that the soul, beginning to vent itself in tears and lamentations, seems to free and disengage itself from the sudden oppression, and to have obtained some room to work itself out at greater liberty.
Michel de Montaigne (1533–1592), philosopher of the French Renaissance[52]

Give sorrow words; the grief that does not speak,
whispers the o'erfraught heart and bids it break.
William Shakespeare (1564–1616)[53]

Grief and creativity

Grief has been described since ancient times, among all nations, and finds expression in religion, literature, philosophy, and art. Grief can be defined as the process of giving intrapsychic significance to the experience of loss.

In the context of bereavement, loss, trauma, or deprivation there is always a potential crisis of meaning and a necessity for mourning. Grief work is a lengthy process that must deal with three different themes of mourning. The *first* is mostly concerned

[52] Montaigne (1910).
[53] *Macbeth*, Act 4, Scene 3.

with a loss, such as the death of a loved person but could also relate to the loss of one's health or the loss of one's homeland. The *second theme* in the process of mourning is to address the fact that the experienced loss cannot be replaced. Adults who were emotionally deprived in their childhood often clamor with infinite longing and deep yearning for all they feel they have missed: love, attention, care, being held, and being contained. Also, sometimes health cannot be recovered or the return to one's homeland is impossible. There are manifold questions around grief: Why did I had to suffer these events? Am I responsible for what happened to me? Do I feel guilty about this situation? Would it have been possible to avoid or prevent the event? Could I have been aware of this situation earlier and changed the outcome? These questions are the *third theme* that has to be elaborated in grief work.

There are situations where a traumatized person enters into a mourning process by asking all these questions—often becoming desperate and disappointed not to find the expected answers. This is, for instance, the case in adoptees with traumatizing lived experiences in their early childhood, often representing an accumulation of multiple deprivations, of personal loss of biological parents, homeland, culture, ethnicity, and language.

In other situations, these questions may partially be answered when the traumatized subject begins to understand the lived experiences of the mother's or father's own family situations. The comprehension of the subject's implication in a transgenerational transmission may favor mourning work.

In each mourning process with an adult, it is essential to elaborate the subjective lived experiences of the person's intrapsychic child—in the developmental trajectory from birth through adolescence— sometimes only expressed through nonverbal communication.

Russian novelist **Fyodor Dostoevsky** (1821–1881) suffered from epilepsy as discussed in chapter 7. For him, "the soul is healed by being with children." According to his second wife Anna and his second daughter Lyubov, also known by the name Aimée, Dostoevsky wrote to a friend at the birth of his first daughter: "It is the greatest joy a man can know here on earth" and seemed to have "wept and sobbed like a woman in despair" at her death, at the age of only three months. "To save a child is to save the world." For Dostoevsky, "much unhappiness has come into the world because of bewilderment and things left unsaid." "Beauty will save the world." "Beauty is mysterious as well as terrible. God and devil are fighting there, and the battlefield is the heart of man." "Pain and suffering are always inevitable for a large intelligence and a deep heart. The really great men must, I think, have great sadness on earth."[54] Dostoevsky, a deeply religious Christian, never separated truth from goodness and beauty.

[54] Quotations are all from letters written by Fyodor Dostoevsky.

Alexandre Dumas (son) (1824–1895), born illegitimate, was a French author and playwright. His romantic novel *The Lady of the Camellias*, published in 1848, is the text that was adapted for Giuseppe Verdi's opera *La Traviata*. Dumas was admitted to the French Academy in 1874 and awarded the Legion of Honor in 1894. At the age of seven his father legally recognized him and took him away from his mother, her agony about this separation becoming the source of his writing about tragic female characters. In *The Illegitimate Son* (a play from 1858), Dumas defends his conviction that a man who fathers a child has to marry the mother and legitimize the child. Profoundly influenced by his family situation he writes: "I have experienced everything that I have presented. I can say that since I held the pen, I have not written down a word that was not an excitement and a memory of my own life, a conviction of my mind, my observations, and my conscience. I have sought where I could to associate this excitement, this memory, this conviction with the cause of humanity, and out of these rapprochements arose my works" (np).

Marcel Proust (1871–1922), best known for his monumental novel *In Search of Lost Time,* notes: "We cannot be taught wisdom, we have to discover it for ourselves by a journey which no one can undertake for us, an effort which no one can spare us. … But it is sometimes just at the moment when we think that everything is lost that the intimation arrives which may save us; one has knocked at all the doors which lead nowhere, and then one stumbles without knowing it on the only door through which one can enter—which one might have sought in vain for a hundred years—and it opens on its own accord" (Proust 1981, 898).

Proust was regarded as a frail child; he suffered from asthma throughout his life and died from pneumonia at the age of fifty-one. In writing Proust was able to address his need to understand the sense and meaning of his past, as well as express his emotions, thoughts, representations, and fantasies, thus working through the process on a semantic and symbolic level. He linked his creative work to his mourning process, describing a book as a "vast graveyard where on most of the tombstones one can no longer read the faded names" (Segal 1952, 198). He was compelled to create by his need to recover his lost past" (Bell 2015, 182).

Antoine de Saint-Exupéry (1900–1944) wrote: "And when your sorrow is comforted (time soothes all sorrows) you will be content that you have known me. You will always be my friend" (Saint-Exupéry 1946, np).

Saint-Exupéry was born into an aristocratic family in Lyon, France. He was the third of five children and lost his father before the age of four. His mother moved him and his four siblings to a relative's castle in the east of France. In 1912 he took his first trip in an airplane—an experience that would have a profound and lasting impression on him. His father's death affected the entire family, transforming their status to that of "impoverished aristocrats." He is said to have written: "I know but one freedom and that is the freedom of the mind."

While attending Villa St. Jean during World War I, a Marianist international school in Fribourg, Switzerland, with François, his younger brother of two years, his brother, at the age of fifteen, contracted rheumatic fever and died with Saint-Exupéry at his bedside. He wrote that his brother "remained motionless for an instant. He did not cry out. He fell as gently as a (young) tree falls," an image that would much later be recrafted into the climactic ending of *The Little Prince*. As the only male in the family, Saint-Exupéry assumed a protective role for his mother and three sisters.

In 1896 at the age of forty, **Sigmund Freud** (1856–1939) lost his own father; he discussed the death of his father and the mourning process in many of his writings with various comments. In the preface to the second edition of *The Interpretation of Dreams* (1900–1901) he wrote: "For this book has a further subjective significance for me personally—a significance which I only grasped after I had completed it. It was, I found, a portion of my own self-analysis, my reaction to my father's death—that is to say, to the most important event, the most poignant loss, of a man's life. Having discovered that this was so, I felt unable to obliterate the traces of the experience" (xxvi).

According to Nicolas Abraham (1919–1975), a Hungarian-born French psychoanalyst, **Leonardo da Vinci** (1452–1519) finished his painting the *Mona Lisa* at the moment when his old father united with his already deceased mother in heaven. Her smile was the smile of one dead person to another and was also Leonardo da Vinci's motivation to live. Only with the death of his father was his mother's happiness—impossible on earth—fulfilled and realized. "The Mona Lisa is looking at something in you, but who is behind you. She looks at the child you have been, as a mother looks at her child" (Mathon 2011, np).

Original mourning

For Racamier (1999), *original mourning* consists of the indispensable renunciation of possession of the primary object[55] (the mother or the primary caregiver) and is essential for disengaging from the narcissistic baby-mother union of the very early life stages. The basic development of the capacity for intimacy in relationships depends on the differentiation between self and other, and the ability to be in touch with one's own intrapsychic space. A separation process from primary significant caretakers is imperative for the individual person in order to find joy and resources in the secrecy of a personal inner world. If awareness of one's own and others' limits are missing, the creation of true intimacy in relationships, of authentic relatedness remains unrealizable.

[55] The notion of primary object corresponds to the constitution of the object of satisfaction of needs and wishes resulting from the first mother-infant encounter, even before questions of inside/outside, subject/object have been raised.

Romain Gary (1914–1980), pen name Emile Ajar, comments on the lived loyalty bond with his mother: "I could not find anything that matched my strange need, nothing worthy of my mother, of my love, of all that I wanted to give her." He was—as he describes it himself—confronted with his mother's narcissistic over-investment and idealization, and at the same time, the unfulfilled emotional and personal realization in her own life. She maintained an intense, exclusive, and intimate symbiotic relationship with her son, inhibiting his developmental processes of individuation, differentiation, and separation, but favoring his ambitious striving and intellectual development. Gary's mother predicted for her son a future as an aviator, a famous writer, an ambassador of France—all of which Gary actually did become, thus satisfying his mother's narcissistic expectations and need. Gary grew up without a father, who had abandoned his family and was then excluded by Gary's mother. He learned only much later about the death of his father in a concentration camp.

Romain Gary was born Roman Kacew in Vilnius, Lithuania (which at that time was still part of imperial Russia), the son of a Jewish merchant of skins and furs, Arieh Kacew, and Mina Owczynska, daughter of a Jewish watchmaker. In 1925, Arieh left his wife and child, and Mina raised her only son, in whom she placed the wildest hopes of grandeur and glory—she who had never been the great actress she had dreamed of being. Fleeing the pogroms of communism, she took Roman to Nice, France, where they settled in 1928. Roman, who changed his name to Romain, was at this time fourteen years old. His mother died from cancer in 1941.

His novel *The Life Before Us,* written under the pseudonym of Emile Ajar, won the Goncourt Prize in 1975. The hero in the story is fourteen years old and his Jewish foster mother defends her "adopted" son like a lioness, thus suggesting a parallel with Romain's biography; the story is a tribute to his mother, as well as a representation of life, old age, death, tolerance and love: "Happiness, I'm not going to throw myself into that, before I have tried everything to pull me through."[56] In this novel, the main characters are Momo (Mohammed), an Arab living in Paris, and Madame Rosa, an old Jewish woman who survived Auschwitz; she is a former prostitute and raises children of prostitutes. Momo's father killed his mother, a prostitute, and ends up in prison and then a psychiatric institution. Momo is fourteen years old, but Madame Rose tells him that he is only eleven. Momo recounts his life with her and his profound love for her, asking: "Is it possible to live without someone to love?" Once out of prison, his father begins looking for his son, but Madame Rose persuades him that Momo is not his son; he is a Jew and his name is Moses. Momo accompanies Madame Rose, his courageous and proud mother, as she becomes increasingly sick at the end of her life: "The first thing I can tell you is that we lived on the sixth floor and that for Madame Rosa, with all the weight she bore and only two legs, it was a real part of daily life, with all its worries and sorrows." She continually reminded him that she did not complain because she was also Jewish. "Her health was not good either, and I can tell you

[56] All the quotations in this paragraph are our own translations.

from the beginning that this was a woman who deserved an elevator." He fights for life because life "does not forgive" and because it is "not necessary to have reasons to be afraid." He helps her to hide in her "Jewish hole," so that she will not have to die in the hospital as a "vegetable" and will thus benefit from the sacred right "of people's disposing of themselves," which, according to Madame Rose, is not respected by doctors. He keeps her company until she dies, and even beyond her death.

In *Promise at Dawn* (1962) Gary tells the story of a mother's sacrifice, his own mother and her unquestionable, unconditional, absolute love for him, his love for her, and their shared life together. "Born out of a mother's murmur into a child's ear, a promise whispered at dawn of future triumphs and greatness, of justice and love" (np).

> In your mother's love, life makes you a promise that it will never keep. You have known something that you will never know again. You will go hungry to the end of your days. Leftovers, cold titbits, that's what you will find in front of you at each new feast. After that first encounter, so early in the dawn, each time a woman takes you in her arms and presses you to her heart and murmurs sweet words into your ear, you will always do your best to forget and to believe, but you will always know better. You will always crawl back to your mother's grave and howl like a lost dog. Never again, never again, never again (Gary in Hirsh 2018, 173).

It was only around 40 that I started to understand. It is not good to be loved so much, so young, so early. It gives you bad habits. One believes that it happened. One believes that it exists elsewhere, that it can be found. One counts on it. One looks, one hopes, one waits. One is then forced to eat cold until the end of one's days. Wherever you go, you carry the poison of comparisons and you spend your time waiting for what you have already received. I'm not saying that mothers should be prevented from loving their little ones. I'm just saying it's better if mothers still have someone else to love. If my mother had a lover, I would not have spent my life dying of thirst at every fountain (Gary in Goldman 2007, 29–30).

The inability to mourn

When someone dies, it is not only death, death is when someone lives and ignores it, death is when it is impossible for someone to die.
Rainer Maria Rilke (1875–1926)

The consequences of severe psychic trauma can under certain circumstances be transmitted from one generation to another, like a cultural heritage. The history of the parents is not separable from the personal history of their child, and the parental past becomes the present for the child. If a person denies a traumatic loss and mourning of the loved one is impossible to fulfill, that person may be emotionally unavailable and affectively empty for his or her own children. A parent may then envy the child's emotional competencies and often have a depreciative, disqualifying attitude toward the child, even being verbally violent or acting aggressively. The child will feel responsible for filling a parent's emptiness with his or her own emotional skills; at the same time tending to feel guilty for the envy and aggression of the parent. The consequences of this enduring situation can be that the child gives up on personal self-development, represses or turns the aggressive feelings toward the parent upon him- or herself, and out of loyalty, feelings of hopelessness, helplessness, and shame remain silent.

Silence is the child's key protection mechanism against a parent's abuse, the parent's violence, for which words are missing; unbearable feelings cannot be addressed with language, especially since no one is present to perceive, hear, share, or understand these intolerable emotions. This imposed silence spares the parent, whose pathology and abuse are never recognized and who is instead idealized, while leaving the child in infinite loneliness and with feelings of worthlessness, defenselessness, and an eternal yearning for closeness and intimacy.

Closeness in this situation requires fusion with the parent, acceptance of the parental pathology, becoming a prisoner of envy and abuse, and, in addition, an obligation to nurture the parent—a duty to fill his or her emptiness. Separation is associated with a simultaneous dreadful fear of not being able to survive on one's own. Pain must be endured without complaints; anger and sadness are not to be perceived. This learned and interiorized relationship-constellation and interaction will be repeated in relationships with others. Therefore, closeness and intimacy are often linked with the abolition of one's own difference, individuality, and separateness. The building up of a private self remains insufficient and subjectively felt experiences of losing self-consistency are repeated. Consequences can include recurrent suicidal attempts in order to escape painful internal experiences. There is an intolerance to grief, a state of annihilation, and an impoverishment of fantasy activity. The entourage is left in an inextricable situation (Racamier 1999, 128).

Marina Abramovic (1946) a performance artist of Serbian origin,[57] presents in her artworks her lifelong struggle to free herself from intensely violent, painful, and frightening traumatic life experiences with her parents.

> My parents were both partisans and national heroes. They were very hardcore and were so busy with their careers that I lived with my grandmother until I was six. Until then, I hardly even knew who my parents were. They were just two strange people who would visit on Saturdays and bring

[57] Performance art is an art form that combines visual art with dramatic performance, presented to an audience within a fine art context.

> presents. When I was six, my brother was born, and I was sent back to my parents. From that point on, my childhood was very unhappy. I grew up with incredible control, discipline, and violence at home. Everything was extreme. My mother never kissed me. When I asked why, she said, "Not to spoil you, of course." She had a bacteria phobia so she didn't allow me to play with other children out of fear that I might catch a disease. She even washed bananas with detergent. I spent most of my time alone in my room. There were many, many rules. Everything had to be in perfect order. If I slept messily in bed, my mother would wake me in the middle of the night and order me to sleep straight. I never felt at home in my own home and I never feel at home anywhere. When I was growing up, my private life was not valued. The noblest thing one could do in my family was to sacrifice everything for a cause. Art became my cause and it's still everything to me. I dedicate all the energy in my body to my work and have completely sacrificed a more conventional personal life for it. I have no partner and no children, but I'm very proud of myself for always doing what I want, no matter what the cost and no matter how long it's taken. … I wake up in the morning with this urge to create; it's almost like I am in a fever. Every single day is structured. I work, work, work, and my curiosity never ends (Popova 2015, np).

The Artist Is Present was an extraordinary exhibition in 2010 of her performance art in the Museum of Modern Art in New York. Abramovic sat immobile and silent for over 700 hours, while spectators took turns in sitting and facing her. In the interviews of Abramovic and psychoanalyst Jeannette Fischer, she remembers that she expended the same energy as a child, when her father left her in the water, alone with her destiny, and rowed away with his boat; she did not know then if she would survive. "I swim. I am alone. I am unloved and abandoned and—survive" (Fischer 2018, 57). Torturing herself and suffering pain releases her from fear. She repeats in this performance what she has experienced all her life, what it is to be abandoned and to have to rely on herself. "I did not know anything else" (65).

Chapter 11

GRIEVING PROCESSES

The replacement or substitute child

The death of a child affects the whole family. The adaptation process that the parents and siblings of a dying child undergo is described as "anticipatory grief." The more the healthy siblings sense that their parents can endure their feelings of sadness and anger, the more likely they are to tolerate their own emotions. When parents are unable to fulfill a mourning process for the loss of their child—a loss that represents a traumatic event—then a living sibling often assumes the grief work of the parents. The surviving child may unconsciously be designated to alleviate the parents' feeling of guilt or may be compared with the lost idealized child and never be able to fulfill the parents' expectations. The replacement child has to build up an identity and origin myth around a "foreign body" that the parents have deposited in him or her, due to their ambivalent attachment to another child, whose loss they deny and whose aliveness they maintain in their intrapsychic world (in "Crypts" through incorporation fantasies, according to Abraham and Torok 1987). The replacement child tries to identify him- or herself (by endocryptic identification) with the lost love object—the parents were not able to mourn—and to internalize it, even if the child did not know the lost sibling. This conduct is motivated by the child's desire to understand the parents yet is often accompanied by uncanny feelings (Hirsch 1999). To be a substitute child means having a serious handicap in the development of one's own identity. The child is constantly compared to the idealized dead sibling. Thus, the replacement child faces a lifelong search for a personal identity, as well as for that of the dead sibling.

Parents may select and reinforce some expressions of their child, which then become part of a specific parent-child communication system. For example, when a baby is expected to replace a deceased person (a brother, sister, or even a grandparent), whose mourning has not been elaborated, the infant runs the risk of becoming a substitute. The mother's or father's need to cling to such a substitute child, who also represents their lost love, is above all expressed by their gaze, voice, attitude, and gestures, and less by their words.

Vincent van Gogh (1853–1890) wrote in a letter to his brother Theo: "Three big pictures ... boundlessly outstretched fields under a cloudy sky, and it is not difficult for me to express in them all my sadness, the utmost loneliness. ... I believe that these pictures tell you what I cannot express in words, namely what I find healthy and comforting in country life"[58] (Misteli 2014, 16).

Van Gogh was a replacement child, having a stillborn brother with the same name—including the middle name Willem—and the same birth date. Both boys were named after their paternal grandfather. As the son of a pastor he grew up next to the cemetery where his brother was buried. He called himself a secondary, a substitute. The replacement theme appears in van Gogh's correspondence. His self-portraits are considered to be connected to his identification of being a substitute child. Van Gogh suffered from fantasies that he was expected to represent the lost brother. His fantasies of death and rebirth, of being a double and a twin, certainly contributed to his creativity, but were also the expression of his melancholy. In 1885 van Gogh's father died suddenly, too early for Vincent to gain the hoped-for acknowledgement of his father.

Looking back at Van Gogh's unique artistic talent and his extraordinary productivity—he created over two thousand paintings—one wonders about his various motivational forces; one driver might have been to outdo his double (his stillborn brother) and fulfill his immense potential. Over the course of a lifetime, replacement children may search for their own and their dead brother or sister's identity and throughout the development experience mysterious feelings around the intrapsychic representation of the dead sibling.

Van Gogh's artistic genius is often diminished by those who see his paintings as mere visual manifestations of his troubled mind. While this may in part be true, in reality his innovative and unique artistic style was of enormous importance to a host of artists who followed in his wake. Even when influenced by his predecessors or contemporaries, his art remained identifiably his own, as he developed a distinctive style that failed to be accepted by the art-buying public in his own time.

Camille Claudel (1864–1943), a French sculptor, was born eighteen months after the death (shortly after his birth) of her brother. She did not fulfill her mother's wish of a boy to replace the lost first son. "There is always something missing that torments

[58] Our translation.

me," stated Camille in a letter to Auguste Rodin in 1886. One may wonder whether she was tormented by the missing brother she was unable to replace.

While her father encouraged and supported Camille in her art, her mother never accepted her daughter's life choices. At age nineteen she started working in Auguste Rodin's (1840–1917) atelier and became his lover. Rodin, twenty-four years her senior, was not willing to end his relationship with Rose Beuret, the mother of his son, also called Auguste. Camille's rage and jealousy in this love triangle may have made a significant contribution to the deterioration of her mental health. In 1892 Camille definitively separated from Rodin, and, through her experiments in marble and bronze combinations, was highly creative, producing novel and outstanding pieces of sculpture. She created *The Implorer* (Fig. 11.1). One may wonder if the sculpture represents herself, on her knees, humiliated and imploring.

Camille Claudel gradually fell mentally ill, destroying her sculptures out of overwhelming feelings of rage and despair. In 1913 her father died, but the members of her family did not inform her of his death, instead deciding to admit her into an asylum.

Figure 11.1 Camille Claudel. *The Implorer* (L'Implorante) (ca. 1898–1910). Bronze statuette.

In 1917, in a letter to a physician, hoping to be released from the asylum, she wrote: "I am reproached (what a terrible crime!) for having lived alone, spent my life with cats, and for having felt persecuted! It is based on these accusations that I have been imprisoned for five and a half years like a criminal, deprived of freedom, deprived of food, warmth, and the most basic essentials." Camille abandoned sculpture work entirely and was held for thirty years in the asylum. The question of whether her internment was justified remains highly controversial, as she continued to be lucid, writing letters to family and friends. On two occasions at least, physicians were in favor of her release. In a letter to a friend in 1935 she wrote: "I live in a world that is so curious, so strange. Of the dream, which was my life, this [life in the asylum] is the nightmare." She died alone at the age of 78 and was buried in the asylum's mass grave because her family did not request her body. The following quotes demonstrate her tormented feelings and struggle with life: "I am in no mood to be deceived any longer by the crafty devil and false character whose greatest pleasure is to take advantage of everyone." "I am scared; I don't know what is going to happen to me. What was the point of working so hard and of being talented, to be rewarded like this? Never a penny, tormented all my life. It is horrible; one cannot imagine it." "I would prefer to have a more appealing job. If I could still change careers, I would prefer it. This unfortunate art is made for long beards and ugly faces rather than for a relatively well-endowed woman." "I am like Donkey Skin or Cinderella condemned to keep the ashes of the heart, never hoping to see the Fairy Godmother or the Prince Charming who must change my clothes made of skin and ash into dresses the color of time. How can you sleep soundly while so many women shout: Help, I am drowning!"[59]

Even when the root is ignorant of the fruits, it nourishes them nevertheless
Rainer Maria Rilke[60]

Rainer Maria Rilke (1875–1926), an Austrian poet and novelist, was a replacement child for a sister who had died in childbirth. His mother dealt with her death by insisting that he wore girls' clothing until he was five years old. "Death, that's so many things, as long as we cannot bury ourselves" (Rilke 1988, 139). "Death is the side of life turned away from us, unilluminated by us: we must try to achieve the greatest possible consciousness of our existence, which is at home in both of these unlimited provinces, and inexhaustibly nourished by both" (Rilke 1988, 144).

Rilke wrote in his poem "Farewell":

How did I feel what is called farewell? How do I still know it: a dark, unwound, cruel something that shows a beautiful bond once again and holds it up and tears it apart.[61]

59 These quotations are from "Camille Claudel," The Art Story, accessed 10 December 2020, https://www.theartstory.org/artist/claudel-camille.

60 Rilke (1988, 10). Our translation.

61 Our translation.

The marriage of Rilke's parents failed when he was nine years old. This early experience of the finite nature of relationships and the problem of mourning are evident in much of his future writings. In his *Letters to a Young Poet*, Rilke (1993) wrote:

> The point of marriage is not to create a quick commonality by tearing down all boundaries; on the contrary, a good marriage is one in which each partner appoints the other to be the guardian of his solitude, and thus they show each other the greatest possible trust. A merging of two people is an impossibility, and where it seems to exist, it is a hemming-in, a mutual consent that robs one party or both parties of their fullest freedom and development. But once the realization is accepted that even between the closest people infinite distances exist, a marvelous living side-by-side can grow up for them, if they succeed in loving the expanse between them, which gives them the possibility of always seeing each other as a whole and before an immense sky. … I hold this to be the highest task of a bond between two people: that each should stand guard over the solitude of the other.

Rilke's abstract definition of his own marriage was of "a love like two solitudes greeting and saluting each other" (1992).

Rilke's *Letters to a Young Poet* were addressed to **Franz Xaver Kappus** (1883–1966), an Austrian military officer, journalist, editor, and writer of poetry, short-stories, novels, and screenplays. In the introduction to *Letters to a Young Poet*,[62] Franz Xaver Kappus writes:

> It was late autumn of 1902, I was sitting under some ancient chestnuts in the park of the Military Academy in Wiener-Neustadt, reading. So deeply was I absorbed in my book, I scarcely noticed when the only civilian among our professors, the Academy's learned and kindly Parson Horacek, came to join me. He took the volume from my hand, contemplated the cover, and shook his head. "Poems of Rainer Maria Rilke?" he asked reflectively. He then turned the pages here and there, skimmed a couple of verses, gazed thoughtfully into the distance, and finally nodded. "So, our pupil Rainer Rilke has become a poet."

[62] Published in German in 1929.

Kappus wrote several letters from 1875 to 1926 to Rilke, also the following *Sonnet*[63]:

> Through my life trembles without plaint, without a sigh a deep-dark melancholy. The pure and snowy blossoming of my dreams is the consecration of my stillest days. But oftentimes the great question crosses my path. I become small and go coldly past as though along some lake whose flood I have not hardihood to measure. And then a sorrow sinks upon me, dusky as the gray of lusterless summer nights through which a star glimmers—now and then: My hands then gropingly reach out for love, because I want so much to pray sounds that my hot mouth cannot find…

Rilke sent the sonnet back to Kappus with this handwritten comment: "Read the lines as if they were unknown to you, and you will feel in your inmost self how very much they are yours."

In his lifetime Rainer Maria Rilke wrote thousands of letters showing not only a unique linguistic and stylistic capacity, but an immense sensitivity, human empathy and critical self-awareness.

The following are excerpts from Rainer Maria Rilke's *Letters to a Young Poet*, which demonstrate his perception and compassion for the suffering subject and his infinite expressive creativity in recounting a narrative of embracing uncertainty, of perseverance in self-recognition, and of the acceptance of loneliness leading to a process of personal growth and self-knowledge. His answers to the poet Kappus testify to his deep wisdom.

His guidance for life: "Only someone who is ready for everything, who doesn't exclude any experience, even the most incomprehensible, will live the relationship with another person as something alive and will himself sound the depths of his own being." "So you must not be frightened if a sadness rises up before you larger than any you have ever seen; if a restiveness, like light and cloud shadows, passes over your hands and over all you do. You must think that something is happening with you, that life has not forgotten you, that it holds you in its hand; it will not let you fall. Why do you want to shut out of your life any uneasiness, any miseries, or any depressions? For after all, you do not know what work these conditions are doing inside you."

[63] Original text: Durch mein Leben zittert ohne Klage, ohne Seufzer ein tiefdunkles Weh.
Meiner Träume reiner Blütenschnee ist die Weihe meiner stillsten Tage.
Öfter aber kreuzt die große Frage meinen Pfad. Ich werde klein und geh
kalt vorüber wie an einem See, dessen Flut ich nicht zu messen wage.
Und dann sinkt ein Leid auf mich, so trübe wie das Grau glanzarmer Sommernächte,
Und dann sinkt ein Leid auf mich, so trübe wie das Grau glanzarmer Sommernächte,
die ein Stern durchflimmert – dann und wann—: Meine Hände tasten dann nach Liebe,
weil ich gerne Laute beten möchte, die mein heißer Mund nicht finden kann

Of love he writes: "Perhaps everything that frightens us is, in its deepest essence, something helpless that wants our love." "Believe in a love that is being stored up for you like an inheritance, and have faith that in this love there is a strength and a blessing so large that you can travel as far as you wish without having to step outside it."

Rilke's advice on searching and finding: "Don't be too quick to draw conclusions from what happens to you; simply let it happen. Otherwise it will be too easy for you to look with blame … at your past, which naturally has a share with everything that now meets you." "I beg you, to have patience with everything unresolved in your heart and to try to love the questions themselves. … Live the questions now. Perhaps then, someday far in the future, you will gradually, without even noticing it, live your way into the answer."

On solitude Rilke has comforting words: "Just in the deepest and most important things, we are unutterably alone." "Embrace your solitude and love it. Endure the pain it causes and try to sing out with it." "But your solitude will be a support and a home for you, even in the midst of very unfamiliar circumstances, and from it you will find all your paths."

Rilke's understanding of art: "Things aren't all so tangible and sayable as people would usually have us believe; most experiences are unsayable, they happen in a space that no word has ever entered, and more unsayable than all other things are works of art, those mysterious existences, whose life endures beside our own small, transitory life."

Salvador Dali (1904–1989), a Spanish surrealist painter, was born nine months after the death of his brother at the age of two years; he was also named Salvador. Dali wrote that he had already experienced the tragedy and despair of his mother about the loss of her first child in the womb. When he was five years old, at his brother's grave, his parents told him that he was his brother's reincarnation. Dali recalled, we "resembled each other like two drops of water, but we had different reflections."[64] He "was probably a first version of myself but conceived too much in the absolute."[65] When Dali was sixteen years old, his mother died.

Dali has called many of his works "hand-painted dream photographs." At the age of twenty-seven he painted his most famous paintings *Persistence of Memory* (also called *Clocks*), regarded as a surrealist masterpiece (Fig. 11.2). It was inspired by the surrealist idea of visual interpretations of dreams or dream impressions, giving rise to uncanny feelings in the viewer. With the melting and distorted clocks in the painting, Dali plays with the idea that our concept of time becomes arbitrary when we are in a dream state.

In the *Diary of a Genius* (Dali and Ballard 2007) Dali states: "One day it will have to be officially admitted that what we have christened reality is an even greater

64 "Salvador Dali," Biography, January 16, 2020, https://.biography.com/artist/salvador-dali.

65 Ibid.

illusion than the world of dreams." Dali read Sigmund Freud and used what he called a "paranoiac-critical method" to access his subconscious, thus enhancing his artistic creativity; he painted out of his dreams and subconscious thoughts. Might the death of his brother, whose memory persists, have played a role in the numerous factors underlying the title of the painting?

Figure 11.2 Salvador Dali. *The Persistence of Memory - Soft Clocks - Melting pocket watch, detail* (1931). Oil on canvas.

Loss of a sibling in childhood

My mother, dressed in black, absorbed by her state of mourning, dreamed about the absent child, her passion for the dead child making her at moments a stranger—yes, even, silently hostile to the living. The young mother in mourning shut herself away in a dungeon of solitary and armed faith, and she shut her son in there with her.
Romain Rolland.[66]

Various artists have lost a sibling. The siblings of dying children are regarded as one of the most neglected groups in bereaved families. Children, adolescents, and young adults intensively mourn a sibling lost during childhood. After losing a sibling, a child also loses his or her "former" parents, since they are occupied with their own grief work. A child's close emotional relationship with a sibling before his or her death increases the mourning reaction. Feelings of rivalry among siblings may turn to feelings of guilt after the death of the sibling. The grief reaction may be accompanied by anger, shame, relief, blame, or remorse.

Sigmund Freud (1856–1939) and Romain Rolland (1866–1944)

Both Freud and Romain Rolland were adored by their mothers, which, according to Freud, is an advantage, as it may contribute to becoming an extraordinary person. Both suffered the death of a sibling in early childhood and lived through their mother's mourning, which may have influenced their creative work. Rolland visited Freud in 1924 in Vienna (together with Stefan Zweig), which was their only meeting. Their creative minds and their shared need to write represented the profound interest in their encounter. "A common feature of their destinies was the struggle against death through the act of creation: 'die or create', as Rolland wrote" (Vermorel 2009, 1242).

Rolland's younger sister, Madeleine, died of illness when he was five years old. At the age of two, Freud lost his then only six-month-old brother Julius. The loss of her son was accompanied by Freud's mother's emotional absence and seems to have provoked in Freud a transitory psychic shock.

In the letters between Freud und Rolland, reading, admiring, and commenting on each other's work, the early loss of a sibling and the mourning state of their mothers contributed to their intimate resonating relatedness. According to Rolland, "oceanic feeling,"[67] a concept developed by him and continued by Freud, can be considered as a form of defense denying the destructive aspect of trauma. Freud interpreted the oceanic feeling as an instance of the primary narcissistic union between mother and infant.

66 *Le voyage interieur. Songe d'une vie* (1959, 84–6).

67 Rolland thought true religion arose from what he called *un sentiment océanique* and extended an invitation to Freud to analyze it.

> Geniuses, who have suffered exceptional wounds, such as bereavements in childhood, an early confrontation with death, have to fight against their internal destructiveness to build an oeuvre aiming at immortality. "The summit meeting"[68] at which Freud invites Rolland on the "hill of the Acropolis," the high place of antiquity, symbolizes the fight that led these two heroes of culture to survive against destruction by creation.
>
> The feeling of strangeness (the uncanny feelings) on the Acropolis revealed the inner conflict of the psychoanalyst within the paradox of his atheistic Jewish identity, between his unbelief on the one hand, and the affirmation of his connection to Jewishness, anchored in an established religion on the other hand (Vermorel 2018, 568).

In 1925 Freud writes: "Nor is it perhaps entirely a matter of chance that the first advocate of psychoanalysis was a Jew. To profess belief in this new theory called for a certain degree of readiness to accept a situation of solitary opposition—a situation with which no one is more familiar than a Jew" (222).

Parents who lose a child face a threefold task: besides their own grief, they have to help their dying child and the surviving siblings with their mourning processes. Siblings' angry feelings toward parents, who are unable to grieve the loss of their child and therefore are incapable of helping the surviving brothers and sisters, are an additional source of guilt. The enhanced and generalized anxiety of losing someone dominates and modifies social interactions. For each child or adolescent, mourning a deceased sibling will be an individual process, sometimes carried out only years later. As adults, they may consider the loss of a sibling during childhood as one of their most important life events, one that has left traces and will persist throughout their life, demonstrated by the following expressions: "Why should we continue to live without my sister" or "I do not believe that my brother is dead." Parental grief work after the loss of a child is only partially or not at all achieved in about half of parents.

[68] Sigmund Freud was eighty years old when he offered his friend Romain Rolland a travel memory in the form of an open letter, on the occasion of the writer's seventieth birthday in 1936.

PART V

Chapter 12

ADVERSITY AND RESILIENCE

And as the ordinary mortal falls silent in his torment,
a god gave me the power to say what I suffer.
Johann Wolfgang Goethe (1749–1832)[69]

Illness was no doubt the final cause of the whole urge to create.
By creating, I could recover; by creating, I became healthy.
Heinrich Heine (1797–1856)[70]

Artists have fought madness, ill-health, penury, and humiliating exile
—political, cultural, religious—in order to do their work.
Toni Morrison (1931–2019)[71]

These words demonstrate the artist's gift for expressing their affects and seeking emotional relief in creating, mastering, and integrating their subjective lived experiences. Artists invent and create throughout their lifetime from an inner original source; the desires and suffering of their personal life are represented, and feelings and emotions shared in their artwork.

Trauma resulting in a deeply distressing or disturbing experience represents "an event in the subject's life, defined by its intensity, by the subject's incapacity to respond adequately to it and by the upheaval and long-lasting effects that it brings about in the mental organization" (Laplanche and Pontalis 1973, 465). The notion of trauma represents a conceptual bridge between an event and its impacts. It tries to

69 The "Marienbad Elegy" (1908, 143) is a poem by Johann Wolfgang von Goethe. It is named after the spa town of Marienbad where Goethe, seventy-three years old, spent the summer of 1821. There he fell in love with the seventeen-year-old Ulrike von Levetzow.

70 Heinrich Heine (1797–1856), German poet, writer and literary critic (Neue Gedichte, Schöpfungslieder 7). Original text: Krankheit ist wohl der letzte Grund des ganzen Schöpferdrangs gewesen; erschaffend konnte ich genesen, erschaffend wurde ich gesund.

71 *The Source of Self-Regard* (2019, 64).

connect the external reality, life events, with their consequences on the inner world of an individual, and thus establishes a relationship between the external and internal reality experience of a subject. Traumatic experience is defined as a vital experience of discrepancy between threatening situational factors and individual coping abilities, which is accompanied by feelings of helplessness, abandonment, and defenselessness (Fischer and Riedesser 1999).

Adversities due to human aggression; atrocities such as war, terrorism, or displacement; disasters caused by human error in technical matters, for example, aircraft accidents and industrial disasters; and natural disasters such as earthquakes, floods, hurricane, or fire must be distinguished from traumata occurring within the family framework, such as abuse, neglect and deprivation, the loss of loved ones through abandon, separation, death or suicide, multiple placements, parental chronic somatic or mental illness for offspring, accidents, operations, serious injury or life-threatening or chronic illness, violence, witnessing cruel acts, and cultural uprooting.

Stress and trauma research demonstrate how traumatic experiences in early life affect the coping capacity of an individual and influence development. The long-term mental consequences of traumatic events are an inability to regulate, control, and verbally express feelings of anger, fear, and sadness, as well as an inability to perceive stimuli appropriately and adapt to the environment. The neurobiological consequences of stress events at early ages, such as bereavements, are reflected in molecular and cellular changes not only in the limbic system (in particular in the amygdala and hippocampus) but also in the prefrontal cortex. Dysfunction of the hypothalamic-pituitary-adrenal axis is postulated to play a key role in stress-related disorders such as depression and post-traumatic stress disorder.

Multiple or repeated traumatization—cumulative traumata—in childhood may have severe outcomes and affect multiple developmental domains such as regulation of affect and impulses, memory, attention, consciousness, self-perception, and interpersonal relationships. What cannot be integrated mentally is imprinted in the body and manifests itself in psychosomatic symptoms, which are constantly repeated. It is as if the body "remembers" and the subject inscribes into his or her body what is unbearable to feel, what is psychically intolerable. Adults who have experienced multiple or cumulative traumata in early childhood often present not only symptoms of a post-traumatic stress disorder (PTSD), but additional symptoms, including difficulties in affective and interpersonal situations and disturbances in self-regulation skills. Recent research (Mary et al. 2020) suggests that subjects suffering from PTSD present a deficit in memory suppression. This dysfunction in memory regulation may explain the persistence of traumatic memories, impairing the ability to develop the necessary coping resources.

Resilience refers to a relative resistance to environmental risk experiences, or to the overcoming of adversity or stress, such as traumatic events, challenging life circumstances, or life transitions. Underlying psychosocial and biological processes, risk and vulnerability factors, and gene-environment interactions are important contributions.

Resilience may be constrained by damaging effects of stress or adversity on neural structures. A secure attachment represents part of the mediation process in which resilience is observed. Notably, interest in the role of oxytocin as a "resilience-hormone" is derived from its effects on fostering attachment. Resilience is responsible for the individual variations in the response of children and adolescents to similar experiences. The exposure to stress and not its avoidance may in certain circumstances strengthen the resistance to later stress, known as the "steeling" effect, in other words when risk experiences have been mastered by successful coping. Longitudinal studies concerning the effects of psychosocial constraints on the development of resilience demonstrate that indicators of child resilience such as adequate behavioral and emotional self-regulation contribute to later competence. The effects of single environmental burdens become quite strong when accumulated into multiple risk scores; they may even affect the development of offspring in the next generation. Good intellectual functioning and parenting resources are associated with good outcomes across competence domains, even in the context of severe, chronic adversity. Individual differences in temperament can increase vulnerability or facilitate resilience. Children with different temperament styles seek out environments that may increase risk or promote resilience. The quality of interpersonal relationships between infant and caregivers is essential in view of intergenerational transmission and resilience development.

Building blocks for creativity in children

Playing

"It is a sophisticated game of hide-and-seek, in which it is a joy to be hidden
but a disaster not to be found"
(Winnicott 1963, 186)

Children love to play hide and seek. Playing hide-and-seek may well be for the sake of playing and not to reach any specific goal, but one cannot exclude a reward-oriented behavior in hiding and then being found. This hide-and-seek play necessitates complex mental representations such as game understanding and behavioral aspects, including rapid, directed locomotion in hiding, followed by the joy of being found. Children will often try to hide again, after they were found, thus extending the game, and really playing for the fun of it. Developing good hide-and-seek strategies requires cognitive abilities for strategically thinking in order to know where the playmate will most likely search or which hiding place works best.

In an animal study, scientists have shown that rats can quickly learn a version of the hide-and-seek game and can easily switch between the different roles of hiding and searching (Reinhold et al. 2019). The rats squealed with joy when the experimenter found them, executing joy jumps. In contrast, they were very quiet when hiding. They carefully chose their hiding places and, when found, they often went off to hide again as they seemed to enjoy the game. To address what is going on in the rat's brain during play, the scientists studied the neural activity in the medial prefrontal cortex, a brain area that in humans is involved in planning and social cognition. Neuronal recordings revealed intense prefrontal cortex activity that varied with game events such as hiding and seeking, clearly suggesting that the rats understood the rules of the game.

It is well known that animals play in the wild. They chase each other and engage in mock fights, readily adopting different roles, probably also playing hide-and-seek, taking turns in seeking each other. From an evolutionary behavioral point of view, the ability to hide well and to search effectively is essential for survival. We thus can assume that play games like hide-and-seek are evolutionarily very old.

"It is in playing, and only in playing, that the individual child or adult is able to be creative and to use the whole personality, and it is only in being creative that the individual discovers the self" (Winnicott 1971, 54). "In the case of children's play we seemed to see that children repeat unpleasurable experiences for the additional reason that they can master a powerful impression far more thoroughly by being active than they could by merely experiencing it passively" (Freud 1920, 35).

Spontaneous play allows an expression of inner psychic processes and may therefore contribute to variations in representations. Without requirements or constraints, play provides an abundance of creativity. "Within the inner life of the child, play is a mental process which takes its stand along with, intermingles with, builds upon and integrates with many other mental processes in the developing child's mind—thinking, imaging, pretending, planning, wondering, doubting, remembering, guessing, hoping, experimenting, revising and working through" (Cohen 2006, 137). In the area of play (Winnicott 1971, 102), a potential space between an individual and his environment, two persons can create new representations together, offering different solutions and significant meanings, sometimes out of chaotic and senseless elements. In the mother-child interaction mutual play is of essential importance. Already in the second month of life, eye contact and vocal accompaniment are significant interactions between mother and infant.

With repetitive play the child tries to master past experiences. Children explore their relationship with significant others and show—in their fantasy play—their expectations and wishes, as well as how these meaningful persons should answer their needs and desires. The therapeutic and restorative functions of playing have already been discussed by Anna Freud (1965). Later Winnicott (1971) considered playing as an important feature fostering development. Playing allows a child to experiment with identification of and solutions to intra-psychic conflict situations and to gain self-understanding and self-awareness. "Just pretend play" facilitates the emergence of unconscious wishes and conflicts; their verbalization in play—that is on a displacement level—may be less anxiety-provoking and more acceptable for a child, later allowing a referring of the play-story to him- or herself and to personal difficulties.

Baby-mother (or caregiver) interaction[72]

The Latin term *infans*,[73] meaning "one who does not speak," refers to the baby before the acquisition of speech, that is, to its preverbal communication; for the infant, the mother holds the role of a "word-bearer." She verbalizes the baby's expressions and provides meaning for the infant's manifestations (Castoriadis-Aulagnier 2001).

According to Winnicott (1971) there is no baby without a mother. For the baby to be recognized visually by mother's face and acoustically by mother's voice are the building blocks for intrapsychic representations, self-constitution, and subjective awareness. Learning the language and its meaning takes place in the emotional interaction with primary caregivers. The process of acquiring speech has been called "the emotional history of words" (Rizzuto 2003).

Bollas (1979) considers the infant's earliest experience of the mother as a process: the mother's psychic attitudes and corporal handling of her baby continuously transform the infant's emotional state and bodily being. When the child has acquired language and thought capacities, a self-narrative[74] process begins in which the child addresses him- or herself as an object in inner discourse: "'I said to myself'" (Bollas 1982, 348). "From this moment on, the child constructs fantasized self-other scenes based on previous and current experiences and uses language retroactively (*nachträglich*) to give affective meaning to earlier experiences" (Rizzuto 2003, 305).

Parents transmit their unconscious desires and fantasies to their children through nonverbal communication, the variants being of a sensorimotor nature, tactile, visual, and auditory modalities. During breast- or bottle-feeding, for example, multiple modes of communication are used: the gaze; the respective postures of the mother and her baby and their mutual adjustment; the prosody and tonality of the dialog; the holding, the contact, and the touch; the speech and vocalizations; as well as the gustatory and olfactory experiences of the baby. The child will react to the fantasies expressed by the communicative behavior of his or her parents according to his or her own motivations, in particular a desire for communication and a need for relationship and holding, deriving from his or her own impulses and defenses. The newborn disposes of an important number of skills brought into play for the "parentalization" of the parents. A baby already has the ability to establish triadic exchanges[75] (Fivaz-Depeursinge and Corboz-Warnery 1999).

When mothers or parents are not able to empathetically mirror their child's inner experiences, the child will then tend to avoid engagement with its true self. "What does the baby see when he or she looks at the mother's face? … Ordinarily, the mother is

72 Numerous authors use for the importance of the primary care of an infant and child the expression "mother-baby" or "mother-infant" or "mother-child relationship or interaction," a role which can of course be assumed by a father, a parent, or another significant caregiver.

73 *Infans* derives from the Greek φημί, phēmí "I speak", in = not.

74 A story to construct meaning.

75 The capacity of the infant to distribute its attention between both parents as early as three or four months old demonstrates an early aptitude for managing a multiperson context.

looking at the baby and what she looks like is related to what she sees (in her baby). … The baby whose mother reflects her own mood or, worse still, the rigidity of her own defenses" (Winnicott 1967, 27). This baby does not see itself in its mother's face and will not develop a sound perception of self as a desiring, thinking, and confident subject. Infants and young children search the face of their primary caretaker; they depend upon the containment and reflected feedback of an emotionally attuned significative adult person in order to be able to identify themselves with these intersubjective relational experiences and to integrate them as part of their representational world. When this existential mirroring-need of every infant is not met, the building up of its own mind, identity, and self are insufficient or inadequate. If the infant internalizes a caregiver's defense mechanisms, adequate representation and expression of personal emotional experiences will not occur. An infant or young child who internalizes emotionally unresolved representations of the mother into a personal self-image on mental and bodily levels will develop inadequate representations of the intentional self, resulting in distorted body- and self-images. The infant or small child's experience of self and self-awareness— markedly influenced by early perceptions of thoughts and feelings of the mother—then has no connection to present or actual emotions, feelings, and experiences. The developmental task of the process of individuality, independence, and separateness cannot be fulfilled. At the adolescent stage, the subject may be overwhelmed by fears of falling, disintegration, and depersonalization and will search to free the core or true self through self-destructive, even suicidal behavior, or establish mental representations through somatization, a predisposition to eventually harm his or her body.

Child and adolescent creativity

The gifted child

Greenacre (1957, 1962) speculates for the gifted child an "innate equipment," which consists of a special degree of sensitivity, empathy, and perceptiveness. He believes that this peculiar capacity of perception is inborn, but that the sensitivity may be increased by early traumata. An inherent richness of stimulation with corresponding responsiveness may be confusing or even overwhelming but leads to an abundance, variety, and diversity of spontaneous symbolism and imagery. Personal relationships are invested with great interest, as are alternate figures and forms, which may appear in media, or as humans or animals, or as senses, for example, odors and sounds, lights and shadows. They represent some sort of contemplated animation and meaning and are linked with lived earlier subjective experiences. The content of the creative work does not express nor represent a solution, but a relief in the associated emotions of lived traumatic experiences. In a highly creative person experiences are multifold, resonating with intuitively inspired imagery and presenting a relationship between creative and personal lives.

Children's creativity at the World Trade Center

"Silence is the real crime" wrote British psychoanalyst Hanna Segal (1987). The following lines written by her are placed at the site of the destroyed twin towers in New York City and serve as a motto on the mural in the lobby of an insurance company building near Ground Zero (Alford 2012): "It is when the world within us is destroyed, when it is dead and loveless, when our loved ones are in fragments, and we ourselves in helpless despair—it is then that we must recreate our world anew, reassemble the pieces, infuse life into dead fragments, recreate life" (Segal 1952, 199).

Art therapist and clinical social worker Marygrace Berberian[76] was present on September 11, 2001 in the World Trade Center in New York City at the moment of the first plane-attack by the Islamic terrorist group al-Qaeda. While dealing with her own trauma, she recognized the need to help affected children throughout the city of New York express their fears and hopes. She developed a project, in which over three thousand children's self-portraits of grief are represented at the site of the destroyed twin towers in New York City.

"Children were recreating life in their art. Creativity allows for describing, building and reconfiguring an injured object so that mourning can begin" (Berberian 2003, 33). "It is only when the loss has been acknowledged and the mourning experienced that recreation can take place" (Segal 1952, 199).

French pediatrician and psychoanalyst **Françoise Dolto Marette** (1908–1988) was the fourth child of a family of seven. At the age of eight years her maternal uncle and godfather Pierre Demmler, to whom she was very much attached, died in World War I (Pignon and Potin 2018). Four years later her older sister died, and she lost at the age of twelve not only her sister, but also the emotional availability of her deeply depressed mother.

At the age of sixteen, she wrote the following poem: "The Dead"[77]

> I live with the dead more than with the living,
> Around me I feel, I see, I hear their soul,
> And their plaintive call keeps calling me
> A remnant of the love I had for them… before!

[76] Marygrace Berberian, an art therapist at New York University, has established school-based art therapy initiatives throughout New York City for at-risk children and families for almost twenty years.

[77] "Les morts," poem by Françoise Marette in her personal diary, April 1924. Association Archives et Documentation Françoise-Dolto.

I love this quiet and silent place
Where does some rose, some bloomed flower
Mark their home until Eternity…
It's a graveyard, yes, but it's happy.

And yet it is not in cemeteries
Only that I go when I want to talk to them
Approach them and then tenderly listen
The worried murmur of familiar shadows.

And I do not need to be on my knees either…
Often in the screaming crowd that brushes against me
I felt a hand hitting my shoulder,
An invisible being said to me: "Think of us!"

Chapter 13

ARTISTS' EXPRESSIONS AND REPRESENTATIONS OF THEIR CHILDHOOD EXPERIENCES

Growing up I witnessed all the ugly facets of war. That and the death of my father when I was three and a half years old marked my childhood.

Tomi Ungerer[78]

Childhood memories of the first years of life are modified or constructed at later developmental periods by the process of *Nachträglichkeit*,[79] that is, by means of "retrospective attribution" (Modell 2006, 36). A constant recontextualization of events takes place from earlier developmental phases into later stages. Thus, critical experiences endured in early childhood may have effects and be understandable only at a later age. This processing of events afterward introduces a special dimension to temporality: it does not influence the sequence of time but the significance of the event. Unassimilated past affective experiences are brought into the present and seek retranscription in a new context and within new relationships. Repetition can thus be considered as a form of memory (Freud 1920). When these events and the associated emotions are not inscribed in a time sequence (past–present–future) they appear as an everlasting presence. "The past is not the passive container of things bygone. The past, indeed, is our very being, and it can stay alive and evolve; the present is the passage where the retranscription and recontextualization of our past continually occur" (Scarfone 2006, 814). "For any significant mental event, there is an après-coup effect (*Nachträglichkeit*), a

[78] Ungerer (1991).

[79] *Nachträglichkeit* is a term used by Freud from 1890 on, translated in English as "deferred action" and in French as *après-coup*.

re-organizing of the mind that lets new forms show up or, conversely, that may bury ideas and affects that had emerged" (Scarfone 2011, 759).

Georges Prosper Remi (1907–1983), better known under his pen name **Hergé**,[80] was a Belgian cartoonist and author of *The Adventures of Tintin,* a series of twenty-four comic albums, considered as one of the most popular comic books of the twentieth century in Europe. Hergé was born near Brussels, but his family history is mysterious as he never knew the identity of his paternal grandfather, who was probably of illustrious origin. His paternal grandmother was Marie Dewigne, a servant to the countess Dudzeele, who owned a castle. While unmarried, Marie Dewigne gave birth to twins in 1882, Hergé's father Alexis and his twin brother Leon; in 1893 she married Philippe Remi, a workman employed by the countess. They had no children, but Remi gave his family name to Alexis and Leo. The countess bought fine clothes for Alexis and Leo and supervised their schooling. Hergé's father Alexis worked in a children's clothing house. His mother Elisabeth did not have any profession. He had little contact with his brother, who was five years younger.

The analysis of Hergé's comics by Serge Tisseron (1948–), French psychoanalyst and psychiatrist, addresses themes related to the secrets in the family of Georges Remi (or Hergé), the creator and designer of Tintin. In 1978 Tisseron, who was very interested in comic strips, published a comic book on the history of psychiatry. He later discovered the secret of Hergé's family after reading the albums of Tintin. He wrote:

> While studying all these strange stories, *The Adventures of Tintin,* I finally acquired the conviction that a second secret story ran behind the "official" representations of the characters of Hergé, and that the mystery masked the sufferings of a boy born of an unknown but probably illustrious grandfather. When I made this hypothesis in 1981, nothing was known about Hergé's life. All this could have remained unchecked, but some journalists discovered, a few years later, that this secret really existed in Hergé's family![81]

In 1993 Tisseron published *Tintin and the Secret of Hergé* and in 1996 *Secrets of the Family*. According to Tisseron, *The Adventures of Tintin* represent all the hypotheses around the family secret that Hergé was constructing as a child. He had probably tried to answer some of these questions in a conscious way, but to a large extent, probably unconsciously. In both cases, drawing was his way of keeping his questioning about

80 Hergé is derived from the French pronunciation of his reversed initials R. G.

81 Serge Tisseron, "Serge Tisseron a découvert le secret de Hergé," Psychologies, January 8, 2010, https://www.psychologies.com/Famille/Relations-familiales/Parents/Articles-et-Dossiers/Les-secrets-de-famille-ils-pesent-sur-notre-destin/Serge-Tisseron-a-decouvert-le-secret-de-Herge (our translation).

his origins alive. He reinvented stories from anything he could imagine, as it is often the case when a child is subjected to a family secret. The presence of a secret can occur in any meaningful relationship. An "enigmatic message" is "a perplexing and impenetrable implicit communication that is overloaded with significance. Such messages implant themselves as foreign bodies, haunting questions in the child's psyche" (Laplanche 1999, 242).

As outlined by Tisseron, the different protagonists in Hergé's books are the following: The Castafiore represents both the mysterious countess and Hergé's grandmother, Marie Dewigne. Thomson and Thompson embody Alexis and Leo, Hergé's father and uncle. Tintin, Captain Haddock, and Professor Calculus symbolize three aspects of Hergé's personality: Tintin strives to solve every enigma, Haddock despairs and sinks into alcoholism, and Calculus retires into himself through deafness and his solitary work.

Thomson and Thompson are the father and the uncle of Hergé, Alexis and Leon. They are police inspectors, in other words, professional investigators. They are always searching for something, and although they seem to approach the truth, they never find it. Thomson and Thompson always fail when it comes to finding out what they would like to know. From this point of view, they therefore resemble Alexis and Leon, who must always have wondered about their father's identity without ever discovering it. Are they brothers? Hergé seems to ask. One is called "Thomson" without the "p" and the other is "Thompson" with the "p." So, if they are twins, what is their father's name? Is it "Thomson" without the "p" or "Thompson" with the "p"? Do they have two fathers? The spelling game reflects the staging by Hergé of the family mystery of Alexis and Leon's "two fathers": the secret father—the man who made Marie Dewigne pregnant—and the workman named Remi, who gave his name to the twins when they were eleven years old. Clothes play an essential role; they recall the importance of the annual gift of new clothes that Alexis and Leon received from the Countess of Dudzeele. Thomson and Thompson attract all the attention, their clothes revealing the identity they want to hide. Are they not the twins Alexis and Leon, blamed for wearing "beautiful clothes," that contrast with their modest origins, thus designating them as "bastards," natural children of a prestigious father? Alexis and Leo, Thomson and Thompson, are condemned to wander without ever discovering what they seek, forever wrong, and mocked by all.

The Castafiore represents the guardian of the secret, both Hergé's grandmother and the famous Countess, at least as he imagined them from family stories, since he had, of course, never seen them. The Castafiore is a great lady, a diva, who often turns into Marguerite, the heroine of *Faust* in Gounod's opera. Hergé did not choose this opera by chance. Indeed, Marguerite, from a modest background, falls in love with a man of a much higher social condition … just like Hergé's grandmother, Marie Dewigne. But the comparison does not stop there. Marguerite accepts the seduction of Faust and becomes pregnant without any marital link. Marguerite seduced, Marguerite pregnant, Marguerite abandoned, this is also the destiny of Marie Dewigne.

But let us go back to Hergé's story. He often said that he was represented by Haddock. By never addressing Captain Haddock by his real name, the Castafiore embodies the guardian of the secret. Neither his grandmother nor the famous Countess ever entrusted to anyone the name of the father of Alexis and Leon, a name that should have belonged to Hergé himself.

The brothers Jacob (1785–1863) and **Wilhelm Grimm** (1786–1859) were born in Hanau, Hesse, Germany. In 1791 the Grimm family moved to Steinau, where the family lived in an office building, their father being an esteemed magistrate. At the age of eleven and ten, the brothers Grimm lost their forty-four-year-old father, who died of pneumonia. Their father's death led to the impoverishment of the family and the separation of the brothers from their family, events which affected them seriously. The brothers were sent to high school in Kassel, where they were brilliant students, following their father's example. They had to support themselves and, in the future, also their family. In 1808, during their adolescence, their mother died as well.

The brothers lived a childhood and adolescence marked by the losses of their father and mother; they seem to express their experienced consecutive hardships through animals, which are exposed, rejected, and dependent, but which resist and succeed in mastering their seemingly helpless and hopeless situation as did the two brothers. Their identification with innocent animals is reflected by the fact that the emotions of their suffering in their critical life experiences are translated into written words by the animals.

The brothers[82] collected and recorded fairy tales. The first edition of *Children's and Household Tales*, published in 1812, contained eighty-six stories; its preface reads: "When a storm, or some other catastrophe sent from the heavens, levels an entire crop, we are relieved to find that a small patch, protected by tiny hedges or bushes, has been spared and that some solitary stalks remain standing."

Death and the Goose-Shepherd[83] is the story of a poor goose-shepherd who guards a flock of white geese on the shores of a stormy lake. He encounters death coming out of the water, who says he wants to leave the world behind. The shepherd, tired of life, begs death to take him with him, but death says it is too early, as he still has things to do, and instead pushes a miser into the water, who drowns with his dogs and cats following after. Days later, death comes to the cheerful shepherd and asks him, if the time is now right. The shepherd is willing and crosses over with his white geese, all of which are turned into white sheep. The goose-shepherd looks at the beautiful land around him, while the patriarch-shepherds Abraham, Isaac, and Jacob come to meet him, set a royal crown upon him, and lead him into the shepherd's castle, where he is still to be found.

82 They heard many tales from Dorothea Viehmann (1755–1816), a German storyteller.

83 The parable *Death and the Goose-Shepherd* (German *Der Tod und der Gänshirt*) figured only in the first edition of 1812 and was replaced in the second edition by *The Town Musicians of Bremen*.

The Town Musicians of Bremen tells the story of a donkey, a dog, a cat, and a rooster, who after a lifetime of hard work are neglected and mistreated by their former masters. One by one they decide to run away and become town musicians in the city of Bremen, according to the saying: "We go to Bremen, something better than death you find everywhere; you have a good voice, and when we play music together, that's the way it must be." On the way to Bremen, they see a cottage and when they look inside, they see four robbers enjoying their dishonest gains. Standing on each other's backs, they scare the robbers with such loud threatening noises that the robbers run away. The animals take possession of the house and enjoy a meal. At night, the robbers return. One enters, but the cat scratches his face, the dog bites him, the donkey kicks him, and the screaming rooster chases him out the door. The shocked robber then describes to his companions in detail how he had been assailed by a horrible witch, and the robbers abandon the cottage, where the animals live happily for the rest of their days.

An alternate version involves the animals' masters being deprived of their livelihood (the thieves stole their money or destroyed their farm or mill) and were therefore obliged to send the animals away, unable to take care of them any longer. After the animals dispatch the thieves, they take the ill-gotten gains back to their masters, thus providing them with the means to rebuild their farm or mill.

All three stories or version of stories deal with death, impoverishment, deprivation, abandonment; challenges that can be met by maintaining hope, strong commitment, courage, perseverance, hard work, strength, and never giving up, and finally lead to solidarity, friendship, restoration and reparation, reward and success.

Tomi (Jean-Thomas) **Ungerer** (1931–2019) was an artist and writer who published over 140 books ranging from children's books to adult works and from the fantastic to the autobiographical. Ungerer wrote in English, French, and German.

He was born with a heart defect and suffered from numerous illnesses, with which he coped mainly by working and a great sense of humor, taking them as something unexpected, an "adventure." He was born in Strasbourg, in the Alsace region of France, on the German border; at the age of three, he lost his father, the co-owner of a factory that produced astronomical clocks. The early death of his father represented a traumatic experience and influenced him throughout his whole life. He and his three older siblings were brought up by his mother, Alice Ungerer Essler, who taught her children to face, experience, master, and overcome fear, and never to look away, to always stand strong, and to understand the importance of experiencing fear and not letting it destroy you.

During World War II, Ungerer experienced the occupation of Alsace by German soldiers and the confiscation of his family's possessions. Alsace was divided in two—half Germany, half France. His family was Protestant—a minority in Catholic Alsace. "I was brought up and educated with hate," Ungerer said in an interview: "Hatred of the neighbors, hatred of the Germans, hatred of the Catholics. It was nothing but hate, hate, hate."[84]

84 Gary Groth, "Comics Journal #303: The Tomi Ungerer Interview (Excerpts)", *The Comics Journal*, February 5, 2019, http://www.tcj.com/comics-journal-303-the-tomi-ungerer-interview-excerpt/.

In *Tomi—A Childhood Under the Nazis* (1998), Ungerer recounts his childhood memories.

> From an early age, I was encouraged to develop my drawing skills—it seems that I was born with my father's artistic talents. During the war most of my drawings were aimed at making fun of the Nazi occupiers. A dangerous pursuit! Then in the winter of 1944–45 we were caught in the Colmar pocket, the last bridgehead the Germans had over the Rhine. The battle raged for three months and I recorded what I saw with pencil and paper. The scenes of war and the waste of destruction became a leitmotif for the rest of my life. By the age of fourteen my outlook on the world was clearly defined by a loathing and abhorrence of violence, prejudice, injustice and fanaticism of any kind. I was born an emigrant in my own country and have remained one all my life. I was born in Alsace, a region torn between France and Germany. I was French before the Second World War, then the Nazis arrived, and I was German. After the war, I was French once again.

Ungerer learned to cope with feelings of being different and not belonging, issues represented in his children's books, where fear is a central theme, for example, in *The Three Robbers* (1961), where the presence of dangers and threats are in opposition to safety. In these narratives Ungerer wants to frighten, challenge, and at the same time delight children; he knew and respected the seriousness of children's sensitivities. For his successful stories, he was awarded the Hans Christian Andersen Prize in 1998. In 2003 the Council of Europe nominated Ungerer as the first Ambassador for Childhood and Education.

Norwegian **Edvard Munch** (1863–1944), Scandinavia's most famous painter, answered, when told he could rid himself of much suffering: "My fear of life is necessary to me, as is my illness. My afflictions belong to me and my art—they have become one with me. They are indistinguishable from me, and their destruction would destroy my art. I want to keep those sufferings. Without illness and anxiety, I would have been a rudderless ship. My art is really a voluntary confession and an attempt to explain to myself my relationship with life. … My art is rooted in a single reflection: why am I not as others are? … My art gives meaning to my life (Munch 2005, np).

In his paintings Munch wanted to represent living people who express their feelings of love, fear, melancholy, sorrow, and despair, as he himself had experienced during his lifetime. His composition of landscapes with figures exemplify the unique relation of mood and atmosphere between nature and human beings. He was compelled to elaborate over and again through his paintbrush his own suffering, a kind of working through process, which he described: "When seen as a whole, art derives from a person's desire to communicate himself to another. I do not believe in art that does not stem from man's need to open his heart. All art, literature and music must flow through the blood of the heart. Art is the very blood of the heart" (Munch in Cordulack 2002, np). "What is art really? The outcome of dissatisfaction with life, the point of impact for the creative force, the continual movement of life. … In my art I attempt to explain life and its meaning to myself" (Munch in Prideaux 2007, 35).

Munch was the second of five children. "Dying I came to the world," he said of birth (Bjornstad 1995, 8). When he was five years old, his mother died of tuberculosis. One of his mother's sisters cared for the family, and it was to her and Inger, Munch's sister, that he later addressed his letters. The loss of his mother had a serious impact not only on Munch, but also on his father, who turned with fervor to religion. Munch's father was a military doctor, and he sometimes took the boy with him on visits. Munch was often ill during childhood and was frequently unable to attend school. At the age of fourteen, he lost his older sister Sophie.

In a conversation with his physician, Munch at an advanced age spoke of his early memories. The father "had a difficult temper, inherited nervousness with periods of religious anxiety which could reach the borders of insanity as he paced back and forth in his room praying to God. … When anxiety did not possess him, he could be like a child and joke and play with us. … When he punished us … he could be almost insane in his violence. … Disease and insanity were the black angels on guard at my cradle. … In my childhood I felt always that I was treated in an unjust way, without a mother, sick, and with threatened punishment in Hell hanging over my head … twin black angels of insanity and disease" (Deknatel 1950, 10).

Munch's comments on three of his paintings demonstrate his endured sufferings with the tragic losses he had experienced as a child and his never-ending mourning process.

The Sick Child is a painting by Edvard Munch's older sister Johanne Sophie (1862–1877), who died at age fifteen from tuberculosis. "Few painters have ever experienced the grief of their subject as I did in the sick child. It was not just I who was suffering; it was all my nearest and dearest as well" (Munch in Prideaux 2007, 85–86).

On his famous painting The Scream (Fig. 13.1), he writes: "I was walking along a path with two friends—the sun was setting—suddenly the sky turned blood red—I paused, feeling exhausted, and leaned on the fence—there was blood and tongues of fire above the blue-black fjord and the city—my friends walked on, and I stood there trembling with anxiety—and I sensed an infinite scream passing through nature."[85] "Far out there—that soft line where the air meets the sea—it is as incomprehensible as existence—it is incomprehensible as death—as eternal as longing" (79). "There should be no more pictures of interiors, of people reading and women knitting. There would be pictures of real people who breathed, suffered, felt, loved."[86]

85 Quote from a diary entry (January 22, 1892), on the experience which inspired his famous painting, *The Scream* ("Shrik"), originally entitled "The Cry of Nature."

86 Quote about Edvard Munch's oil-painting *Melancholy*, taken from his artist's credo "St Cloud Manifesto" of 1889.

Figure 13.1 Edvard Munch. *The Scream* (1893). Oil on canvas.

The Vampire was one painting in a series of drawings, pastels, and paintings on the theme of emotion; he gave these works the title *The Frieze of Life*, which also included *The Scream*. He exhibited the first sequence of images of this cycle in Berlin in 1893 under the title *Love:* innocence, passion, jealousy, despair, love, and pain.

When Munch's friend Stanislaw Przybyszewski saw the painting for the first time, he called it *Vampire*; Munch decided to keep the title.

Munch felt haunted by death and—continuously overwhelmed by anxieties, fear and nostalgia he could no longer bear—was beset with suicidal thoughts

"The fire in the fireplace is my only friend—The time I spend sitting in front of the fireplace gets longer and longer. When I suffer most, I lean my head against the fireplace—then I suddenly feel a desire overwhelm me—Kill yourself and then it is all over, why live? … You will not live much longer anyway. And dragging through the world like this, in this miserable body … and with this constantly cautious fear. When I light the candle, I suddenly see my huge shadow across half the wall, clear up to the ceiling—And in the large mirror over the fireplace I see myself—the face of my own ghost" (Munch in Prideaux 2007, 115). Growing older and suffering from illness, with his dead family members continually present, Munch withdrew into himself entirely. "From my rotting body, flowers shall grow, and I am in them, and that is eternity. And I live with the dead—my mother, my sister [Sophie], my grandfather, my father [who died in 1889, when Munch was in France]. Every day is the same—my friends have stopped coming—their laughter disturbs me, tortures me … my daily walk round the old castle becomes shorter and shorter, it tires me more and more to take walks" (Munch in Stang 1979, np).

Balthasar Klossowski de Rola (1908–2001), known as **Balthus**, said: "I guess my childhood memories played a bigger role. It's really like in a dream" (Zeki and Balthus 1995).

Balthus was a Polish-French modern artist. In 1914 when he was six, his family moved from Paris to Switzerland, just after World War I had been declared. At the age of nine, his parents separated, and about a year later his mother became the lover of poet Rainer Maria Rilke, whom Balthus met in 1919. The "replacement" of his father and his mother's new love relationship may have, for the young Balthus, represented critical life events, bringing feelings of abandonment and jealousy.

Two years earlier at Christmas, he had welcomed, taken care of, and adopted a stray cat, but at the age of eleven, his cat Mitsou ran away. Desperate, desolate, and inconsolable, Balthus turned to drawing in order to overcome the loss of his beloved cat and his feelings of abandonment. In his memoirs, he writes that he illustrated the various life phases he had experienced with Mitsou, thus keeping alive his friendship with the cat. This was the beginning of Balthus's love for and interest in cats. In 1935 he painted *Le roi des chats* (The King of Cats) representing himself and a ferocious cat he called Frightener (Fig. 13.2).

Rilke showed a great interest in the story of Mitsou, told in forty ink drawings, and recognized the young boy's talent. In 1921 Rilke organized the publication of a small book entitled *Mitsou* with a preface by himself. It was Balthus's first entry into painting. In secret, Balthus felt himself to belong to the world of cats; he appreciated their independence and, as Rilke said, the impossibility of truly knowing a cat's nature. In

Figure 13.2 Balthus. *King of Cats* (1935). Oil on canvas.

1921 Balthus's mother moved to Berlin with her two sons, and Balthus lost Rilke's guidance and watchfulness.

In his *Memoirs*, collected by Alain Vircondelet, Balthus describes Rilke as a man endowed with the faculty for having a great familiarity with children: "A secret grace united us." Rilke—as Balthus wrote—helped him in his vocation as a painter, as he was convinced that "painting was my way, this trace of truth."

In 1921 Rilke wrote to Balthus:

> Many years ago I knew an English writer in Cairo, a Mr. Blackwood, who in one of his novels advances a rather attractive hypothesis: he claims that at midnight there always appears a tiny slit between the day ending and the day beginning, and that a very agile person who managed to insert himself into that slit would escape from time and find himself in a realm independent of all the changes we must endure; in such a place are gathered all the things we have lost (Mitsou, for instance) … children's broken dolls, etc. etc.
>
> That's the place, my dear Balthus, into which you must insert yourself on the night of February 28, in order to take possession of your birthday, which is hidden there, coming to light only every four years! (Just think how worn out, in an exhibition of birthdays, other people would be compared with this one of yours which is so carefully tended, and which is removed only at long intervals, quite resplendent, from its hideaway.) (Vircondelet 2001, 92).

Rilke refers to the "Crac" which he identifies with Balthus's mysterious missing birthdays on February 29. In letters to Balthus he told him that to catch up with those lost dates, all he needs do is slip through the "Crac."

In this tiny gap (the "Crac," when day gives way to night and vice versa) Balthus wanted to glimpse the "other splendors" that Rilke spoke of, maintaining that he had to accept this enchantment, an entry into the marvelous world of painting, into the profound earth where light is to be found—the wonderland as Balthus later called it. Balthus was overwhelmed by Dante's force of imagination and power of vision in the *Divina Commedia*—a present from Rilke. Influenced also by a book with Chinese reproductions of the great Song dynasty and Rilke's narrations, he also intended to write a play on the Buddhist civilization; his mother recalled him holding a figurine of Buddha against him like a cat, refusing to give it back to her (Vircondelet 2001).

Balthus was sixteen years old when Rilke died, which reinforced—as he recounts in his memoirs—his somber and skittish character, feeling that a kind of guardian had disappeared. Rilke's awareness and openness to the universe represented for him as a painter a vast investment whose source and center he felt he had to reveal.

Balthus also evoked his passion for Mozart's music, especially operas, which he savored each and every day—in his view, Mozart had achieved the highest expression of the human soul, whose resonating emotions reached the world's secret and most hidden mysteries. For Balthus, music and painting must merge to attain infinite sacredness—he wished to paint Mozart's music. Balthus made the decorations for the opera *Cosi fan tutte* in Aix-en-Provence in 1950. Famous for his paintings of nubile adolescent girls, their bodies' tumultuous excitation communicates—according to Balthus—the ambiguity of light and shadows, traces of pure nature.

Balthus recalled his design in 1948 of the set and costumes of *L'état de Siège*, the play Albert Camus said most resembled him and who declared: "My avowed aim was to extract the theater out of its psychological speculations, and to make resound on our murmuring scenes, the loud cries, which today bend or release crowds of men."

Balthus lived through the death of his only son Fumio (to his second wife Setsuko Ideta, a Japanese painter), who was born in 1968 and died at the age of two and a half, in the Villa Medici in Rome, in the sudden golden light of the Turkish room. This was—as Balthus writes—for him a revelation and an assumption, the reason for his fervent faith in the certainty of light, which he wanted to seize in its full brightness. This is why painting is a grace (Vircondelet 2001).

In interviews with neurobiologist Semir Zeki (Zeki and Balthus 1995) Balthus reminisces about his experience as an artist and the act of creation. Here are a few quotes:

> In musical terms, painting is a long process of ensuring that notes produce the right tone (12). My painting is a kind of prayer because I am religious (14). I never talk about my painting. Painting is a language that cannot be expressed in other words (21). Of course, we are like a child when we paint (39). I am not a modern painter. A modern painter seeks to express himself. I never want to express myself, myself does not exist (49). I am a craftsperson (73). I do nothing consciously. It's unconscious. I feel that I am always guided by something; I do not know what it is (75). We paint because we have an inner vision of things; we paint because we try to reach this inner vision. This desire may be that of a child, but the child could not paint (120).

Edward Franklin Albee (1928–2016) was an American playwright who seems to have learnt about his adoption at around six years of age. However, it was only after his adoptive mother's death in 1989 that he learnt that his biological father had abandoned his mother Louise Harvey, who gave her son Edward up for adoption two weeks after his birth. Reed and Frances Albee became his foster parents when he was only eighteen days old; they officially adopted him in 1929 and changed his name to Edward Franklin Albee III. His adoptive mother is described as emotionally cold and authoritarian, his adoptive father as distant and unengaged in his son's development. As a young adult, Albee left his home, and the relationship with his adoptive parents was interrupted for almost twenty years.

Adoption is associated with many personal and familial variables; its consequence is unpredictable and may bear fateful outcomes. For Edward Franklin Albee it led to the achievement of an outstanding literary oeuvre. Adoption constitutes a potential risk situation for psychic traumatization, and relationship dynamics can be considered a lifelong process for the persons involved in this triangle of birth parents, adoptive parents, and the child. Children experience this relationship constellation as a psychic trauma if they are not able to cope with their feelings of having been abandoned or rejected by their biological parents.

Albee's immensely creative body of work demonstrates what Moro (1989) describes as the destiny of abandoned children; they are faced with a breakdown of family ties and are confronted with an extremely threatening event. They preserve memories of these lived experiences in the form of interactive phantasms between themselves and their surroundings. The abandoned child develops in an environment that shares the child's conviction of radical strangeness. Their phantasmatic productions often demonstrate an oscillation between two poles: an extreme psychic vulnerability or the development of an extraordinarily creative potential, the latter being the case for Albee.

Albee's play *Who's Afraid of Virginia Woolf* (1962) represents an impressive example of parental phantasms: the "son" of the two protagonists George and Martha reveals himself as a phantasm. For Martha and George fulfilling the parental role is the most noble task of all humanity's endeavors, their sterility being their mutual failure, a narcissistic injury, a tragedy. They create an imaginary idealized child who has all the most wished for qualities, some of which even differed: George giving the baby blue eyes and Martha green eyes like her father's.

Edward Franklin obviously did not represent this idealized child for his adoptive parents Reed and Frances Albee; he was not able to assume the task of healing his adoptive parents' narcissistic wounds due to their infertility. In the play Albee shows the game of Martha and George around their fictional son and demonstrates their defensive strategy of intellectualization against their feelings of narcissistic rage,[87] sadness, and despair. They avoid facing, sharing, and engaging in a mourning process in order to work through their own loss of a biological child. Both adoptive parents and adoptive children need to mourn the loss of their fantasized biological child and their fantasized biological parents—only then can an authentic significant relatedness be built up, which apparently never happened for Albee nor for his adoptive parents, ending in the breakdown of their relationship.

Charlie Chaplin (Sir Charles Spencer Chaplin 1889–1977) created silent films in which he was simultaneously the script writer, composer, and actor. The comic character "The Tramp," created a century ago at the beginning of the cinema age, presented

87 Narcissistic rage (Kohut 1972) is the reactive anger following a narcissistic injury (Freud 1920), a threat to a person's self-esteem.

a childlike and generous "little fellow," as Charlie Chaplin called him. He may be considered as a particularly resilient child, as he was able to successfully cope with his experiences of multiple familial, social, and environmental adversities. Again, and again he mastered and overcame stressful life situations, as if his resistance had been strengthened by the fact that he was continuously exposed to psychosocial high-risk conditions. At an early age he seized any opportunity for creative acting, helped by his half-brother Sydney,[88] who was four years older and who later gave up his own profession as an actor to serve his brother as business manager.

Chaplin grew up in nineteenth-century London; his early years were marked by extreme poverty. His parents separated when he was about two years old. The following year, his mother, Hannah, gave birth to a third son, who at six months was taken away by Leo Dryden, his father. With his mother in and out of mental institutions, Chaplin was placed twice—at age seven for eighteen months and then again at age nine—in institutes for destitute children. He lost his alcoholic father, whom he had hardly known, at the age of eleven. When he was sixteen, his mother was confined to a mental institution. As an adult, Chaplin had the unique ability to represent autobiographical details and childhood memories in his films.

Freud had watched Chaplin's films and referred to him as "a great genius." He had wished to meet him during his visit to Vienna, but Chaplin had had to cut his trip short. In a letter to his friend Max Schiller, Freud wrote in 1931:

> You know for instance, in the last few days Charlie Chaplin has been in Vienna. Almost I, too, would have seen him, but it was too cold for him here and he left again quickly. He is undoubtedly a great artist; certainly, he always portrays one and the same figure; only the weak, poor, helpless, clumsy youngster for whom, however, things turn out well in the end. Now do you think that for this role he has to forget his own ego. On the contrary, he always plays only himself as he was in his early dismal youth. He cannot get away from those impressions, and to this day he obtains for himself the compensation for the frustrations and humiliations of that past period of his life. He is, so-to-speak, an exceptionally simple and transparent case. The idea that the achievements of artists are intimately bound up with their childhood memories, impressions, repressions and disappointments, has already brought us much enlightenment and has, for that reason, become very precious to us.

Charlie Chaplin in *My Autobiography* (1964) contradicts Freud's view on the prevalent influence of sexuality in development, stating: "Contrary to Freud, I do not think that sexuality constitutes the most important element of behavior. The cold, hunger and shame born out of poverty are more likely to affect psychology." "I was hardly

[88] Sydney John Chaplin (born Sydney John Hill) 1885–1965.

aware of a crisis because we lived in a continual crisis; and, being a boy, I dismissed our troubles with gracious forgetfulness" (10). Children's psychosexual development, as stated by Freud, is shaped by their libido (sexual energy). Insufficient fulfillment of children's libidinous (affective) needs may have negative consequences in later life. According to Freud each human being's childhood experience becomes his or her inner law and has a determining influence on the path life takes. "The Child is the father of the Man" (Freud 1909–1939, 412), a sentence in which Freud emphasizes "of what extraordinary significance for the whole later direction of a person the impressions of his childhood are, especially of his first childhood years."

Michael Ondaatje (1943–), famous for his novel *The English Patient*, once said: "I'd lost my childhood, so I had to reinvent it." "There's a need to write about family when there's a break-up." Ondaatje was born in Colombo, the capital of the British colony of Ceylon;[89] he is of Tamil, Sinhalese, and Dutch origins. "My background is a real salad, so it's difficult to know who I am." "I am a mongrel of place. Of race. Of cultures. Of many genres." "Ondaatje was probably a Tamil name, originally from India, but I'm not much of a Tamil now." "I can't speak the language, apart from a few rude words." Of Ceylon's oral tradition, in which he was brought up, he says: "Tall stories, gossip, arguments and lies at dinner."

From his mother, he states, "I got a sense of the dramatic, the tall stories, the determination to now and then hold the floor." "My father was in tea and alcohol; he dealt in tea and he drank the alcohol."

At the age of five, his parents separated and a year later his mother left Colombo for England with his brother Christopher and his sister Janet, leaving Michael and his sister Gillian behind. "My memory is very vivid, of being quite solitary, though not alone—I was scattered with uncles and aunts."

At eleven he travelled on board the ship *Oronsay*, anxious and unsure if his mother would "know when exactly I would arrive. And if she would be there. … I heard 'Michael,'" he writes, "and it was a voice scared of being wrong. I turned and saw no one I knew. A woman put her hand on my shoulder and said 'Michael.' When I saw her face, I knew it was her face." "When I did meet my mother eventually, on the docks at Tilbury near London, she had become 'another,' a stranger."

After having been separated from his mother for six years, when he meets her again in another country, she is a stranger. His losses of his homeland, significant persons, culture, language, and ethnicity plunges him into deep distress.

"When I came to England, I had to change everything." "In London, I didn't have a clue, I was lost." "Going to places starts you remembering things."

[89] Ceylon gained independence in 1948 and changed its name to Sri Lanka when it became a republic in 1972.

Ondaatje's prolific writings may be viewed in the context of a continually evolving presentation of his coping with and memorizing his lived deprivations and adversities, as well as his need to find meaning and integrate his lived experiences.

Running in the Family (1982) is a semi-autobiographical and fictional narrative, in which Ondaatje, who returns to Sri Lanka for the first time in twenty-five years, tries to connect himself to a lost time and place. He uses memories, fantasies, and family legends to recreate his own and his family's history.

Ondaatje's father died of a brain hemorrhage. "My loss was that I never spoke to him as an adult. … He was a sad and mercurial figure. There was a lot I didn't know about him, and that was recurring in my books: trying to find the central character. It became a habit. In all my books there are mysteries that are not fully told."

The narrative *Anil's Ghost* (2000) shows the various multiple and individual subjective reactions to war traumatization, the context being the civil war of Sri Lanka. The most dramatic descriptions are flashbacks, but also the nonverbal expression of unspeakable, unutterable feelings and ineffable, indelible emotions. The traumatic grief finds expression in bodily postures, in an embodiment, in gestures, mimics, in the gaze, and it is this visual perception of the unbearable pain and sadness that leads to the resonance of readers' emotions, evoking empathy and compassion with the victims. The following example shows the nonverbal expression of a women: "Her legs under her as if in formal prayer. … There are no words Anil knows that can describe, even for just herself, the woman's face. But the grief of love in that shoulder she will not forget, still remembers" (4).

Twelve-year-old Lakma had seen her parents killed. "The shock of the murder … had touched everything within her, driving both her verbal and her motor ability into infancy." She remained silent and nonreactive, except for any sudden sound, and slept hidden underneath her bed. She "was scared of the evidence of anything human" (99–100). The description of the girl's reaction demonstrates her regression on a verbal and motor level, which often takes place after a traumatic event.

Sarath Diyasena, an archaeologist assigned by the government says: "Most of us can be broken by just the possibility of what might happen…. I wanted to find one law to cover all of living. I found fear" (131). Anil used "to believe that meaning allowed a person a door to escape grief and fear. But she saw that those who were slammed and stained by violence lost the power of language and logic" (51).

If traumatic experiences remain unspoken, that is, withdrawn from verbal discourse, secrets of unimaginable or non-pronounceable events emerge. When trauma-processing work cannot be accomplished, the nightmare of the past is lived in the present and becomes the unique perspective of the future.

In the book *Divisadero* (2007), the significant characters of the story are a father, his daughter Anna, his adopted daughter Claire, and Coop, a foster son: the three children growing up together on a farm in California. Even twenty years later their interwoven personal life experiences influence their existences and shape their fates, shadowing their past.

"The person formerly known as Anna" gives the explanation of the novel's title: "I come from Divisadero Street. *Divisadero*, from the Spanish word for division, 'the street that at one time was the dividing line between San Francisco and the fields of the Presidio. Or it might derive from the word *divisar*, meaning to gaze at something from a distance'—after a nearby height called El Divisadero. Thus, a point from which you can look far into the distance. It is what I do with my work, I suppose. I look into the distance for those I have lost, so that I see them everywhere" (142–3). "For we live with those retrievals from childhood that coalesce and echo throughout our lives …. We live permanently in the recurrence of our own stories, whatever story we tell" (136). "There is the hidden presence of others in us, even those we have known briefly. We contain them for the rest of our lives, at every border that we cross" (16). "We relive stories and see ourselves only as the watcher or listener" (158). "Anna, who keeps herself at a distance from those who show anger or violence, just as she is still fearful of true intimacy. Her past is hidden from everyone. Just as she herself works in archives and discovers every past but her own, again and again, because it will always be there. … We fall in love with ghosts" (75–6). "We enter art to hide within it" (164). "I work where art meets life in secret. Perhaps it was the unknown life of my mother, her barely drawn portrait, that made me an archivist, a historian. Because if you do not plunder the past, the absence feeds on you…. An awkward, solitary man, hungry for the family he had brought together and then lost—his wife in childbirth, this orphan son of a neighbor, and Anna" (141).

Anna seems to maintain an inner relation with her lost mother. A mourning process barely took place. She identifies with the disappeared mother and is haunted by her presence, like a ghost, searching for her throughout her life. Yet her unfulfilled grief hinders her from engaging in an intimate relationship. Her need to distance herself shows her fear of suffering a breakdown, the one she had endured—overwhelmed by unbearable existential fears of annihilation—after the loss of her mother.

Ondaatje was motivated to write the novel *The Cat's Table* (2011) (which is the least important table in the ship's dining room) by his children, who asked questions about their father's childhood. "Although the novel sometimes uses the coloring and locations of memoir and autobiography, it is fictional." "I read somewhere, that people who lose their childhood eventually have to retrieve it."

Warlight (2018) is a story of two teenage children in London in 1945, who are left by their parents in charge of a strange person. "Warlight," according to the author "is an invented word. At one moment in the book, I describe the River Thames at night during the war. … I wanted to write a tone or a kind of light to suggest that time for those around before and after the war." "I was eleven years old, rather like the boy in the novel, I went from Ceylon (or Sri Lanka) to England, and I had no parents watching over me so I felt tremendously independent for the first time in my life."

Chapter 14

WRITERS' TESTIMONIES

Holocaust survivors

I moved heaven and earth, I risked fall and dementia by questioning
the memories of the living and the dreams of the dead in order to live the lives
of beings who, near and far, continue to haunt me: but when, yes,
when will I finally start to live my own life?
Elie Wiesel[90]

Children deported during the Holocaust often went on for many years to endure the traumatic consequences of these past events; each child has his or her subjectively felt sensations, flashbacks, nightmares, and the accompanying everlasting emotions and fears. In these situations, words are insufficient to express the lived feelings of traumatic loss situations: for example, to write "horrible" or "unbearable" never expresses what an individual person has suffered.

Elie Wiesel (1928–2016) in *Some Questions That Remain Open* (1988) writes: "Only those men and women who lived through the experience know what it was, and others—to my great distress—will never know. Hence, here lies the tragedy in the survivor's mission. He must tell a tale that cannot be told, he must tell a story that cannot be communicated. We have no tools, we have no vehicles, we have no methodology. We don't even know where to begin" (12).

[90] *Le cinquième fils* (1983, 252). Translated in English as *The Fifth Son* (Schocken Books: Berlin, 1985).

Wiesel spent all his life listening to the victims of the holocaust. "The enemy wanted to be the one who speaks. And I felt, I still feel, we must see to it that the victim should be the one who speaks and is heard. Therefore, all my adult life I always try to listen to the victim" (np).

Elie Wiesel was born in 1928 in Sighet, a border town with a long and complicated history. After World War I, it was part of Hungary, then handed over to Romania, and then taken back by Hungary at the beginning of World War II. During the war, the town became part of Hitler's Third Reich. After the war, it was under Russian rule for a time and was then turned over to Romania.

Wiesel and his three sisters grew up in the Jewish section of Sighet. His father Shlomo, who was closely involved in the Jewish community, was a shopkeeper. Elie's mother, a well-educated woman, encouraged him to be pious. She would have liked for her son to become a rabbi. As a boy, Wiesel felt closer to his mother than his father. He immersed himself in religious studies and dreamed of becoming a scholar. Then in March of 1944, the Germans entered Hungary and Wiesel's life changed forever. Within a month, the Nazis were deporting thousands of Jews from Transylvania, including about fifteen thousand from Sighet and eighteen thousand from neighboring villages. Wiesel, at the age of fifteen, was among those shipped to Auschwitz along with his parents and sisters. There his mother and youngest sister were immediately sent to the gas chambers. His two older sisters managed to survive, but he did not know their fate until after the war. Wiesel and his father clung to one another from their arrival at Auschwitz to their entry into Buchenwald. There his father developed dysentery and died just three months before the liberation.

After the war, Wiesel was sent to France along with four hundred other child-refugees. At the border, the children were asked if they wanted to become French citizens. Wiesel, unable to understand the question, did not respond. As a result, he was stateless until 1963, when he became a US citizen. Over the next few years, Wiesel learned French, continued his Jewish studies, and took classes in philosophy and literature. He supported himself by tutoring in Yiddish, Hebrew, and the Bible.

For Wiesel, the French language offered a new beginning, a new possibility, a new world. Although he eventually became a reporter who wrote articles in Hebrew, Yiddish, and English, all of his books except *Night* have been written in French. On one assignment in 1954, he met the French Catholic writer François Mauriac who not only urged the young reporter to write about his experiences but also helped him find a publisher. Two years later, Wiesel completed the first version of *Night*. After it was condensed and translated from Yiddish into French, Mauriac wrote the foreword.

Wiesel understood silence as its own form of action, as he writes in referring to Juliek, a young man from Warsaw, also deported to Buchenwald:

> I heard the sound of a violin. A violin in a dark barrack where the dead were piled on top of the living? Who was this madman who played the violin here, at the edge of his own grave? Or was it a hallucination? It had

to be Juliek. He was playing a fragment of a Beethoven concerto.[91] Never before had I heard such a beautiful sound. In such silence. … All I could hear was the violin, and it was as if Juliek's soul had become his bow. He was playing his life. His whole being was gliding over the strings. His unfulfilled hopes. His charred past, his extinguished future. He played that which he would never play again. … Out of the darkness emerges the pale and melancholy face of my Polish comrade bidding farewell to an audience of dying men. … When I awoke, in the daylight, I could see Juliek, opposite me, slumped over, dead. Near him lay his violin, smashed, trampled, a strange overwhelming little corpse (Wiesel 2008, 94–95).

You can be a silent witness, which means silence itself can become a way of communication. There is so much in silence. There is an archeology of silence. There is a geography of silence. There is a theology of silence. There is a history of silence. Silence is universal and you can work within it, within its own parameters and its own context, and make that silence into a testimony. Job[92] (Hebrew name Iyyov, meaning persecuted, hated) was silent after he lost his children and everything, his fortune and his health. Job, for seven days and seven nights, he was silent, and his three friends, who came to visit him, were also silent. That must have been a powerful silence, a brilliant silence (Wiesel 2001, np).

The silence in me is sometimes so heavy that my heart is about to explode, however I do not want to undo myself of this silence. I am looking for a special way: between speech and silence. As I seek a particular time: between life and death. No, I correct myself: between the living and the dead (Wiesel 1983, 11).

Most of the students who came to me, were children of survivors. I realized they came to me because their parents didn't talk to them. I became a surrogate father. Then the parents came to me, and I became to them a surrogate son—a bridge between the father and the son. And it was very moving to tell the children: "You now become the parents of your parents.

91 Beethoven Violin Concerto in D Major, op. 61, 2nd movement.

92 Elie Wiesel: "Whenever Holocaust survivors attempt to tell our own story, we transmit Job's story. At one point, Wiesel quoted a midrash (an ancient commentary on part of the Hebrew scriptures, attached to the biblical text) from the Talmud, where the rabbis attempted to explain why Job, a supposedly upright man, could have deserved such a horrible fate. In that story Job was in fact one of three advisers that the Pharaoh consulted, prior to taking action against the increasingly multiplying 'Children of Israel.' Balaam gives evil advice urging the Pharaoh to kill all Hebrew male new-born babies. Jethro opposes the Pharaoh and tells him not to harm the Hebrews at all, and Job keeps silent and does not reveal his mind even though he was personally opposed to the Pharaoh's destructive plans. It is for his silence that God subsequently punishes him with his bitter afflictions" (Witnessing Wiesel: TBE @ the Y," One on Foot: Joshua Hammerman's Blog, October 16, 2009, https://www.joshuahammerman.com/search?q=witnessing+wiesel).

> They see in you their own parents, and you must them help more than they can help you (Wiesel and Heffner 2001, 166).

According to Elie Wiesel the opposite of good is not evil but indifference. To be indifferent—for whatever reason—is to deny not only the validity of existence, but also its beauty. Betray, and you are human; torture your neighbor, you're still human. Evil is human, weakness is human; indifference is not. Our indifference to evil makes us partners in the crime. "I owe them (the dead) my roots and memory. I am duty-bound to serve as their emissary, transmitting the history of their disappearance, even if it disturbs, even if it brings pain. Not to do so would be to betray them, and thus myself" (Wiesel 2008, 76).

In 1986, when he received the Nobel Peace Prize, Elie Wiesel described his feelings of being compelled to bear witness to the dead as, for example, to the little seven-year-old girl who, hugging her grandmother, whispered: "Don't be afraid, don't be sorry to die... I'm not."

For Wiesel "hope without memory is like memory without hope. Just as man cannot live without dreams, he cannot live without hope. If dreams reflect the past, hope summons the future." (Semprun and Wiesel, 2019).

In presenting the award, Egil Aarvik, the chair of the Nobel Committee, said the following of Wiesel:

> His mission is not to gain the world's sympathy for the victims or the survivors. His aim is to awaken our conscience. Our indifference to evil makes us partners in the crime. This is the reason for his attack on indifference and his insistence on measures aimed at preventing a new Holocaust. We know that the unimaginable has happened. What are we doing now to prevent its happening again? Through his books Elie Wiesel has given us not only an eyewitness account of what happened, but also an analysis of the evil powers which lay behind the events. His main concern is the question of what measures we can take to prevent a recurrence of these events (Aarvik 1986).

Imre Kertész (1929–2016) in his novel *Kaddish for An Unborn Child* explains: "I write because I have to write, and if one writes, one engages in a dialogue; … as long as God existed, probably one engaged in a dialogue with God, but now that He no longer exists most likely, one can only engage in a dialogue with other people or, in the better case, with oneself, or in other words talks or mumbles, as you like, to oneself" (Kertész 2004, 18–19).

Kertész, a Hungarian author, was deported at age fourteen to the Auschwitz concentration camp and later to Buchenwald; he was liberated in May 1945.

In his 2002 Nobel Prize in Literature speech he described how he had received—from the director of the Buchenwald Memorial Center—"a copy of the original daily report on the camp prisoners for February 18, 1945."

> I learned about the death of prisoner #64,921—Imre Kertész, factory worker, born in 1927. The false data: the year of my birth and my occupation were entered in the official registry when I was brought to Buchenwald. I had made myself two years older so I wouldn't be classified as a child and had said worker rather than student to appear more useful to them. In short, I died once, so I could live. Perhaps that is my real story. If it is, I dedicate this work, born of a child's death, to the millions who died and to those who still remember them. When we write about Auschwitz, we must know that Auschwitz, in a certain sense at least, suspended literature. One can only write a black novel about Auschwitz, or—you should excuse the expression—a cheap serial, which begins in Auschwitz and is still not over. By which I mean that nothing has happened since Auschwitz that could reverse or refute Auschwitz. In my writings the Holocaust could never be present in the past tense. Being a Jew to me is once again, first and foremost, a moral challenge. If the Holocaust has by now created a culture, as it undeniably has, its aim must be that an irredeemable reality gives rise by way of the spirit to restoration—a catharsis. This desire has inspired me in all my creative endeavors (Kertész 2002).

Kertesz's internal dialogue with memories and his self-awareness led to the painful recognition of an unconscious element of destructiveness and shame. Shame reveals vulnerability or injury, is painful and impedes empathy and guilt. Kertesz acknowledges that as human beings we might be both victims and perpetrators. He kept his creativity alive in his writings, thus overcoming destructiveness and creating life in the next generation. The following quotation is from Kertész's semi-autobiographical book *Kaddish for An Unborn Child* (2004).

> "No!" something bellows, howls, within me, I don't wish to remember … remembering is knowing, we live in order to remember what we know, because we cannot forget what we know … not out of some kind of "moral duty" … it's simply not at our discretion, we are not able to forget, that is the way we are created,… the reason why we know and remember is in order that somebody should feel shame on our account … in any case you're always partly to blame, that's all there is to it, I have stuck around and therefore I am, I thought; no, I didn't even think, I just was, simple as that, like a survivor from Warsaw, like a hanger-on from Budapest who sets no store on his hanging on, who feels no need to justify his sticking around, to attach notions of purpose to his having hung on, yet, to turn his having hung on into a triumph, however quiet, however discreet and intimate, yet essentially still the only genuine, the only possible triumph, as the prolonged and propagated perpetuation of this hung-on-to existence, namely my own self, in descendants—in a descendant (27–28).

Aharon Appelfeld (1932–2018) was born in Cernăuți, Romania (in today's Chernivtsi, Ukraine) and died in Petah Tiqwa, Israel. He is above all recognized for his novels in Hebrew about the Holocaust.

In his 2014 interview with Alain Elkann, he said: "I was very alone. No parents, no friends. I asked myself: What do I need? Why am I working in the fields? What will happen to me? Where is my life going? I had nothing. So then one day I made a list. My father, his name, Michael—I wrote that. My mother, Bunia. My grandfather, Meir Joseph. I wrote, I was born in Czernowitz and my mother was killed. This list gave me a ground I understood. I was not alone. I still had my family. They exist in me. I made myself a family on paper. I wrote it down, and they became real."

He went on to describe the loss of his parents, his survival, and his writing in Hebrew:

> We were with my grandmother at the farm. The Romanians and Germans came, and they shot my mother and my grandmother. It was in the summer of 1941. I was nine and a half years old. She was thirty-one. I am now eighty-two. My mother will always remain young and I am going to be very old. She was a beautiful woman. … I had just finished first grade when it happened. When I was in first grade, my mother used to read a story to me every night, converse with me, and so on.
>
> I was ill with the mumps, and suddenly I heard shooting. My mother was in the courtyard. My father was with some people outside. When I heard shooting, I jumped out the window. There was a field of corn, and I jumped into the field of corn.
>
> And then I found my father. And both of us went to Czernowitz, on foot. We stayed in the ghetto. Then we were taken to the camp, and I was separated from my father. I was alone with women and children. Every day some of them died. I escaped the camp. When I escaped it was 1941, before electric fences were erected.
>
> It was a kind of transformation—I became a small animal. It was the wish for life, the wish to survive. When I lived in the woods, my conception of the world was totally existential. Food, a coat, shoes, shelter—these were the problems. Other thoughts were not in my mind. They came later when I began to write. My life was blind, it could not have any words, but when I began to write about my childhood—and I have written a lot—it came up.
>
> I was fourteen years old when I came to Israel. I was alone, in a group of young people, and totally disoriented. Everyone was speaking a different language, but slowly. What can you say after seeing so many dead people, after seeing so much pain? After a big catastrophe, you lose words. Every word is a stupid word when you use it.

> I felt myself as a beaten person, who had been beaten for many years. And I couldn't explain it. I could not understand what had happened to me.
>
> German could not be my language anymore. Even though it's my mother's language and even though, in my dreams, I still sometimes speak German, Hebrew became my adopted mother tongue. And with it, I became very free, maybe because it's not my language.
>
> Also, I wanted to become a Jew, a full Jew. To be a Jew, the first stage was to acquire Hebrew. … I wanted to acquire knowledge, the biblical Hebrew, the medieval Hebrew, the Hebrew of Kabbalah, the Hasidic Hebrew, the philosophical Hebrew, and so on.[93] I wanted to know everything that is connected with Jewish belief, the Jewish way of life, law, the rabbinic law, the mystical law. I had a feeling that my generation—and me, also—we were naked. We did not belong to anything.

The following notes are excerpted from his autobiographical book *The Story of a Life* (2004).

> Literature is an enduring present—not in a journalistic sense, but as an attempt to bring time into an ongoing present (125).
>
> Everything that happened is imprinted within my body and not within my memory. The cells of my body apparently remember more than my mind, which is supposed to remember. As a rule, I am not given to crying, but even the most casual partings can reduce me to tears. I say, "I don't remember" and yet I still recall thousands of details. Sometimes just the aroma of a certain dish or the dampness of shoes or a certain noise is enough to take me back into some middle of the war, and then it seems to me that it never really ended, but that it has continued without my knowledge. For a child, memory is a reservoir that doesn't empty. It replenishes over the years, clarified. It's not a chronological recollection but overflowing and changing (90-92).

Appelfeld experienced several traumatic separations; the emotions dating from past events are stored in implicit memory and reactivated later, again and again, even in ordinary separation situations. Intolerable feelings, which cannot be named with

[93] The history of the Hebrew language is usually divided into four major periods: Biblical, or classical Hebrew, until about the third century BC, in which most of the Old Testament was written; Mishnaic, or Rabbinic Hebrew, the language of the Mishna (a collection of Jewish traditions), written about AD 200 (this form of Hebrew was never used among the people as a spoken language); Medieval Hebrew from about the sixth to the thirteenth centuries, when many words were borrowed from Greek, Spanish, Arabic, and other languages; and Modern Hebrew, the language of Israel in modern times. Historically, Kabbalah emerged after earlier forms of Jewish mysticism, in twelfth- to thirteenth-century Spain and southern France. Lurianic Kabbalah was popularized in the form of Hasidic Judaism from the eighteenth century onward.

words, nor mentally integrated, are inscribed in the body, that is, the body takes over the function of expressing the unbearable emotions. One can assume that Appelfeld as a child was overwhelmed by existential fears and threats during and after the war. Later on, stimuli, such as a certain odor or noise, bring back intrusive memories of the past, so-called flashbacks.

> For about two years I lived out in the fields and surrounded by forests. There are sights that have been engraved into my memory and there is much that I have forgotten, but distrust has remained engraved on my body; even today I stop and listen every few paces. Anyone who was in the ghetto, in the camp or hiding in the forests knows silence in his body. During the war, words had less currency than faces and hands. From the faces you learned to what extent the person next to you wanted to help you or intended to harm you. Words did not help one understand. Words are powerless when confronted by catastrophe; they're pitiable, wretched, and easily distorted (102).

The human being is a unity of soma and psyche, both are closely related and affect each other. Children left alone without care, learn to survive on their own. They mistrust people but are at the same time highly vigilant and competent in reading people's nonverbal expressions.

> For weakness is our essence and our humanity. A man who is aware of his weaknesses is far more likely to be able to overcome them. A moralist cannot face his own weaknesses; instead of criticizing himself, he criticizes his neighbor (106).
>
> As an instructor insisted to know where I had been during the war … I felt trapped, caught. And mute. A great anxiety gripped me, and my memory shut down. During the war, when I was forced to hide my identity, the first rule was silence (122–3).
>
> Contemplation made me forget about the hunger and the fear, and visions of home would return to me. These hours were perhaps the most joyful ones, if one can use this description to describe life during a war. The little boy who was on the verge of getting lost—or even killed—in that savage foreign land could go back to being the child of his father and his mother (138).

One can assume that Appelfeld as a child enjoyed significant and secure affective relationships within his family. Remembering his earlier life experiences and feelings shared with his family, seemed to have helped him to resist and overcome multiple adversities. As a writer he worked through his perceptions, fantasies, and emotions of the past traumatic events. In recounting his affective history, he processed and found understanding and meaning of his past. Personal narratives help a subject to be connected to the past, live in the present and anticipate the future.

> The old Jewish saying that the world continues to exist only by virtue of a few righteous people is as true today as it was back then. … The world I had left behind—parents, home, street, and city—was alive within me. Everything that had happened to me or that was about to happen to me was connected to the world from which I had sprung. The moment I realized this, I ceased being an orphan dragging his orphanhood behind him and became someone who was able to confront the world.
>
> … I did not know how to deny my past. The past lived inside me with a burning intensity, demanding that I give it my attention. … My consciousness as an individual began to take shape for the first time. … I began to figure out where I came from and where I was headed. True literature engages what is concealed in fate and hidden in the human soul; it exists in the metaphysical realms (148).

Events and intrapsychic experiences of the past, which the child was not able to accommodate, only later find meaning and interpretation. Childhood memories of the first years of life are modified or constructed at later developmental periods by means of recontextualization. This process does not influence the sequence of the dimension of time, but the significance of the event, reframing it in a different context.

Refugees confronted with cultural uprooting

Refugees are people who have been forced to cross national boundaries and are no longer able to return to their homeland safely. Their cultural uprooting represents social mutation, discontinuity from ancestry, and loss of family identification references. They are confronted with processes of adaptation in a new cultural environment, of recovering from multiple losses, and developing a new personal and family identity by keeping family and socio-cultural references alive.

Hilde Domin (-Löwenstein) (1909–2006) said: "The loss of belonging is a wound that never completely heals" (Domin 1993, 15). Domin, of Jewish origin and born in Köln, was a German lyric poet, author, and translator. She published her poems under the pseudonym "Domin," taken from the name of the island, the Dominican Republic, where she started to write. Her first poem was written in 1951, after the death of her mother. Domin's poems in German are often the expression of her biographic history, her life of tremendous suffering as a refugee in Italy, London, and Argentina, while fleeing from Nazi persecution, but they also refer to her interpretation of Jewish and biblical knowledge and tradition. This is eloquently illustrated by the following poem entitled in German "Bitte" (1987), meaning "please":

We were deluged
and washed with the waters of Noah's flood
we were soaked through
to the skin of our hearts
Longing for a landscape
this side of the border of tears
doesn't work
longing to hold on to spring blossom
longing to remain unscathed
doesn't work
What works is to ask
please
that at sunrise the dove
will bring the olive branch
that the fruit will be as colorful
as the blossom
that even the rose petals on the ground
can become a shining crown
And that we, out of the flood
out of the lion's den and the
fiery furnace
will be released
renewing ourselves
even more wounded and even more healed.

At a press conference on January 27, 1969 in Zurich, Switzerland, Domin said: "I was a dying person who was writing against dying. And as long as I wrote, I lived." "That was a gift or, if you will, you can say a grace. It was a redemption."

"My parents have provided me with the trust, the trust that seems indestructible and from which I take the power of 'nevertheless.' I'm known as a human of the 'nevertheless'" (Domin 1992, 32).

In resilient families a child benefits from reliable relationships and communications based on trust, empathy, and tolerance and learns to adapt to challenges and find solutions in problematic situations. In the 1969 press conference, Domin said: "I have never lost faith in people, and this is something quite unique that I was able to keep faith in people, despite all the terrible things. That's luck."

The first lines of Hilde Domin's first book of poems are the following:

You have to be able to walk away
And yet be like a tree
As if the root in the ground remained

As if the landscape moved
And we would stand firm
Do not get tired
But to the miracle
Quietly
Like to a bird
Hold out your hand

"The 'miracle' … is for me not to abandon. Not oneself and not others. And not to be abandoned. That's the minimum of utopia, without which it is not worth being human" (Domin 1978, 406). Domin may have been strengthened by her own experiences and mastering stress and painful adversities, motivating her to continue fighting and overcoming her death impulses. Her poems not only furthered her own development, growth, and personality, but also led her to engage with others. "Through the poem, selfhood, one's own identity, becomes intensified to an extraordinary extent" (Domin 1987b, 252). For Hilde Domin, a poem is a moment of freedom.

"The message of the not—or hardly—communicable: that is the task of the lyricist. His poem is 'used' for this purpose. It is no longer his poem when it is needed. It is no longer about his self-encounter but about the self-encounter of others, whom the poem helps: about the encounter of these others with their own experience" (Domin 1968, 15).

Tobie Nathan (1948–) writes in *Les âmes errantes* (1986): "I am blaming the migration for having been separated from my parents. … We were separated on this bridge of the boat … in the port of Alexandria. Something was broken there. … I happened to think that this separation resulted from the loss of our dead. … In their moments of fury against the Jews, the Egyptians desecrated the tombs, smashed the stelae. … Just like me, the migrant children are far away from their dead. Perhaps their disorders only remind us how much the dead are essential to life" (55).

Nathan, a French psychologist and writer, is one of the pioneers of ethnopsychiatry. In 1979, he opened the first center for ethnopsychiatry in Paris. Ethnopsychiatry is the study of mental illness from a cross-cultural perspective; it takes into consideration the fact that Europeans or Americans are not the only ones with effective knowledge in classifying and treating mental disorders, as the diversity of social and cultural factors must always be recognized.

Tobie Nathan's parents are Italian Jews, who settled in Cairo. His family was forced to leave Cairo in 1957 following the Egyptian revolution and the expulsion of the Jews. They lived in Italy, then settled in France, where Tobie Nathan studied psychology in Paris and obtained French citizenship at the age of twenty-one.

Nathan considers the unthinkable and unspeakable loss of the cultural environment as a psychological trauma, as each individual relies on his or her specific cultural environment in order to decipher reality. He sees the identity of a subject as a kind of memory, a memory that gives the subject a temporal continuity and a spatial unity. When family and personal histories are characterized by deficits such as the loss of cultural affiliation, that is, a first-generation failure to belong and an insecure, perturbated filiation due to parental unavailability or familial disturbances in the second generation, then the risk for the offspring developing disorders is high: they are uprooted from familiar places, from their languages, ethnicities, divinities, rites, and traditions, and the formation of their identity with regard to their future, projects, aims, and relatedness is impaired.

In *La folie des autres. Traité d'ethnopsychiatrie clinique* (1986), Nathan presents the theoretical concepts and basic clinical features of ethnopsychiatry. According to him, ethnic identification is composed of various overlapping components such as personal identification, self-esteem, and identification with various social groups. The significance of ethnic identification seems to be mediated by environmental factors, such as the family structure, the community, and ethnic groups.

In an article in the *New York Times* on February 27, 1949, **Arthur Asher Miller** (1915–2005) commented on his most well-known novel, *Death of a Salesman*: "The quality in such plays that does shake us … derives from the underlying fear of being displaced, the disaster inherent in being torn away from our chosen image of what and who we are in this world. Among us today this fear is as strong, and perhaps stronger, than it ever was. In fact, it is the common man who knows this fear best."

Miller, an American playwright, was born in Harlem, New York; he was the son of an immigrant family of Polish and Jewish descent. His father, abandoned by his parents in Poland, was illiterate; he later joined his family on his own. In New York, he built up a coat manufacturing business, which he lost during the Great Depression, after the Wall Street Crash of 1929. The family was forced to move from Manhattan to Flatbush, Brooklyn. To contribute financially to his family's income, Miller delivered bread at four o'clock in the morning, seven days a week, for four months. After graduating from high school, Miller worked in a warehouse for two years and was thus able to enroll in the college of the University of Michigan, where he worked as a dishwasher and fed laboratory mice in order to finance his studies. He wrote for the student paper and completed his first play, *No Villain*, for which he won the school's Avery Hopwood Award in 1936, making him financially secure.

Miller lived through the Great Depression and the accompanying enormous existential insecurity, which highly influenced his creative writing. Christopher Bigsby in his biography of Arthur Miller (2008) recounts that "Miller wrote letters to himself, which were never addressed to anyone. They were simply a way of making sense of what he was seeing and feeling, giving order to what seemed a numbing irrelevance of work that meant nothing to him" (71). "His plays were not so much imagined as recalled lived experiences, which he considered as a guarantee of authenticity, and not of a failure of imagination" (101). His unpublished plays, stories, and novels would often express even closer private truths, one of the reasons for their remaining unpublished.

The following are citations from the book *Arthur Miller* by Christopher Bigsby (2008):

> I had my own career from the time I was six years old. I had my own space, psychologically. Kemit [his older brother] was totally occupied by them [the parents]. He was the man they relied on to carry on (75). Depression was my time, when you are fourteen or fifteen, you walk into a moment of history. It's your most sensitive moment of consciousness (40).
>
> Playwriting was an act of self-discovery from the start and would always be; it was a kind of license to say the unspeakable. ... It was a sort of blessing I invented for myself (94). All writers were first formed as sons or daughters; and built into that relationship ... a battle for mastery and identity and for independence. The character comes from inside yourself (101).
>
> One of the strongest urges in the writer's heart, and perhaps most specially the American's, is to reveal what has been hidden and denied, to rend the veil. Poems or novels lack the significance of a shared event. The temporal limits of drama conveyed the urgency of a process that rushed to conclusion, that relied on revelation, on thought and language into action (73).

African Americans

If you try to suppress the arts, then you suppress the deepest dreams and aspirations of a people.
Barack Obama[94]

African Americans or Afro-Americans, the second largest racial group in the USA, are the descendants of enslaved black people from the African continent. There is a high likelihood that they are undercounted, as they share characteristics of poverty and housing insecurity. Accurate census numbers are important, as the collected data affect the nation's ability to ensure equal representation and equal access to important governmental and private sector resources for all Americans, including across racial and ethnic lines.

Toni Morrison (1931–2019), born Chloe Anthony Wofford, was an Afro-American novelist, essayist, editor, and teacher, known for her studies of black American experience within the black American community. The main theme of her novels expresses the life of black characters, struggling for their personal and cultural identity in an unjust society. At Cornell University she wrote her thesis on William Faulkner and Virginia Woolf, and later became a professor at Princeton University.

[94] Remarks by President Obama at YSEALI Town Hall on May 25, 2016.

"What was driving me to write was the silence—so many stories untold and unexamined."[95] "The writing is—I'm free from pain. It's where nobody tells me what to do; it's where my imagination is fecund, and I am really at my best. Nothing matters more in the world or in my body or anywhere when I'm writing,"[96] said Morrison.

In 1993 she received the Nobel Prize in Literature for her book *Beloved* and in 2010 was made an officer of the French Legion of Honor. In 2012 she was awarded the US Presidential Medal of Freedom. The National Memorial for Peace and Justice in Montgomery, Alabama, includes this quote by Morrison in the section commemorating individual victims of lynching: "And O my people, out yonder, hear me, they do not love your neck unnoosed and straight. So love your neck; put a hand on it, grace it, stroke it and hold it up. Your inside parts that they'd just as soon slop for hogs you got to love them. The dark, dark liver—love it, love it and the beat and beating heart, love that too. More than eyes and feet. More than lungs that have yet to draw free air. More than your life-holding womb and your life-giving private parts, hear me now, love your heart. For this is the prize."

In her book *The Origin of Others* (2017), Morrison traces the history of black slavery, which haunts all African Americans, a past unable to be erased, the traces as ghosts still present. She describes how the same racial attitudes are at work today.

> Race, class, gender, color, religion, wealth, culture are means to separate, judge others as arbiters of difference, using and abusing power and control with the aim to gain ascendance. Fundamentally there is a profound need—psychologically and socially—to define the other as an outsider, a stranger in order to define one's self. One of the consequences of these strategies is an exaggerated fear of the stranger. For example, the urge to consider the other as foreign seems to be an indispensable effort to confirm one's own self as to be all right. It is easier to alienate the other than trying to meet and understand him. … There are no strangers. There are only versions of ourselves, many of which we have not embraced, most of which we wish to protect ourselves from (38).

According to Morrison, the Other is unpredictable, not a foreigner, but meeting the Other confronts us with our own self, with our unawareness and especially with profound associated emotions within our self, which we tend to project onto others, thus denying their personal individuality and identity. Media's perverse representations render our perceptions and visions of human values hazy and obscure, as the notion of truth is no longer respected.

95 Hilton Als, "Toni Morrison and the Ghosts in the House," *The New Yorker*, October 20, 2003.

96 "'I Regret Everything': Toni Morrison Looks Back On Her Personal Life," *NPR*, April 20, 2015.

The Bluest Eye is Morrison's first novel, published in 1970, was a book she had long wanted to read, and as no one had written it, she thought that maybe she would. In the foreword to a later edition, she writes: "What it is like to be actually hated—hated for things we have no control over and cannot change."

While researching her novel *The Black Book* (1974), Morrison came across a nineteenth-century article about a fugitive black slave named Margaret Garner who escaped in 1856 with her husband and their children from a Kentucky plantation. On the verge of being recaptured by her enslavers, she killed her infant daughter to prevent her child from returning to slavery. This historical background inspired Morrison's best-known novel *Beloved* (1987), for which she received the Nobel Prize in Literature. She writes of the book: "I inserted a speaking, thinking dead child whose impact—and appearance and disappearance—could operate as slavery's gothic damage" (2017, 83). Morrison never ceased to illustrate the transgenerational transmission of the heritage of slavery; even today black people are being haunted by the effects of racism.

"Beloved the girl, the haunter is the ultimate Other. Clamoring, clamoring forever for a kiss" (1987, 91). The need to be loved, the name Be-loved given to the dead girl, symbolizes the infinite void the nameless and oppressed slaves suffered.

Beloved's "footprints come and go, come and go" (324). The dead girl continues to live in her mother's mind. If mourning cannot be fulfilled, secret intrapsychic crypts or enclaves are formed by incorporation fantasies, which allow the preservation of an irreplaceable representation of a highly significant person, whose loss is radically denied.

"What I remember is a picture floating around out there, outside my head. I mean, even if I don't think it, even if I die, the picture of what I did, or knew, or saw is still out there. Right in the place where it happened" (43). Haunted by the traumatic experience, a "picture" of the moment of the event is recorded, along with associated feelings of shock, fear, pain, anger, guilt, and shame.

"Everybody knew what she was called, but nobody anywhere knew her name." Beloved "cannot be lost because no one is looking for her, and even if they were, how can they call her if they don't know her name"? As a ghost, Beloved searches to be seen, heard, loved, and to find an identity, allowing her to come alive and then finally find peace in death.

"The girl who waited to be loved." In a nightmare, traumatic experiences are reactivated, remembered with overwhelming frightening feelings; only confrontation and working through these traumatisms help to overcome and integrate the lived events.

"It took longer for those who had spoken to her, lived with her, fallen in love with her, to forget, until they realized they couldn't remember or repeat a single thing she said, and began to believe that, other than what they themselves were thinking, she hadn't said anything at all. So, in the end, they forgot her too. Remembering seemed unwise." Traumatic memories are powerful, long-lasting and repeat themselves; in recounting traumatic events, the accompanying painful affects are reexperienced; therefore, denial is a survival strategy in order to forget the cruel and threatening past.

"It is not a story to pass on" (323–324). The shadow of the past is represented by Beloved and will continue to haunt future generations. In 2006, after polling hundreds of writers, editors, and critics, the Book Review section of the *New York Times* named *Beloved* the best American work of fiction of the previous quarter-century.

Of her family Morrison writes: "The world back then didn't expect much from a little black girl, but my father and mother certainly did."[97] Losing her father, she felt that the world disappeared with him.

The high esteem of her grandmother can be read in the following lines from the foreword to *Tar Baby*: "She told us stories to keep us working at tedious tasks, picking through baskets of wild grapes to sort out the bruised; to take our minds off pain and chickenpox; to split open the dreary world to expose an enchanted one."

According to Morrison the cruelty, brutality, and savagery of the lives of slaves can never be healed, nor forgotten, nor erased, and will haunt their descendants unto their death, forever a remainder of racism, an invincible shadow of the past. For African Americans who have never visited Africa, belonging is colored by feelings of secret familiar bindings to their land of origin and at the same time of deep unknown strangeness.

Barack Obama (1961–) was the 44th president of the United States, the first African-American to be elected to the position. His father Barack Hussein Obama Sr. studied in the United States, after winning a scholarship. He later went on to become a senior governmental economist in Kenya. He met Obama's mother Ann Dunham at the University of Hawaii. She grew up in the USA before her family moved to Honolulu. Obama's father left his wife and son when Obama was two years old, to study at Harvard University. Obama's parents divorced in 1964. At the age of six, Obama moved with his mother—then married to an Indonesian geologist—to Indonesia. Years later he returned to Hawaii to live with his maternal grandparents. Obama saw his father only once more, at the age of ten. He is the main character in Obama's book *Dreams of my Father* (2004).

Of his mother during their time in Indonesia, Obama writes: "Five days a week she came into my room at 4:00 in the morning, force-fed me breakfast, and proceeded to teach me my English lessons for three hours before I left for school and she went to work." When he resisted, "she would patiently repeat her most powerful defense: This is no picnic for me either, buster" (47–48). The meaningful significant loving relationship with his mother, as well as her engagement and commitment for the future of her son and her consistent rigor in his education can be considered to have enhanced resilience and contributed to the achievements of her son.

[97] Quoted in Paul Gray, "Books: Paradise Found" *Time*, January 19, 1998, http://content.time.com/time/subscriber/article/0,33009,987690-6,00.html.

For Obama, a family is a store of shared memories. In his book he narrates the dreams he had of his father. In one of his dreams he weeps as his father tells him: "Barack, I always wanted to tell you how much I love you" (129). He realizes "how even in his absence his strong image had given me some bulwark to grow up to live up to or disappoint" (129). He also writes of having struggled all his life with nothing more than a ghost, trying to find his balance and thus paying the price for the silence around his father. Silence kills and betrays one's faith, faith in other people, a silence that arises out of fear and shame. "At the time of his death, my father remained a myth to me, both more and less than a man." He had the impression he was living someone's else story, not his own, as if the incomplete narrative of his life stood between himself and others. "Inside myself … I found only a great emptiness" (302). Later he writes that "the fantasy of my father had at least kept me from despair" (221). "Where once I'd felt the need to live up to his expectations, now I felt as if I had to make up for all his mistakes. Only the nature of those mistakes still wasn't clear to my mind. … My image of him remained so contradictory" (227). Obama was afraid of not recognizing warning signs and becoming "captive to his father's tragedy, as if living out a preordained script" (227). "My fears were always internal, the old fears of not belonging" (253). "It was as if I couldn't escape him" (265).

In trying to understand what happened to his family, in the perspective of a transgenerationally maintained silence, Obama writes:

> Oh, father, I cried. There was no shame in your confusion. Just as there had been no shame in your father's before you. No shame in the fear, or in the fear of his father before him. There was only shame in the silence fear had produced. It was the silence that betrayed us. If it weren't for that silence, your grandfather might have told your father, that he could never escape himself or recreate himself alone. Your father might have taught the same lessons to you. And you, his son, might have told your father. … You could never forge yourself into a whole person by leaving those things behind" (429).

It may take generations for an event to awaken awareness. "I saw that my life in America—the black life, the white life, the sense of abandonment I'd felt as a boy … all of it was connected … by more than the accident of a name or the color of my skin. The pain I felt was my father's pain" (430).

What does a child need? According to Obama the promise of sharing, a sense of being able to master one's environment, an understanding of oneself, one's world, one's culture, one's community. The black child learns "someone else's history. Someone else's culture" (258), the same culture that rejects him or her, denies his or her humanity. How then should children be interested in learning? Half of these children do not know their own fathers. "There's nobody to guide through the process of becoming a man … to explain to them the meaning of manhood. And that's a recipe for disaster" (258).

Africa was the promised land, full of ancient traditions. Only from a distance, could Obama embrace Africa. In returning to his homeland, to the place of his ancestors, he writes: "For the first time in my life, I felt the comfort, the firmness of identity, that a name might provide, how it could carry an entire history in other people's memories. … My name belonged and so I belonged drawn into a network of relationships and alliances … that I did not yet understand" (305). "The worst thing that colonialism did was cloud our view of the past" (434). For Obama, the opposite of culture is not ignorance, it is indifference; the opposite of faith is not atheism, it is indifference; and the opposite of morality is not immorality, it is indifference.

Chapter 15

TESTIMONY FROM ARTISTS MISSING THEIR MOTHERS

I carry her in my memory, my mother.
Giovanni Segantini[98]

Artistic creation can be regarded as an artist's struggle with intrapsychic pain and despair, and the ability to endure torment and suffering. Art permits the confrontative expression of the conflict between denial and recognition of loss and at the same time the attempt for its reparation and restoration (Segal 1952).

In the following section, artists who lost their mother through death or emotional unavailability are described.

Pablo Neruda (1904–1973), who lost his mother at the age of two months, wrote: "I love you without knowing how, or when, or from where" (Neruda 2004, Sonnet XVII).

Pablo Neruda, Chilean poet, diplomat and politician, whose birth name was Neftalí Ricardo Reyes Basoalto, adopted his pen and later legal name in memory of the Czech poet Jan Neruda. His mother, a teacher, died when he was an infant; his father was a railway employee. At the age of thirteen he published his first poem "Enthusiasm and Perseverance," which can be regarded as a recurring theme throughout his life.

In 1971 he received the Nobel Prize in Literature. In his acceptance speech he said: "I believe that poetry is an action, ephemeral or solemn, in which there enter as equal partners solitude and solidarity, emotion and action, the nearness to oneself,

98 Abraham (1911, 214).

the nearness to mankind and to the secret manifestations of nature. … We must pass through solitude and difficulty, isolation and silence in order to reach forth to the enchanted place where we can dance … and sing our sorrowful song."

In the following lines of "Poem 15," Neruda (2004) seems to address his mother—whom he has never known—and at the same time portrays his grieving engagement.

> I like you quiet because it's as if you are absent.
> Distant and painful as if you had died.
> A word then, a smile would do.
> And I'm happy, happy that it isn't true

Pablo Neruda's poems can be viewed as expressions of his ongoing mourning process with respect to the early loss of his mother. "As if you had died" expresses his knowledge of the permanent and irrevocable death, but at the same time "happy, happy that it isn't true" shows his denial of the loss, the refusing to recognize it. His maintaining of an inner dialog with the loved mother can be found in the following verses in Sonnet XVII:

> I love you as certain dark things are to be loved,
> in secret, between the shadow and the soul.
> I love you as the plant that never blooms
> but carries in itself the light of hidden flowers…
> I love you without knowing how, or when, or from where.

The denial of the loss of a parent exists simultaneously with the awareness and knowledge of the reality of the loss. Children's fantasies and internal dialogs with the deceased person are considered as survival strategies and may therefore be helpful in the mourning process. The construction of the human personality is shaped by ongoing losses; at birth, the infant experiences its first loss, namely, the warmth and well-being in utero. Infant and early childhood development is accompanied by loss and gain, specifically, the fact that growing up goes hand in hand with loss. During the growth process, the child gains an ever-greater autonomy. This simultaneous gain may allow a parallel grieving process for experienced losses. At each new developmental phase, a child must mourn significant losses.

One might wonder what role the dog played in the mourning process of Pablo Neruda when we read the following lines of his poem "A Dog Has Died":

> No, my dog used to gaze at me,
> paying me the attention I need,
> the attention required
> to make a vain person like me understand
> that, being a dog, he was wasting time,

but, with those eyes so much purer than mine,
he'd keep on gazing at me
with a look that reserved for me alone
all his sweet and shaggy life,
always near me, never troubling me,
and asking nothing.

For children, animals serve not only as protectors and guardian angels, but as intimate confidants with whom to engage in dialog, ready to hear every sorrow and receive all pain, always understanding and alleviating any feelings of distress and grief through their presence and their nonverbal communication, for example, their gaze. They provide comfort and represent a support-giving companion.

Maternal depression

Various artists, painters, creative writers, and musicians have experienced their mother's emotional unavailability, for instance, due to the loss of a child. Their relationship with a profoundly depressed mother evokes the concept of Green's (1997) dead mother complex. He describes an infant or young child's response to a chronically depressed, emotionally absent mother. The mother is physically present, but psychically "dead" for her young child, who is terrified and confused. This interaction has been observed by Stern (1994) who states: "Compared to the infant's expectations and wishes, the depressed mother's face is flat and expressionless. She breaks eye contact and does not seek to reestablish it" (12). "After the infant's attempts to invite and solicit the mother to come to life, to be there emotionally, to play, have failed, the infant, it appears, tries to be with her by way of identification and imitation" (12–13).

Psychoanalysts like Bion (1962, 1970), Winnicott (1974), and Ogden (2014) describe the consequences of a rupture of the mother-infant bond, which leaves the infant or young child in a state of primitive agony with feelings of "endless falling," "nameless dread:" a threat of nonexistence. The depressed mother's mental or emotional disinvestment leaves a void, a hole, and is linked with a negative, even malignant identification of the infant. The consequences are manifold: in a state of dependency the child's separation-developmental needs are accompanied by a fear that if separated, he or she will not be able to survive. A mother's unpredictability and nonreliability inhibit the child's developmental process and capacity to establish significant relatedness. Winnicott's concept of the "fear of breakdown" refers to "the fear of a past event that has not yet been experienced" (1974, 107) and tends by compulsive repetition to be reactivated; the emotions associated with the original critical event are continually relived on an interpersonal level and may represent over and over again a retraumatization. An infantile event of "primitive agony,"[99] of an original break-down, remains actual, unrepresented, and can only be inscribed into the past if taken up by the ego in present experiences and having been worked through, integrated, and remembered. For Freud, impressions from early childhood that produced no effect on the child may attain traumatic power at a later date as vivid memories (Breuer and Freud 1895).

Donald Woods Winnicott (1896–1971) testifies in his "Poem The Tree"—written at the age of sixty-seven—to his subjective emotional experience in his relation with his mother, which may have influenced his immense creativity in life and work.

> Mother below is weeping weeping weeping,
> Thus, I knew her.
> Once, stretched out on her lap as now on dead tree
> I learned to make her smile, to stem her tears
> to undo her guilt, to cure her inward death.
> To enliven her was my living.

Winnicott's mother had to cope with depressive episodes; his much-occupied father apparently unconsciously delegated his son to care for his mother (Kahr 1996, 10). According to his wife Clare, Winnicott—already advanced in age—said: "I was left too much to all my mothers. Thank goodness I was sent away at thirteen!" (25). Winnicott lived in a very feminine domestic universe as the only boy with two older sisters, a nanny, and a governess.

Winnicott's musical talent would have allowed him to become a professional musician, but he chose the medical profession, specializing in pediatrics. "His infantile need to repair the depression of his mother drove him inexorably into the helping professions" (24).

In the paper "Hate in the Countertransference" (1949) Winnicott writes: "Analysis is my chosen job, the way I will best deal with my own guilt, the way I can express myself in a constructive way" (196), and in *Through Pediatrics to Psycho-Analysis* (1975): Their [the children's] task is first to deal with mother's mood. If they succeed in the immediate task, they do no more than succeed in creating an atmosphere in which they can start on their own lives" (92).

For Winnicott (1986) we live in the inner, the outer, and the transitional world. Cultural experience takes place in the transitional area and begins with play, leading to "the whole area of man's inheritance, including the arts, the myths of history … also all the accumulated culture of the past five to ten thousand years" (36).

[99] "Primitive agonies" are characterized by the "return to an unintegrated state," the sensation of "falling forever," "the failure of indwelling," the "loss of the sense of the real," and the "loss of the capacity to relate to objects" (Winnicott 1974, 104).

Giovanni Segantini (1858–1899) wrote of his mother: “She was beautiful … like a sunset in spring.” He not only experienced the depression of his mother due to the death of his brother but suffered from subsequent losses and adversities.

Segantini seemed to have been able to express and transcend his early childhood traumatic experiences through his paintings. According to Abraham (1911), the shadow of death accompanied Segantini throughout his life. Giovanni was born in Arco in Trentino in 1858, the year in which his brother Lodovico, who was five years older, died in a fire. He lived with his mother, his father being mostly absent in search of work as a tradesman. His early childhood was marked by poverty and his mother’s depression following the death of his brother. When he was seven his mother died, and from then on, he was in the care of Irene, a daughter from his father’s previous marriage. He lost his father, whom he had hardly known, at the age of eight. With Irene, he moved to Milan, but he soon ran away and was taken in by a family, where he worked as a swineherd; but he had to return to his half-sister. He fled once again and was finally institutionalized. He learned reading and writing only in adult life.

In his paintings, Segantini dealt with the traumatic events of his childhood, one being the abandonment by his mother. In numerous paintings there is an idealization of mother, motherhood, and mother with infant. The painting *Two Mothers* (Fig. 15.1), represents mother and infant, and sheep and lamb.

Figure 15.1 Giovanni Segantini. *Two Mothers* (1899). Oil on canvas. After the death of the artist, the painting was finished by Giovanni Giacometti.

In a letter to the poetess Neera,[100] Segantini recounts that as a young boy he was asked to draw the dead infant of a young mother who said: "If only I had a picture of my baby." This was his first drawing; he worked for several hours in order to fulfill the wish of the mother, producing a drawing that represented the girl as if she were still alive. One wonders about Segantini's wish for his mother to still be alive. Drawing became his art, an art to call the dead back to life.

Segantini found consolation in nature, saying that sounds accompanied what his heart narrated, the quiet harmonies of sunsets, the innermost essence of life. "Thus, my mind was nurtured by a great melancholy, which resounded in the soul in infinite sweetness. … Yes, I am a passionate lover of nature. At sunny, sunny spring days in these home-made mountains, when the blossoming alpine roses are made of the grey of the granite rocks or the soft green of the drifts delicately emerge, when the blue heavenly arch is reflected in the clear eyes of the earth, I feel an endless jubilation. … I love the sun the most, after the sun the spring, then the springs that are gushing crystal clear out of the rocks in the Alps. … I get high on this love that never saturates me, I bend myself to the earth and kiss the blades of grass, the flowers, while high up in the blue sky the larks sing. Man is not abandoned when he feels himself in union with nature" (Zehder-Segantini 1912, 29).

> One day, when I was about four years old, I was crossing a narrow little bridge over a mill stream which worked several flour mills, leading to some dye-works. Another boy, a little bigger than myself, was crossing the bridge in the opposite direction to draw water; so we met half way. He bent down to fill his pitcher from the stream; the bridge was narrow, and he knocked up against me so that I fell in. I remember being carried down under a stone bridge; the stream was rapid; beyond the bridge there were some washerwomen along the bank: I can still see them with their arms upraised and their scared faces, shrieking madly. Whenever my head rose above the waters, I saw my cap, a red woolen cap which my mother had made; and lastly, I saw the great wheel of my godfather's mill looming ever nearer. When I again opened my eyes, a brilliant white light struck me: it was the sun beating on our garden wall. In the blue sky the larks were singing. This too I remember well that a man with long legs was carrying me on his shoulders towards home (Villari 1901, 6).

With what emotions of threat, fears of annihilation and death, the four-year-old Segantini, abandoned and helpless, must have been overwhelmed! He remembers in details this traumatic event; early childhood memories are often extremely strong. In narrating his experience, Segantini attributes meaning and significance, permitting an understanding of what took place and contributing to a sense of self-continuity.

[100] Anna Radius Zuccari (1846–1918) was an Italian writer who used the pen name Neera.

> I was abandoned and orphaned at the age of six, so alone without love, far from everyone, like a great dog. In such circumstances, I could only become wild, and I was always, towards the existing laws, filled with unrest and turmoil … more so I got strength in the feeling of love for all of us who are miserable. I never shed tears over my pain, neither for my soul, nor my body, never I let the mind, or the heart go idle, for I learned from them the secret of life and worldwide love. I always loved my poor companions, old and young, for it seemed to me that the friendship with them cleans me up a bit. … Art is the mediator between God and our soul. Rather, since our soul is a part of God, the work of art must be an expression of deity. … Art is love enveloped in beauty (Zehder-Segantini 1912, 85).

At the end of his life Segantini worked on the Schafberg,[101] high above Pontresina, on his *Nature-Death-Life* triptych: "Yes, true life is a single dream, the dream of gradually approaching an ideal that is as far away as possible but high, high to the infinite" (Abraham 1911, 48).

Segantini's wife described a dream that her husband had told her twelve days before his sudden death at the age of forty-one: he dreamed that he was the one who was carried on the stretcher from a hut (and he pointed to the painting *The Death*); "one of the women nearby was you and I saw how you were crying" (Servaes 1902, np).

In 1904 Gabriele D'Annunzio (1836–1938) wrote these magnificent lines on the death of Giovanni Segantini:

> Extinguished are the humble and precious eyes greeting the infinite beauty, having left your soul where shadow and light, life and death were only one prayer, and the melody of the stream and the roaring of the herd and the thunderstorm and the eagle cry and the human moan were just a single word (np).

Giovanni Segantini answered Tolstoy's question: "What is art?" in the following way: "Art should glorify and transfigure work, love, motherhood and death" (Abraham 1911, 4), themes that characterized the essence of his life and that he represented in his paintings. In another letter he stated: "In my almost wildlife, in the midst of nature, thinking and art have developed. … Perhaps one would have to descend down to the roots in order to study and analyze all sensations of the soul up to its first, even the most remote movements of childhood" (Abraham 1911, 5).

[101] The Segantini Hütte is a mountain hut above Pontresina in the Upper Engadin in the Swiss canton of Grisons. It is named after the painter Giovanni Segantini, who died there in September 1899. The hut is located on the Schafberg.

Egon Schiele (1890–1918) made the following comment on his painting *The Three Mothers*: "The one in the middle is on fire, the one to the right has burnt out, the one to the left has perished in the fire" (2014, 22). Schiele grew up with a profoundly depressed mother.

Egon Schiele's father was a station master, and as a child fascinated by trains, Schiele would draw them for hours. At age three he lost his elder sister Elvira and grew up with his mother's deep depression after losing two other daughters at birth. He witnessed the deterioration of his father's mental health and finally at age fifteen his father's death from syphilis.

Schiele's major body of work shows his search not only for self-recognition, identity, and insight into his tormented mind, but also for knowledge and awareness of the world. In his representations he expressed his longing for the divine in nature, as well as for self- and world-comprehension. For Schiele, art not only reveals the personality of the artist but also his body as a medium of aesthetically conveyed truth. "Adults have forgotten how much they themselves were attracted by sex when they were children."[102] Schiele's painting was criticized as "macabre eroticism." He stated: "I am human, I love death and love life. Even the most erotic artwork has sanctity."[103]

At the age of twenty he painted *Dead Mother,* a mother with a hopelessly lost child (Fig. 15.2). Later he acknowledged that this painting was one of his best. Two years later he painted a child with a frightened and horrified look in *Mother and Child II* and at age twenty-five, *Mother with Two Children.* The three paintings show very young children left with a lifeless mother unable to show any emotional resonance, evoking uncanny feelings in the viewer. Thanks to his immense creativity, Schiele seems to have been able to convey the terrifying feelings of his lived traumatic experiences in early childhood in his paintings; exploring the uncanny (Kohon 2016) may open up a "potential for greater self-awareness, for being more, not less, in touch with one's inward life" (Parson 2014, 51).

In 1913 he writes: "I mainly observe the physical movement of mountains, trees, water and flowers. Everywhere one remembers similar movements in the human body, similar movements of joy and suffering in the plants."[104] In his painting of a *Small Tree in Late Autumn* Schiele portrays a solitary dry tree, exposed to autumn weather and the wind, like a dancing human figure; a dead dance according to Rössler (1922), where the tree (that is, nature) reflects Schiele's psychic state.

Schiele considered the artist as the savior of the world and as a man of pain. "I brought sacrifices to others, those who had mercy for me, those who were far away or who did not see me, the seeing."[105]

[102] Quotation from the exhibition in the Leopold Museum, Vienna, on the 100th anniversary of Schiele's death in 2018.

[103] Ibid.

[104] Ibid.

[105] Ibid.

Figure 15.2 Egon Schiele. *Dead Mother* (1910). Oil on wood.

Of his painting *Fir Tree Forest,* he wrote: "I return to the red and black cathedral of the dense pine forest, which lives without noise and looks at itself mimically. The eyes of the trunks grip tightly and exhale the visibly wet air—how well—everything is dead alive."[106]

[106] Ibid.

On his painting *A Self-Image* he comments: "An eternal dream full of the sweetest excess of life—restless, with anxious pain inside, in the soul. Flares, burns, grows after fight—heart break. I am the most noble of the noblest—and the most repentant of donors."[107]

It is interesting to reflect on comments by Klaus Albrecht Schröder (1955–) an Austrian art historian:

> Egon Schiele constructs, he stages, and this theater that he performs has not become more superficial, because it does not represent the imprint of life, but rather finds its way ingeniously through a symbolic figure for the state of mind of an epoch that is so close to us today: being alone, being exposed, an existential instability, ultimately also this pessimistic world view of Schiele, that there is no bridge between people, is what probably not only characterize his pictures, but lets him appear today so close to us. … I believe that there is no "modern" art, that there is only art, which is eternal.[108]

Käthe Kollwitz (1867–1945), a German sculptor, wrote of her mother: "I loved her so much, but I could not go to her" (1968, 348).

Kollwitz lived in a deeply religious family; her paternal grandfather was a Lutheran pastor. The religious atmosphere she was exposed to emphasized obedience and the requirement to suppress one's own feelings; Kollwitz wrote: "A loving God was never brought home to us" (Walters and Jarell 2013, 122). She grew up in a family of seven children, of whom three died. At eight years old, she experienced the death of her one-year-old brother and her mother's ensuing profound depression. Not only did she feel guilty and haunted by the death of her youngest brother, but she also sensed that her mother was no longer approachable. She had lost her mother's emotional engagement and availability, leaving her with feelings of abandonment.

In October 1914 Kollwitz lost her own son, killed in World War I. One can assume that the death of her son Peter reactivated the losses that she had experienced earlier in life, along with the accompanying lived affects. Farewelling Peter, her eighteen-year-old son, was like once again cutting her son's umbilical cord, the first time to live, but now to die. From that point onward, she felt as if she was getting old, closer to the grave; it represented an intense breaking point for her, with the impression of being bent to such a degree that she could never again straighten up. Five weeks after the death of her son, she decided to create a sculpture as a memorial for him, a wonderful goal, she wrote, no one else has this prerogative. In sculpting she upheld communication with her son; but almost five years after his death she broke off her work on the sculpture, acknowledging the firm belief with which she had worked,

[107] Ibid.
[108] Ibid.

standing by her son, seeing his dear and devoted smiling face; she thought of all the time she had spent on her sculpture-work, of her love and determination, and all her tears; she promised him she would return to it, to fulfill it for him and others, and that the work was only postponed. Kollwitz named her sculpture *Mother with Dead Son*. She completed it in 1932.

In her diary in 1937, on the twenty-third anniversary of her son's death, she wrote: "I am working on a small sculpture which has developed out of my attempt to make a sculpture of an old person. It has become something like a Pietà (Fig. 15.3). The mother is seated and has her dead son lying between her knees in her lap. There is no longer pain—only reflection." Her following words let us presume a coming to term with the mourning process and may be regarded as an acceptance of her destiny: "The human condition which is subject to the law of life, i.e., separation and death are part of everyone's life" (Kollwitz 1968, 312).

Figure 15.3 Käthe Kollwitz. *Pieta* (1937/1938). Bronze sculpture.

"Kollwitz's art is driven by introspection and self-reflection; a sort of ongoing self-analysis" (Coulter 2016, 486). "The final years of the Second World War brought more hardship for Kollwitz. Her husband died in 1940. Two years later her grandson, named Peter like her son, was killed fighting in Russia. Following this potent reminder of the death of her son, she stopped working altogether. Then her home in Berlin, in which she had lived for over fifty years, was destroyed in an air raid, together with a great number of her works. She finally found refuge at the Moritzburg estate of Prince Ernst Heinrich of Saxony, an admirer of her work. She died there on 22 April 1945 and was buried in Berlin" (488).

Chapter 16

TESTIMONY FROM ARTISTS MISSING THEIR FATHERS

Growing up without a father represents a theme that is widely and controversially discussed. Children are especially vulnerable after the death of a parent. The loss of one's father by death, abandonment, separation, or divorce, represents an experience of bereavement. A father's absence is an issue requiring an approach that is based on the contextual situation and that considers the paternal role and function.

"Without music, life would be a mistake," (1899) said **Friedrich Wilhelm Nietzsche** (1844–1900), born in Röcken (near Leipzig) in Germany, where his father was a Lutheran minister, his mother being eighteen years old at their marriage. His father died in 1849 at the age of thirty-six, and only a few months later, his brother Joseph died, too; thus Nietzsche, at the age of five, was confronted with two significant losses. The family moved to Naumburg, where Nietzsche grew up with his mother, grandmother, two aunts, and his younger sister Elisabeth. On the subject of missing his father, he wrote: "I am convinced that the death of such a distinguished father, on the one hand, really deprived me of paternal help and guidance for later on in life, while on the other, it planted the seeds of seriousness and contemplation in my soul. … Man's maturity: to have regained the seriousness that he had as a child at play. … We have art so that we shall not be destroyed by the truth" (Nietzsche 1994, 66).

At the age of only twenty-four, the future philosopher was appointed professor of classical philology at the University of Basel. After numerous interruptions, he had to give up his chair in 1879 due to illness. In the following years he published his most famous works, such as *Thus Spoke Zarathustra* (1883–5), *Beyond Good and Evil* (1886), and *On the Genealogy of Morality* (1887). He is well known for his criticism of traditional European morality and religion. A central theme in Nietzsche's writings concerns our attitude toward suffering, one of life's constants. His health slowly deteriorated, both mentally and physically, and he died in 1900.

Guillaume Apollinaire (1880–1918), born Guglielmo Alberto Wladimiro Alessandro Apollinare Kostrowitzky of Polish origin, was a French poet and writer, and defender of modern art. Born in Rome, the son of Angelica of Kostrowitzky and of an unknown father. (The paternity attributed to Francesco d'Aspermont, an aristocrat from the Swiss canton of Grisons who disappeared early from Apollinaire's life, is not at all certain.)

Apollinaire (1950) writes: "You cannot carry the body of your father everywhere with you. He is abandoned in the company of the other dead. And, remembering him, regretting him, one speaks about him with admiration. And if you become a father, do not expect that one of our children wants to double himself for the life of our dead body. But our feet come off only in vain from the ground that contains the dead" (9).

Apollinaire lived with his mother and his half-brother in Bologna, Italy, then in Monaco, Cannes, and Nice. When he was nineteen, his mother settled in Paris where he wrote his first poems. Two years later, in Germany, he was impressed by the Rhine, its landscapes and legends. "We must … embrace at a glance: the past, the present and the future. The canvas must present this essential unity that alone causes ecstasy" (10).

Apollinaire returned to Paris in 1902, where for the first time he signed his book *The Heresiarch & Co*, a collection of short stories, with the name Guillaume Apollinaire. He writes: "This is a book for those who love literature, powerful and disturbing, strange and logical."

Working as a journalist, poet, art critic and lecturer, he published *Alcools* (*Alcohols*) in 1913, his first success.

"Farewell" (*Alcools* 1913)[109]

I picked this sprig of heather
Fall is dead, remember
We will not see each other on earth
Smell of time sprig of heather
And remember I'm waiting for you

The first poetic collection of *Alcools* contains written texts from 1898 to 1913, many having appeared previously in various reviews. During this time, Apollinaire was inspired by different art movements such as symbolism, futurism, and cubism,

[109] Original text:
L'Adieu
J'ai cueilli ce brin de bruyère
L'automne est morte souviens-t'en
Nous ne nous verrons plus sur terre
Odeur du temps brin de bruyère
Et souviens-toi que je t'attends

"justifying" the plural of the title *Alcools,* as well as by the fact that each of the poems is an alcohol, that is to say, a metamorphosis of the world into songs, a kind of resurrection, allowing human beings to incorporate the universe instead of being at its mercy. It also represents the universal thirst of the poet, the paroxysm of his desires.

Apollinaire's book *Cubist Painters, Aesthetic Meditations* (1913) is a defense of contemporary art. He is considered a precursor of surrealism whose name he coined. Creation for Apollinaire was not based on any theory but must originate from imagination and intuition and be as close as possible to life, to nature. "I am a fierce supporter of excluding the intervention of intelligence, that is, of philosophy and logic in the manifestations of art. Art must be based on the sincerity of emotion and the spontaneity of the expression: both are in direct relationship with the life they strive to magnify aesthetically."[110]

In 1914, Apollinaire was engaged as an artilleryman in the French army. He sustained a severe head injury in 1916, requiring a long convalescence. He died in 1918 of influenza during the pandemic.

Jean-Paul Sartre (1905–1980), born in Paris to Jean-Baptiste Sartre and Anne-Marie Schweitzer (a cousin of the physician and humanitarian Albert Schweitzer), lost his father, a naval officer who died on duty in Indochina, when he was fifteen months old. He wrote about his father: "In 1904, in Cherbourg, the young naval officer, who was already wasting away with the fevers of Cochin China,[111] made the acquaintance of Anne-Marie Schweitzer, took possession of the big, forlorn girl, married her, begot a child in quick time, me, and sought refuge in death" (Sartre 1964, 15).

Sartre's mother returned with her son to her parents' home and seemed to have established a fusional relationship with her son, sleeping in the same room and enjoying the same childish pleasures. "In truth, the early retirement of my father had gratified me with a very incomplete 'Oedipus': no superego, all right, but no aggressiveness either. My mother was mine, no one denied me the quiet possession: I did not know … jealousy. Against whom, against what would I have revolted: never has the whim of another claimed to be my law" (Sartre 1964, 26).

"Good friends told my mother that I was sad, that I had been surprised to dream. My mother hugged me, laughing: 'You are so joyful, always singing! And what would you complain about? You have everything you want.' She was right: a spoiled child is not sad; he is bored like a dog. I'm a dog: I yawn, tears rolling, I feel them rolling … trembling minutes panicked me, swallow me, and never stop agonizing … my mother tells me again that I'm the happiest of all little boys. How can I not believe it? On my abandonment I never think … there are no words to name it" (94).

[110] Interview between J. Perez-Jorbas and Guillaume Apollinaire on July 24, 1918, published in *La Publicidad.*

[111] Cochin China, or Quinam, is a region encompassing the southern third of modern-day Vietnam whose principal city is Saigon. It was a French colony from 1862 to 1954.

For Sartre, death was shining by its absence. In his book *Les mots* (The Words) (1964) he writes: "These fourteen years were the happiest of my childhood. … My mother and I were the same age … she called me her serving knight, her little man, I told her everything" (217). "I saw death. When I was five, it lay in wait for me. In the evening, it would prowl on the balcony. … In that period, I had an appointment with it every night in bed. … I would wait, all atremble, and it would appear, a very run-of-the-mill skeleton with a scythe. … During the day, I recognized it beneath the most varied disguises: if my mother happened to sing the *Erlking* in French, I would stop my ears " (95).

"The Erlking": poem by J. W. Goethe (1782), song by F. Schubert (1815), translation by Paul Dyrsen (1878):

> Who's riding so late through th' endless wild?
> The father 't is with his infant child;
> He thinks the boy's well off in his arm,
> He grasps him tightly, he keeps him warm.
>
> My son, say why are you hiding your face ?
> Oh father, the Erlking's coming apace,
> The Erlking's here with his train and crown!
> My son, the fog moves up and down.
>
> Be good, my child, come, go with me!
> I know nice games, will play them with thee,
> And flowers thou'lt find near by where
> I live, pretty dress my mother will give.
>
> Dear father, oh father, and do you not hear
> What th' Erlking whispers so close to my ear?
> Be quiet, do be quiet, my son,
> Through leaves the wind is rustling anon.
>
> Do come, my darling, oh come with me!
> Good care my daughters will take of thee,
> My daughters will dance about thee in a ring,
> Will rock thee to sleep and will prettily sing.
>
> Dear father, oh father, and do you not see
> The Erlking's daughters so near to me?
> My son, my son, no one's in our way,
> The willows are looking unusually gray.

I love thee, thy beauty I covet and choose,
Be willing, my darling, or force I shall use!
Dear father, oh father, he seizes my arm!
The Erlking, father, has done me harm.

The father shudders, he darts through the wild;
With agony fill him the groans of his child.
He reached his farm with fear and dread;
The infant son in his arms was dead.

At the death of his maternal grandmother (date unknown) he states: "I did not feel anything. Not even when we followed the coffin to the cemetery" (Sartre 1964, 95).

Sartre is best remembered for his existentialist philosophy—of love, desire, freedom—aspiring to live a more authentic life. However, he recognizes in one of his most famous books, *Being and Nothingness* (1943), the ambiguity of life, realizing what he calls man's absurd situation in the world. His philosophical work has a revolutionary fervor and has to be understood in the context of post-World War II liberation movements and the student uprising of 1968 (Bakewell 2016).

Albert Camus (1913–1960), born in Mondovi, Algeria, was the second son of Lucien Camus and Catherine Sintes, of Spanish origin. Camus's father was mobilized during World War I and died in 1914, when Albert was ten months old. His mother, partly deaf and unable to read or write, settled with her children at her mother's house in Belcourt, one of the poor neighborhoods of Algiers. Thanks to the help of one of his teachers, Louis Germain, Camus obtained a scholarship and studied at Bugeaud high school in Algiers.

In 1957 Camus received the Nobel Prize in Literature "for the whole of a work which brings to light, with a penetrating seriousness, the problems which are posed in our days to the conscience of the men." He dedicated his lecture to his former teacher Louis Germain. In a letter addressed to him on November 19, 1957 he wrote: "Without you, without that loving hand that you have held to the poor little child that I was, without your teaching and your example, none of this would have happened" (Camus 1994, 327).

The First Man[112] (1995), an unfinished autobiographical novel by Albert Camus, is a most beautiful and truthful narrative of the experiences of loss in early childhood. The handwritten manuscript was found in the car in which Camus, at the age of only forty-seven, was killed accidentally. Catherine, Camus's daughter, wrote in the preface to the American edition: "We believed a manuscript of such importance would sooner or later be published unless we destroyed it. Since we had no right to destroy it, we preferred to publish it ourselves so that it would appear exactly as it was."

[112] *Le Premier homme*, Paris, Gallimard, 1994.

In *The First Man* Camus writes:

> Since born on a land without ancestors and without memory, where the annihilation of those who had preceded it, had been … total. … He [the boy] was not even sure that she [his mother] had loved this man [his father] passionately and in any case, he could not ask him … he did not even want to know what had been between them (261).
>
> He [Louis Germain] had succeeded in replacing the father. This is why he [Camus] had never forgotten him, as if, having never really felt the absence of a father whom he had never known, he had unconsciously recognized, first as a child and then throughout his life, the only paternal gesture, at once thoughtful and decisive, which had intervened in his childhood life. Because … his teacher of the certificate class, had weighed with all his human weight, at a given moment, to modify the destiny of this child for whom he was in charge, and he had modified it indeed (129).

Camus could be considered as a resilient[113] child with a high interactive capacity, allowing him to establish a significant relationship with his teacher, a surrogate person, and use him for his development. He writes: "Rescue this poor family from the fate of the poor, which is to disappear from history without a trace. The speechless ones. They were and they are greater than I. … To give up art here is to give up one's self."[114]

In his Nobel Prize lecture, Albert Camus said: "For myself, I cannot live without my art. … It is a means of stirring the greatest number of people by offering them a privileged picture of common joys and sufferings. … It subjects him to the most humble and the most universal truth. … True artists … are obliged to understand rather than to judge. … Truth is mysterious, elusive, always to be conquered. Liberty is dangerous, as hard to live with as it is elating. … It remains for me … to make … the same and ancient promise of faithfulness which every true artist repeats to himself in silence every day."

Per Olov Enquist (1934–2020) in an interview[115] states: "One always hopes for a miracle. … If you do not hope, you are probably not human. … An upbringing like mine marks you like a branding iron."

Enquist was a Swedish author, journalist, playwright and novelist. His autobiographical novel *A Different Life* (2008) is the story of the loss of his father. He states: "Everything I write about me is true. The way I remember it. And I remember well." He was also a replacement child for his brother who was two years older.

113 Resilience comprises a reduced vulnerability to environmental risk experiences, the overcoming of stress or adversity, or a relatively good outcome despite risk experiences (Rutter 2012).

114 "La portée du langage," *L'Argent - Revue Quart Monde,* no. 229, January 2014: 54.

115 With Andrew Brown, July 30, 2016.

Enquist's father, a laborer who worked in local sawmills and also in shipyards miles away from the family home, died when Enquist was six months old. He lived alone with his mother, a teacher, in an isolated house in the forest, near the village of Hjoggböle, in the far north of Sweden, one thousand kilometers away from Stockholm. His first-born brother, carrying the same name, died by umbilical cord suffocation. As a child, he felt he was a "representative" of his stillborn brother. Enquist was raised by his mother in rigorous piety in an environment of isolation. He writes of the silence in this stillness. "When I wrote, my loneliness decreased, and I almost became human."

"There is one existential question: how do things fit together? What I mean, I have a dog, a pretty smart dog, the difference between the dog and me is that he never asks how things fit together, or where is it going? Why?" (Mayer 2009, np).

In *A Different Life,* Enquist writes about his childhood experience, in the third person and part of his narrative can be summarized as follows. The absence of a father is only a strength, a mother's point of view is that he does not miss his father. Four years old he is quite sure that the father is an angel guardian with wings. Even when mother is home, he feels lonely, thinking intensely of father, who almost always reveals himself, answering the child's emergency calls, in moments of extreme distress, fear and boundless abandonment. A secret friend looking down at him with an encouraging smile.

The loss of his father, a significant relationship, aroused in Enquist existential fears and the need for security, protection, and narcissistic gratification. A child has not yet developed the maturity to cope with the intense feelings of sadness, fear, anger, and longing, and therefore denies the loss. Very often, the child maintains—on a fantasy level—the bond to the lost person and thus continues, as Enquist describes, an inner relationship with the father. Such fantasy occupations and internal dialog may be temporarily helpful. In this way feelings of loss can be fended off until a level of development is reached, at which point a child can endure the psychic pain.

Against his intense feelings of fear and abandonment the boy in Enquist's book creates a fantasy world in which his father's presence helps him to feel less lonely and more protected. Thus, he maintains a strong and loyal attachment to his father that is contrary to his mother's intention. Mother does not speak about father, his character, his experiences, no image of his personality is being built up. Thus, mother intends to kill the father after his death out of fear that he could become a partner of the child, his son. Mother wants to possess him only for herself. Only in his heart he can escape her, secretly.

Mother's emotional unavailability to help her son mourning his father results in the boy's secret dialog with him. A child is not able to accomplish a grieving process alone; he needs the help of a meaningful adult person in a continuous relationship, offering a dialog to fulfill a work of mourning. Sitting in a corner, he could speak to his dead father and describe his worries. Father was present and broke through the dreadful darkness and with a reassuring gesture raised his hand. This gesture was wordless. He tried to hear his father's voice and replied. Thus, he had a loyal friend like others had a dog. To share his life with father, to tell and reveal to him the whole truth.

Mourning for children is different to that of adults. The child has to mourn his or her loss at each new developmental phase, as he or she understands it, according to his or her psychological maturity. Only at the age of latency (from the age of six until puberty) is a child able to comprehend on a cognitive level that death is a permanent loss. Often the child imagines that death is reversible as the desire for reunion with a lost parent is so strong that even if the child knows the truth, fantasies have a greater impact. In childhood the capacity to cope with the intense feelings of sadness, fear, anger, and longing is not yet reached; the loss is therefore denied.

No mourning, no loss, the dead father is everywhere, he turns to the father, who looks at him, rejoices with and over him and proudly admires him, an omnipotent fantasy world, serving him as survival strategy.

The ability to accept the reality of an irretrievable loss is indispensable for mourning. Children's grieving can be described as a mental process that a child goes through after a loss and allows him or her to continue developing within a normal range. A child's grief cannot be compared to that of an adult because mourning as such occurs only after adolescence.

Everything changed at the age of thirteen, without any inner anchorage, staring endlessly at the childhood years, receiving no answers, remaining only a tabula rasa forever. Locked up in a ship, which trapped inside a volcano with feelings of panic anxiety, restlessness, hopelessness, frozenness, aggressivity out of vulnerability, hurt and humiliation.

Adolescence is a critical phase for those who have not been able to carry out the work of mourning past traumatic losses. Overwhelming feelings can lead to a psychic breakdown with manifestations of panic anxiety, flight reactions, states of confusion, depersonalization, or severe depression, with hetero- or auto-aggressive behavior, delinquent actions, drug abuse, or promiscuity.

On a developmental level, various identification-, individuation-, and separation processes can be disturbed by the loss of a significant person. Triggered by internal development phases or by external experiences, the child has to go through the grieving process again and again. In order to prevent a perception of ambivalence toward the deceased person and to avoid feelings of guilt, multiple defense strategies are used, for instance, an idealization of the lost parent. Fantasies over the cause of death or preconscious fantasies that contain aggressiveness (e.g., death wishes) can complicate the mourning process, thereby affecting a fresh mental start.

A grieving process is necessary, not only for the child to continue the developmental process but also to prevent him or her from reproducing his or her traumatic experience and undergoing additional traumatization. The working through of loss by a child is particularly difficult when additional events (as in Enquist's life, with the death of his elder brother carrying the same name) complicate and aggravate a mourning process.

Enquist—out of the lived silent and mute burden he carried throughout his childhood and adolescence—put words to his traumatic experiences in his books, as

Shideler (2004) states: "Enquist's profound commitment to humanity, especially to those individuals, good or bad, who cannot speak for themselves and who deserve a voice. From his earlier novels to his most recent works, Enquist has tried to let his characters speak, so that we as readers might hear them and profit from their experiences" (np).

The developmental process of young children may be impaired, especially if one considers the failing or missing paternal functions in very early childhood: the father as the separating third, as a facilitator of the development of psychic structure and of affect management, as well as a harbor of psychic safety (Davies and Eagle 2013). Yet as the life of so many artists cited here proves, the missing father may lead to an extraordinary faculty of abundant creativity.

PART VI

Chapter 17

PSYCHOANALYTIC CONCEPTION OF ART, CREATIVITY, AND AESTHETICS

The artist finds a way of returning from the world of phantasy back to reality, with his special gifts he molds his phantasies into a new kind of reality.
Sigmund Freud[116]

The idea of psychoanalysis as a science as well as an art has always been a controversial subject. Today psychoanalysis is still considered by some as belonging to the biological sciences, but it is mainly a creative therapeutic process of subjective life experiences. Whereas science searches for objective truth, psychoanalysis looks for the subject's truthfulness with him- or herself, for his or her self-integrity. Thoughts and expressions of one's self characterize a subject. Art and psychoanalysis are embedded in the lived moment and enhance self-awareness. All subjective experiences have qualitative features and unfold in time and space.

Sigmund Freud commented on art, beauty, aesthetics, and creation throughout his life in different texts. "We observe that this useless thing which we expect civilization to value is beauty. We require civilized man to reverence beauty wherever he sees it in nature and to create it in objects of his handiwork as far as he is able" (Freud 1930, 59). "The science of aesthetics investigates the conditions under which things are felt as beautiful" (82). "Thus art constitutes a region half-way between a reality which frustrates wishes and the wish-fulfillment world of the imagination—a region

116 "Formulations on the two principles of mental functioning" (1911, 224).

in which, as it were, primitive man's strivings for omnipotence are still in full force" (Freud 1913, 188).

For Freud, who refers to Aristotle's theory of catharsis in tragic Greek theatre, drama corresponds to "opening up sources of pleasure or enjoyment in our emotional life just as, in the case of intellectual activity, joking or fun open up similar sources" (1906, 305). "We remain on the surface so long as we are dealing only with memories and ideas. What is alone of value in mental life are rather the feelings. No mental forces are significant unless they possess the character of aroused feelings" (49). According to Freud, emotions belong to subjective experiences, are important in communication, and need to be regulated. "Mentalized affectivity specifies the value in reflecting on one's own affective experience. Such reflection entails awareness and knowledge of one's own history" (Jurist 2006, 1330).

Freud (1905[117]) stated: "The purpose of drama is to arouse 'terror and pity', as has been assumed since Aristotle, and so 'to purge[118] the emotions,'" by a "process of getting rid of one's emotions by 'blowing off steam'"[119] (1890–1839, 1080). In the book *Studies in Hysteria*, Breuer and Freud (1895) wrote: "For we found, to our great surprise at first, that each individual hysterical symptom immediately and permanently disappeared when we had succeeded in bringing clearly to light the memory of the event by which it was provoked and in arousing its accompanying affect, and when the patient had described that event in the greatest possible detail and had put the affect into words" (6). The concept and method of catharsis and the talking cure originate from these observations, notably of the patient Anna O. (Bertha Pappenheim's pseudonym) who called the treatment "chimney sweeping." Unconscious emotions may be re-experienced by the auditor-spectator of a tragic theatre through deep identification with the character's emotional representations and thus offer an occasion for "working through," a form of self-analysis, according to the interpretation of Aristotle's theory of tragic catharsis (Turri 2015).

Interpretation of art, in a psychoanalytically oriented perspective, always refers to mostly unconscious emotions that need to be felt, expressed, and bound into a meaningful narrative. Considering the artist and the receiver of art, Freud's view is that the artist "produces emotional effects" (Freud 1912, 90). The viewer explores and interprets the multiple significations of any artwork.

Freud (1915) begins his essay "On Transience" by recalling a summer day in 1913. In a countryside in bloom, he is walking with a "taciturn friend" (Lou Andreas-Salomé) and a "young but already famous poet" (Rainer-Maria Rilke). The latter, struck by the beauty surrounding him, is still profoundly saddened by the thought that all that beauty, like all of human beauty and creation after all, is destined to disappear.

[117] In *Psychopathische Personen auf der Bühne*.
[118] In German Freud uses the word *Reinigung*.
[119] In German Freud uses the word *Austoben*.

Freud answers: "Transience value is scarcity value in time. ... A flower that blossoms only for a single night does not seem to us on that account less lovely ... since the value of all this beauty and perfection is determined by its significance for our own emotional lives, it has no need to survive us and is therefore independent of absolute duration" (Freud 1915, 305–306).

Jurist (2006)[120] considers Freud's "Leonardo da Vinci and a Memory of Childhood" (1910) and *The Moses of Michelangelo* (1914), as his "most controversial works on aesthetics. ... Freud makes the struggle for affect regulation central to his interpretation of and personal response to the artists Leonardo and Michelangelo" (1321).

Freud (1910) stated in his text "Leonardo da Vinci and a Memory of Childhood": "Leonardo ... had merely converted his passion into a thirst for knowledge; he then applied himself to investigation with the persistence, constancy and penetration which is derived from passion, and at the climax of intellectual labor, when knowledge has been won, he allowed the long restrained affect to break loose and to flow away freely, as a stream of water drawn from a river is allowed to flow away when its work is done" (74–75). "The wildness in Freud's response to Leonardo is best understood in terms of Freud's own unconscious, creative impulses" (Jurist 2006, 1323).

In his text *The Moses of Michelangelo*, Freud (1914) writes that Michelangelo had given form to "his own inner experiences" (221). Freud's main interpretation of the sculpture focuses on Moses' struggling to regulate his emotions. The extremely personal response to the sculpture marks Freud's own struggle to hold the psychoanalytic movement together and to restrain the rage he felt at the time for Adler and Jung's defection from his movement. "In a letter to Sándor Ferenczi of October 1912, Freud pointedly complained that his current mood made him feel more like the historical Moses than Michelangelo's Moses" (Jurist 2006, 1324). "Freud hoped to be capable of balancing science and art and attempted to have a scientific theory of affects. He was attracted to figures like Leonardo and Goethe who were both scientists and artists, as well as Robert Musil[121] who asked: 'A man who wants the truth becomes a scholar; a man who wants to give free play to his subjectivity becomes a writer; but what should a man do who wants something in between?'" (1330). According to Freud (1914) artists intentions are to "awaken in us the same emotional attitude, the same mental constellation as the one which produced in him the impetus to create" (212). This leads to the possibility of "sharing highly valued emotional experiences" (Freud 1927, 14).

120 For the interpretation of Freud's writings *Moses of Michelangelo* and "Leonardo da Vinci and a Memory of Childhood," see Jurist (2006).

121 Robert Musil, *The Man without Qualities*. Vol. I, Knopf, New York, 1995. Robert Musil (1880—1942) was an Austrian philosophical writer most well known for his novel *The Man without Qualities* (German title: *Der Mann ohne Eigenschaften*).

In "Creative Writers and Day-Dreaming" Freud (1908) writes: "Might we not say that every child at play behaves like a creative writer, in that he creates a world of his own" (143). He compares the imaginative writer with the day-dreamer or poetical creation with day-dreaming and asks how the writer enables us to enjoy our own day-dreams without self-reproach or shame (1908, 153), a "capacity to exchange its originally sexual aim for another one, which is no longer sexual, but which is psychically related to the first aim" (Freud 1908b, 187).

In "The Uncanny" Freud (1919) wrote: "The storyteller has a peculiarly directive power over us; by means of the moods he can put us in, he is able to guide the current of our emotions, to dam it up in one direction and make it flow in another" (251) and in "Delusions and Dreams in Jensen's *Gradiva*" (1907), "creative writers are valuable allies and their evidence is to be prized highly, for they are apt to know a whole host of things between heaven and earth of which our philosophy has not yet let us dream. In their knowledge of the mind they are far in advance of us everyday people, for they draw upon sources which we have not yet opened for science" (8).

Freud in *A Short Account of Psychoanalysis* (1924) seems to summarize his ideas as follows: "We have shown that myths and fairy tales can be interpreted as dreams, we have traced the convoluted paths that lead from the urge of the unconscious wish to its realization in a work of art, we have learnt to understand the emotional effect of a work of art on the observed, and in the case of the artist himself we have made clear his internal kinship with the neurotic as well as his distinction from him" (208).

According to the painter Lucian Michael Freud, "everything is biographical. … What we make, why it is made, how we draw a dog, who it is we are drawn to, why we cannot forget"; he follows thus the idea of his paternal grandfather Sigmund.

Next follow citations of some post Freudian psychoanalysts describing their view and understanding of art, providing an enriching dimension into the creative processes of artists.

For Rose (1999): "Art safely promotes a heightened self-awareness, fosters the reconciliation of primitive and mature self and object representations, and offers a renewed sense of wholeness. Psychoanalysis enables us to link peak aesthetic experiences to the creativity of everyday life—namely the perpetual need to integrate inner and outer worlds, and the eternal pursuit of a fuller human experience" (591–2).

Loewald (1988) supposes that certain "magical" qualities of art, are "connected with the achievement of a reconciliation—with the return, on a higher level of organization, to the early magic of thought, gesture, word, image, emotion, fantasy, as they become united again with what in ordinary nonmagical experience they only reflect, recollect, represent, or symbolize" (80–81).

For Fairbairn (1938), "Aesthetic experience represents a specific emotional reaction which occurs in the beholder when he discovers an object which functions for him symbolically as a means of satisfying his unconscious emotional needs" (173).

According to Kris (1952), artists use regression for their creative activities; he introduced the concept "regression in the service of the ego." An individual fantasy life is intimately related to the artist's personal history and is reflected in the artist's creative imaginations of his art.

For Segal[122] (1952), symbol formation is the outcome of a loss, a creative action involving pain and a mourning process.[123] The creation of symbols is the fundament of art. The artist is withdrawn into his phantasms but conveys and shares his inner world. At the same time, he repairs and restitutes not only his own internal representations, but also the outside reality. According to Segal, all artists aim at immortality. "All creation is really a recreation of a once loved and once whole, but now lost and ruined object, a ruined internal world and self " (199), that is "to restore and recreate the loved object outside and inside" (197). For Segal, creativity requires grief work and is associated with symbolic elaboration. Communication of the subject with an external as well internal reality depends on the ability to symbolize. Aesthetic pleasure resides in the spectator's identification with the artistic work and the representation of the artist's internal world.

Sirois (2008) estimates that art does not attempt to heal but share human conflicts. He considers aesthetic experiences as the sensation of perceiving an external object, such as a melody, an image, or an expression. The external object thus becomes an essential mediation which gives substance to the internal experience, represents it, and invites us to overcome the conflict.

Kohut (1986) considers artistic activity to be part of narcissistic self-representation. Creative artists, and scientists, may be attached to their work with the intensity of an addiction, trying to control and shape it with forces and for purposes that belong to a narcissistically experienced world. They are attempting to recreate a perfection that was formerly a direct attribute of their own personality.

For Winnicott (1971): "It is creative apperception more than anything else that makes the individual feel that life is worth living" (65).

Bollas (1978) values the aesthetic moment as evoking an existential memory in the sense of transferring the affects of being. These moments carry, for instance, familiar, uncanny, sacred, awed, or anxious feelings, which do not belong to coherent cognition. The recorded emotions represent the essential relationship with the primary caretaker, a dialog and being-with of the infant with its mother, who guarantees continuity of being. When a person feels a deep subjective relation with a painting, a poem, the melody of an opera, or a landscape, Bollas (1978) calls this an aesthetic moment. The subject experiences an uncanny fusion with the object, as though feeling an event from his or her earliest experiences, being held by the mother in time and space. "In a generative mood the person goes into himself to contact the mute, unknown child self" (Bollas 1987, 101). Bollas conceptualizes the ongoing subjective feeling experience of being held, cared for, and handled by mother as the aesthetics

[122] On her work, see Steiner (2015).

[123] At the age of two, Hanna Segal lost her older sister, a highly painful experience as she felt genuinely loved by her as a child.

of being, a "maternal aesthetics," the first human aesthetic, which influences the subjective aesthetic experience later on in life. The contentment of the self is built up in this primary encounter and is experienced as a strange pleasure when contemplating a poem, painting, or any object (Bollas 1978, 385). Artworks provide us with occasions to remember and feel such aesthetic moments of our earliest life experiences, a search that continues throughout life (Bollas 1979).

Hagman (2002) states: "Beauty elevates human subjectivity and human values to a transcendent level. The sense of beauty in its reparative and preservative function asserts love over aggression, life over death and harmony over disintegration. It may even be one of the ways that we reconcile our relationship with the world" (672).

The creative process serves to reconcile intrapsychic feelings of subjective experiences and their expression through externalizations in artworks, in aesthetic forms. The intentions (e.g., affects and images) of the artist and setting (context and conditions) can be considered as a kind of holding or containing environment. When the artwork perfectly reflects the intrapsychic lived experience of the artist, the term "aesthetic resonance" is used by Hagman (2000, 286). "It is the elaboration and refinement of the external object—the artwork—that results in the resolution of self-crisis. It is this process that is the true engine of creativity, as crisis is followed by restoration through aesthetic action—something new and beautiful is articulated and given form" (Hagman 2008, 53).

In *Aesthetic Experience: Beauty, Creativity, and the Search for the Ideal*, Hagman (2005) "emphasizes the central role of early childhood experience in the emergence and structuralization of the sense of aesthetic form. As a result of developmentally based processes of idealization, the child's formal aesthetic sense takes on a profound and lifelong concern with form and quality" (10). He considers the roles of relatedness and intersubjectivity as fundamental in aesthetic experience and in creative processes. The internalization of the interpersonal intimate affective relationship between infant and parent is the foundation of aesthetic values and experiences. Creativity is fundamentally intersubjective; the artist externalizes subjective experiences and enters into a relationship with the artwork, which is repeatedly invested with qualities of personal subjective experiences. The artist establishes a unique dialog between internal and external aspects of lived subjectivity. Art is then a new creation that evokes self-experience and represents self-relatedness. The artist's sense of aesthetic resonance emerges when intrapsychic and exteriorized subjective experiences—realized in the artwork—are associated. This is a moment of an idealized and grandiose self-object experience, a euphoric moment, which is easily lost by the artist's constant critical evaluation of the artwork. Beauty, according to Hagman "is a special element in the aesthetic experience in which the investment of reality with subjectivity creates an experience of that reality as both ideal and harmonious with our inner life," while "ugliness is the provocation and projection of unconscious fantasies" leading to the experiences of "most disturbing and repulsive feelings" (7). The latter occurs when artists abandon the achievement of beauty and pleasurable feelings in their work and explore new approaches, within which their creativity may promote transformations of emotions and thoughts. The title of the 2007 Venice Biennale,[124] "Pensa con I sensi, senti con la mente" (Think with the senses, feel with the mind), conveys this idea of a kind of artistic endeavor whose fundamental aim is to promote new thinking through the formal visual and sensual means that are specific to art. "Contemporary art invites us both to think and to feel, but often the very first priority is to think" (Abella 2010, 177).

Art can be considered as creating relatedness with oneself and others and represents a (non)verbal communication to others as spectators or auditors. Through the artist's expression and projection of emotionally lived experiences and the viewer's or listener's response emerges an engagement, which is subjectively different for both parties, a consciously and unconsciously partially shared experience. For Stefana (2019), the psychic process of the audience may be similar but is not identical to that of the artist. "In this sense, artworks can be considered mutual creations in which the aesthetic response of the viewer (who becomes a more active participant) takes shape from what he perceives and feels, what associations are activated and what they represent for him" (144).

[124] In 1893 the Venetian City Council passed a resolution to set up a biennial exhibition of Italian art.

Chapter 18

THE UNCANNY[125]

This uncanniest of all guests.
Friedrich Nietzsche[126]

Your memory is a monster; you forget—it doesn't. It simply files things away. It keeps things for you or hides things from you—and summons them to your recall with a will of its own. You think you have a memory; but it has you!
John Irving[127]

Introduction

The experience of uncanny feelings is associated with confusion and perplexity, where reality appears to be weird, mysterious, threatening. Uncanny (strange or eerie) feelings may arise in traumatic events and post-traumatic stress situations and are related to and emerge in secrets and grief. They may also be evoked by vision, such as in pictures or films; sounds in nature, for example, thunderstorms; music;[128] or narration in literature and dreams.

The concept of the uncanny was elaborated by Freud in 1919. Historically, of course, uncanny phenomena are thousands of years older. In the tragedy of Antigone, the ancient Greek poet Sophocles wrote: "There is much that is strange, but nothing

125 In German, *das Unheimliche*. In French, *inquiétante étrangeté*.
126 "Nihilism stands at the door: whence comes this uncanniest of all guests?" (Nietzsche 1922).
127 In *A Prayer for Owen Meany* (1989), novel by American writer John Irving.
128 Ernst Jentsch (1867–1919) in Jentsch E. (1904 and 1911).

that surpasses man in strangeness. Wonders/terrors (Greek *deinos*[129]) are many, and none is more wonderful/terrible (*deinos*) than man" (Heidegger 1959, 86). The Greek word *deinon* is translated by Heidegger as uncanny. "Manifold is the uncanny, yet nothing beyond the human being prevails more uncannily" (Heidegger 1996, 52).

Uncanny is also what is hidden. For the ancient Greeks, truth (*a-laetheia*) is what is revealed from the hidden (*laethae*). For the ancient Greek philosopher Parmenides, truth is well rounded (*alaetheia eukukleos*), a circle without beginning or end, its origin is not seen, nor is its end predictable. Heidegger commented on Plato's doctrine of truth:[130] "Only the essence of truth understood in the original Greek sense of alaetheia—the unhiddenness that is related to the hidden (to something dissembled and disguised)—has an essential relation to this image of an underground cave" (Hyland 2004, 58).

Freud in his essay "The Uncanny" (1919) stated:

> The German word *unheimlich* is obviously the opposite of *heimlich, heimisch,* meaning "familiar, native, belonging to the home"; and we are tempted to conclude that what is "uncanny" is frightening precisely because it is not known and not familiar. Uncanny is then what once was familiar, such as an infantile wish or the childlike belief in the omnipotence of thought; something familiar that has been repressed and kept hidden in the unconscious. In eerie experiences and ideas, it returns in alienated form. The fearful character of the uncanny is based on the fact that the emotion of every affect is transformed by repression into fear. … The frightening element can be shown to be something repressed which recurs … for this uncanny is in reality nothing new or alien, but something which is familiar and old-established in the mind and which has become alienated from it only through a process of repression (15).

The prefix "un" in this word is the mark of repression. Freud agrees with Jentsch[131] that the effect of the uncanny "doubts whether an apparently animate being is really alive; or conversely, whether a lifeless object might not be in fact animate, the impression of automatic, mechanical processes at work behind the ordinary appearance of mental activity" is frightening (Freud 1919, 225–226).

129 The Greek word *deinos* (**δεινός**) has various significations such as terrible, horrible, fearful, astounding, danger, marvelous, mighty, powerful, wondrous, strange, skillful, clever, shamefully timid, or cowardly.

130 According to his notes, Heidegger's text was composed in 1940 and first published in 1942.

131 *Zur Psychologie des Unheimlichen* was published in the *Psychiatrisch-Neurologische Wochenschrift* 8.22 (Aug. 25, 1906): 195–98 and 8.23 (Sept. 1, 1906): 203–05 (the bibliographical references in the Freud editions do not make it clear that Jentsch's essay is spread over two separate issues of the weekly).

In the story *The Canterville Ghost* by **Oscar Wilde** (1854–1900), the phantom refers to deeply repressed and hidden psychic contents, which have been passed on over generations and cannot be verbalized. Only a verbal exchange and an emotional encounter with the phantom and his destiny leads to its disappearance. In the story it is Virginia, the daughter of the American family Otis that inhabit the haunted house, who takes care of the phantom, mourns for him, and bids him farewell. This experience enabled Virginia to understand "what life is, what death signifies, and why love is stronger than both." *The Canterville Ghost* was the first of Wilde's stories to be published in 1887.[132] Freud commented: "Even a 'real' ghost, as in Oscar Wilde's *Canterville Ghost,* loses all power of arousing at any rate an uncanny horror in us as soon as the author begins to amuse himself at its expense and allows liberties to be taken with it. Thus, we see how independent emotional effects can be of the actual subject matter in the world of fiction" (Freud 1919, 240).

Freud (1900–1901) in his book *The Interpretation of Dreams* remembers one of his dreams, an *anxiety dream* "from my seventh or eighth year, which I submitted to interpretation some thirty years later. ... I saw my beloved mother, with a peculiarly peaceful, sleeping expression on her features, being carried into the room by two (or three) people with birds' beaks and laid upon the bed" (583). Freud associated his dream vision with his Philippson Bible,[133] representing an Egyptian funerary relief, a kind of *revenant* (one who has returned as if from the dead). On his thirty-fifth birthday Freud received a copy of the Bible from his father with a Hebrew inscription:

> My dear son Schlomo (Salomo) in the seventh year of your life the spirit of the Lord began to move you and said to you: Go, read in my Book that I have written. ... You have looked upon the face of the Almighty, have heard and striven to climb upwards, and you flew upon the wings of the Spirit. ... For the day on which you have completed your 35th year I have had it covered with a new leather binding ... and offer it to you for a remembrance and memorial of love. From your father, who loves you with unending love, Jacob, son of Rabbi Sch. Freud (May 6, 1891).

There seems to be a kind of transmission from father to son by *chronology*, which for Guyotat (1980) is an absolute necessity. On his thirty-fifth birthday, when he received the bible and inscription from his father, Freud remembers the dream he had at the age of seven or eight.

132 See D. Bürgin and B. Steck, "Das Gespenst von Canterville (nach O. Wilde) oder Vom Leben und Sterben eines Phantoms in Abhängigkeit von der Adoleszenz einer jungen Frau," *Kinderanalyse*, 4. Jahrgang, Heft 4: 362–384.

133 An illustrated und annotated Hebrew/German Bible by Ludwig Philippson.

E. T. A. Hoffmann (1776–1822), a German author, composer, and music critic, experienced at the age of two the separation from his father, who abandoned him, but took his eldest brother. At the same time, the second oldest brother died. Hoffmann was living with his mother, two aunts, an uncle, and a grandmother: his beloved aunt Charlotte cared for him—replacing his psychic ill mother—but he lost her too when he was three years old.

Hoffmann not only produced fantasy stories evoking uncanny feelings through vision ("The Sandman") but seems to have been able to find consolation for such feelings by listening to music. He wrote of Beethoven's Mass in C major, Op. 68, C minor section of Agnus Dei, written in 1805: "A feeling of inner melancholy that does not tear the heart to pieces, but rather benefits it, and, like the pain that has come from another world, dissolves into supernatural bliss" (Hoffmann 1813, 254). One wonders about the meaning of "the pain that has come from another world" and the supposition arises that this might be an allusion to the numerous losses Hoffmann experienced in his childhood.

In the fantasy story "The Sandman" (Hoffmann 1816), Nathanael, the main character, describes his childhood fear of the Sandman, who is depicted by Hoffmann as "a wicked man who comes when children won't go to bed and throws handfuls of sand in their eyes so that they start bleeding from their heads. He puts their eyes in a bag and carries them to the crescent moon to feed his own children, who sit in the nest up there. They have crooked beaks like owls so that they can pick out the eyes of naughty human boys and girls."

Nathanael's unassimilated affective experiences of the traumatic death of his father are brought up again into the present in various scenes of his life. In a compulsive repetition of the traumatic event, he seeks recovery and recuperation. He falls in love with Olympia, an automaton doll, which is presented as a living person.

Freud refers in his article "The Uncanny" to the wooden doll Olympia as a mechanical doll; he considers "the theme of the doll Olympia, who is to all appearances a living being, by any means the only, or indeed the most important, element that must be held responsible for the quite unparalleled atmosphere of uncanniness evoked by the story" (226).

In the tale of "The Sandman," the curiosity of the child is solicited by a nocturnal, unfamiliar noise: the strangeness of the noise is heightened by the fact that the child cannot, at first, see anything nor know what he or she is hearing, and it is this missing ability to interpret and to name the noise that creates anxiety. According to Freud, the uncanny is at the crossroads of the strange and the infantile, since the "explanations" and "meanings" that render an experience more or less familiar are lacking. The Sandman is foremost a mysterious and unidentifiable being.

Freud (1919) called Hoffmann "the unrivalled master of the uncanny in literature" (233). Freud's interest in the meaning of *unheimlich* issues from the fact that an unconscious part of the self has become visible, a part that is not familiar to the self. "The storyteller has a peculiarly directive power over us; by means of the moods he can put us in, he is able to guide the current of our emotions, to dam it up in one direction and make it flow in another" (251). "The souls in Dante's *Inferno,* or the ghostly apparitions in *Hamlet*, *Macbeth*, or *Julius Caesar*, may be gloomy and terrible enough, but they are no more really uncanny than is Homer's jovial world of gods. We order our judgment to the imaginary reality imposed on us by the writer, and regard souls, spirits and specters as though their existence had the same validity in their world as our own has in the external world" (242). There is "no doubt that the feeling of something uncanny is directly attached to the figure of the Sandman, that is, to the idea of being robbed of one's eyes" (226). Freud quotes Schelling:[134] "Everything is unheimlich that ought to have remained secret and hidden but has come to light" (225).

The uncanny has interested numerous psychoanalysts; according to Rahimi (2013) "uncanny experiences" are associated with themes and metaphors of vision. For Anzieu (1976, 1979), it is a sound or a noise that is responsible for feelings of the uncanny; the fate of sounds is linked with an experience of anxiety and fear. Both authors mention "The Sandman" as a brilliant example of the uncanny—for Anzieu strange noises at night cannot be understood, and this relation with the unknown leads to an encounter with the uncanny. The main topic of interest according to Rahimi is "the relationship between vision and doubling or dualism, and the duality/identity paradox as a significant trope in producing the uncanny effect" (458).

For Terr (1985), "traumatic anxiety *is* a ghost! It moves through the generations with the stealth and cunning of a most skilled specter" (528). Ferenczi (1955) describes a "sudden, surprising rise of new faculties after a trauma" (164–165). For him a traumatic experience "makes the person in question … more or less clairvoyant," as the traumatic event—lived like a death moment—is related to "the supposition that the instant of dying … is associated with that timeless and space-less omniscience" (Ferenczi 1955b, 243).

Parsons (2014) offers the reader a moving description of a personal encounter with the uncanny. He begins by highlighting his important departure from Freud's belief that the experience of the uncanny is indicative of regression to primitive forms of psychic functioning and argues instead that exploring the uncanny may carry the "potential for greater self-awareness, for being more, not less, in touch with one's inward life" (51). He emphasizes the importance of a free-floating listening that is directed both outwardly (to what the subject is saying) and inwardly (to what is stirred up in the analyst in psychotherapy) and to the need for a certain kind of inner space that will allow for this, as well as the value of working not only with regression, but with an ability to face the uncanny. The emphasis, in other words, is on being "sensitive to the level of emotional work that a given moment calls for" (151). Thus, the uncanny may at times feel uncomfortable but being able to face it can open possibilities for new and creative ways of being. "There is a powerful attachment to

[134] In S. Zizek and F. W. F. von Schelling, *The Abyss of Freedom: Ages of the World*, University of Michigan Press, Ann Arbor, MI, 1997, 1–104.

what is secret (*heimlich*). The work of analysis, and the work of creative aliveness in whatever situation, is to question such structures, momentarily opening doors to the uncanny for greater freedom. The terror of passing through these doors is the terror of not going on being the self that is familiar: the terror of dying. It takes courage and time to discover that beyond them may lie a fuller kind of living" (33).

Being able to face the uncanny, the terrifying feelings of lived traumatic experiences in early childhood, which have never been integrated, but repeated during a lifetime, lead to opportunities for creativity, inner freedom, and more joyful and carefree perspectives.

The uncanny in literature

The uncanny, writes Royle (2003), involves feelings "of something strangely beautiful, bordering on ecstasy … of uncertainty, in particular regarding the reality of who one is … one's sense of oneself." These feelings arise "in the uncertainties of silence, solitude and darkness" (22).

The ghost of *Hamlet* (1599–1601) in the play by **William Shakespeare** (1564–1616) is an example of impossible grief, as one of the most difficult aspects of mourning is to endure the continuous internal presence of the loved one and at the same time being confronted with the external absence. In special situations such as the disappearance of a loved person, the grieving process is hindered and takes the form of an "enigmatic mourning." The survivor may idealize the lost person and identify with the disappeared loved one. His or her mind is haunted by the lost person.

Abraham and Rand (1978) in analyzing *The Phantom of Hamlet* suggest that the unspeakable secret of the murdered king was transferred and unconsciously integrated by his son in a kind of crypt housing the ghost, the phantom. "If thou hast uphoarded in thy life / Extorted treasure in the womb of earth / For which, they say, you spirits oft walk in death / Speak of it."[135]

> The shameful and therefore concealed secret always does return to haunt. To exorcise it one must express it in words. But how are we to accomplish this when the phantoms who inhabit our minds do so without our knowledge, embodying the unspeakable secret of … another? This other, of course, is a loved one. The gaps and impediments in our communication with the loved one, wrought by the secret, produce a twofold and contrary effect: the prohibition of knowledge coupled with an unconscious investigation. As a result, the "haunted" individual is caught between two inclinations. He must at all costs maintain his ignorance of a loved one's

[135] Shakespeare (1603), *Hamlet*, Act 1, Scene 1.

> secret, hence the semblance of unawareness (nescience) concerning it. At the same time, he must eliminate the state of secrecy, hence the reconstruction of the secret in the form of unconscious knowledge. This twofold movement is manifest in symptoms and gives rise to "gratuitous" or uncalled acts and words, creating eerie effects: hallucinations and delirium, showing and hiding what—in the depths of the unconscious—dwells as the living-dead knowledge of someone else's secret. So, it is with the "phantom" of Hamlet (Abraham and Rand 1978, 3).

The German writer **Johann Wolfgang Goethe** described in his autobiography *From My Life: Poetry and Truth* (1811–1833) a vision he saw with the eyes of his mind:

> Amid all this pressure and confusion I could not fail to see Frederica[136] once more. Those were painful days, the memory of which has not remained with me. When I reached her hand from my horse, the tears stood in her eyes, and I felt very uneasy. I now rode along the footpath towards Drusenheim, and here one of the most singular forebodings took possession of me. I saw, not with the eyes of the body, but with those of the mind, my own figure coming towards me, on horseback, and on the same road, attired in an outfit which I had never worn; it was pike-gray with somewhat of gold. As soon as I shook myself out of this dream, the figure had entirely disappeared. It is strange, however, that eight years afterwards, I found myself on the very road, to pay one more visit to Frederica, in the outfit of which I had dreamed, and which I wore, not from choice, but by accident. However, it may be with matters of this kind generally, this strange illusion in some measure calmed me at the moment of parting (433).

"Now is the air so full of ghosts, that no one knows how to escape them"[137] (*Faust*, Goethe) is cited in the epigraph to *Psychopathology of Everyday Life* (1901) by Freud.

Ghosts (1881), a play by **Henrik Ibsen** (1828–1906), is called in the original Danish language *Gengangere*, literally translated as "ones who return" or "revenants." In this story, the past—believed to have been mastered—remains effective in the present. Desperate Helene Alving helplessly witnesses how the horrible past haunts the present time:

> I am obsessed by the presence of ghosts that I never can get rid of … I am half inclined to think we are all ghosts. … It is not only what we have inherited from our fathers and mothers that exists again in us, but all

[136] Frederica (German Friederika) Brion had a love affair with Goethe.

[137] Original text: Nun ist die Luft von solchem Spuk so voll, dass niemand weiss, wie er ihn meiden soll. Goethe, *Faust*, Part II, Act V, Scene 5. (Translation: Walter Kaufmann).

> sorts of old dead ideas and all kinds of old dead beliefs and things of that kind. They are not actually alive in us; but there they are dormant, all the same, and we can never be rid of them. There must be ghosts all over the world … I am here, fighting with ghosts both without and within me (34).

When Ibsen asked Grieg in 1874 to write the music for the play *Peer Gynt*, he enthusiastically agreed. However, it was much more difficult for Grieg than he imagined. "Peer Gynt progresses slowly," he wrote to a friend in August 1874, "and there is no possibility of having it finished by autumn. It is a terribly unmanageable subject." His wife wrote of him and his music: "The more he saturated his mind with the powerful poem, the more clearly he saw that he was the right man for a work of such witchery and so permeated with the Norwegian spirit" (Goulding 1982). Even though the première was a "triumphant success," it prompted Grieg to complain bitterly that the Swedish management of the theater had given him specifications as to the duration of each number and its order: "I was thus compelled to do patchwork. … In no case had I opportunity to write as I wanted. … Hence the brevity of the pieces," he said.[138]

Thomas Stearns Eliot (1888–1965), a poet, dramatist, literary critic, and editor, had to overcome physical limitations as a child. Struggling from a congenital double inguinal hernia he could not participate in many physical activities and thus was prevented from socializing with his peers. As he was often isolated, his love for literature developed.

Eliot's poem "The Family Reunion" (1909–1950) describes the atmosphere of families suffering under the burden of secrets. Traumatic experiences of loss that have not been dealt with and overcome may represent the starting point for the development of family secrets. If traumatic experiences remain unspoken, withdrawn from verbal discourse, secrets of unimaginable or unpronounceable events emerge. The existence of a secret interferes with any meaningful relationship. Traumatized and traumatizing families rely heavily on defense mechanisms such as denial, trivialization, and avoidance in order to protect themselves, and family members commit themselves to remaining silent. The dread of revelation of humiliating secrets with regard to the surroundings may be so threatening because of fears of a familial or individual breakdown.

"The Family Reunion" expresses the uncanny:

> REFRAIN:
> In an old house there is always listening, and more is
> heard than is spoken.
> And what is spoken remains in the room, waiting for
> the future to hear it.

[138] The movements Grieg chose for his suites bear no relation to the chronology of the play.

> And whatever happens began in the past, and presses
> hard on the future.
> The agony in the curtained bedroom, whether of birth
> or of dying,
> Gathers in to itself all the voices of the past, and
> projects them into the future.

"We die with the dying: See, they depart, and we go with them. We are born with the dead: See, they return, and bring us with them. … And he is not likely to know what is to be done unless he lives in what is not merely the present, but the present moment of the past, unless he is conscious, not of what is dead, but of what is already living" (Eliot 1919, 11).

The history of earlier generations can be transmitted like a cultural heritage; this is particularly true when the mourning of losses never ends and the non-elaborated past of family members becomes the present for their children, impacting their sense of time and continuity of being.

"Time present and time past are both perhaps present in time future, and time future contained in time past. If all time is eternally present, all time is unredeemable" (Eliot 1936).

Chapter 19

AESTHETIC EXPERIENCE AND PSYCHOANALYTIC THERAPY

The psychoanalytic process contains both artistic and scientific aspects. Aesthetic experience represents an opportunity to approach psychic reality (Holm-Hadulla 2003). Therefore "a psychoanalytic session is an aesthetic experience, because it deals really with the same problem—how to get in touch with terrible things and contain them and sublimate them and lead them to the point of restoration" (Segal, in Quinodoz 2008, 25). "Aesthetic pleasure … is due to an identification of ourselves with the work of art as a whole and with the whole internal world of the artist as represented by his work. What the artist aims at is to awaken in us the same mental constellation as that which in him produced the impetus to create" (Segal 1952, 204).

Art can be considered as a way to contain subjective experience, as well as an active creation of passively endured experiences. Unconscious dissociated or implicitly remembered experiences are represented in artwork symbolically or metaphorically. The viewer explores and "interprets" the probably multiple significations immerged in the artwork. "The artist has a highly developed awareness of the pain of his inner world but also the capacity to endure it and, through his equally highly developed reality sense, he gives form to his struggle, creating through it a real object, always a communication to his fellow human beings" (Bell 2015, 182).

Traumatic experience

In a therapeutic relationship the creation of meaning is a shared build-up between patient and therapist. Nonverbal expression through artwork may be an essential process in order to encourage the later possibility for putting experiences in words, that is, to verbalize the affects in the lived traumatic encounter. The artwork serves as a reference for patients' and therapists' associations by means of metaphors[139] and narratives. At the same time, patient, artwork, and therapist bear witness to the traumatic experience. The emotional engagement of a patient to gradually reveal his lived affects of endured traumatic events demands the continuous containment and relatedness of the therapist, allowing the patient to exercise a certain control and gradually reduce feelings of fear, confusion, and helplessness. The patient will be able to "comprehend" the lived traumatic experience, even if not able to remember what exactly happened in the external reality (Buk 2009).

In psychoanalytic therapy the spoken words aim at revising the relation of the subject to the unconscious psychic experiences by helping elaborate their understanding and meaning and to create a personal narrative, thus linking past to present and with a better psychic self-integrity for envisaging the future. The self-narrative of subjective experience is reorganized by the emotionally engaged, spoken dialog between patient and analyst. Telling a story connects—by means of symbolism—memories, images, and scenes with the associated emotions and language. Narratives reveal un- and preconscious representations and phantasms of individual experiences. Telling a story also serves to ascribe meaning and significance to life events that may have interrupted the continuity of personal experiences. Narratives promote a grieving process and the working through of loss and psychic trauma.

Salmon (2008) compares music and psychoanalytic therapy: they both contain thoughts and feelings and attention is focused on listening. "Music, like the psychotherapeutic process, provides a flexible and creative container; able to hold, express and console, to carry one to breathless heights and darkest depths, and to offer possibilities of increased integration and freedom" (8). According to Erel-Brodsky (2016) "musical reverie, whereby the therapist experiences a kind of daydreaming that includes songs with both lyrics and tunes" allows containment and symbolization of early traumatic areas in a patient's psyche, as it unites the words and the melody and bridges the symbolic and presymbolic. The analytic space formed by music, a "sonorous bath" (Anzieu 1976, 175) corresponds to the infants' needs to hear its mother's voice. It enables an intimate authentic togetherness and contributes to a holding and containing experience.

[139] Metaphor, from Greek *metaphorein*, meaning transmission, unites the event and its meaning. The function of a metaphor is to symbolize an emotional experience. The affect—bound in the metaphor—initiates a thought process. It is as if the metaphor allows the illusion of a common mental space to be shared and works as a kind of mediator between the affect and the representation. A metaphor often triggers surprise and initiates the search for a transferred meaning. It enables a representation of the unknown. The metaphor is openness of meaning, a transfer from one place to another, intrapsychic and intersubjective. It solicits active participation, involving the other in a creative illusion of a common and shared experience.

Transference

Freud (1913) believed that "everyone possesses in his own unconscious an instrument with which he can interpret the utterances of the unconscious in other people" (320). Transference[140] contains the patient's communications in analytical psychotherapy: verbal expression such as dreams and narrations, nonverbal communication such as posture, bodily movements, facial expressions, and gesticulations, and voice, the "musical dimension" of the transference (Mancia 2006). The relationship between patient and analyst represents in part a shared "musical experience," allowing the affective and emotional world to be expressed.

The varied and complex transference and countertransference situations in psychoanalysis can be considered as a creative activity or investment.[141] Often understanding of a patient's personal history has to be elaborated from enactments, by working on transference and countertransference elements, so that recollection can be achieved and psychic continuity created. The three dimensions of aesthetic experience—poiesis (making/creating), aesthesis (sensation/perception), and catharsis (purification/cleansing)—take place during the analytical process. Aesthetic experience and creativity not only serve the recovery of dysfunctional psychic states but are indispensable for the comprehensive understanding of internal and external reality. Comprehending the therapeutic process is based on sensory-aesthetic experiences and on cognitive-dialog processes (Holm-Hadulla 2003). "Being found" by spoken words is often the secret hope of patients with subjective experiences of having felt lost or fallen when their inner emotions were not met by a caregiver's affectionate engagement and attuned speech. The analyst attempts to perceive, sense, and comprehend the intrapsychic lived experience of the analysand and returns in words the meaning of the analysand's experiences. The trusted therapist, who has registered the patient's indirect communication, has to reflect back to his patient the mutual reverberation and resonance. "In these highly specialized conditions the individual can come together and exist as a unit, not as a defense against anxiety but as an expression of I AM, I am alive, I am myself. From this position everything is creative" (Winnicott 1971, 56).

140 In psychoanalytic theory, transference refers to the process in which an analysand's unconscious desires are actualized and projected (transferred) onto the analyst.

141 The process of investment of mental or emotional energy in a person, object, or idea is called cathexis.

Creativity in the transitional or intermediate area

Since Aristotle's Poetics,[142] the earliest human creativity has been associated with play activity.[143] For Winnicott, we live in the inner, outer, and transitional world. Cultural experience takes place in the transitional area and begins with playing, leading to "the whole area of man's inheritance, including the arts, the myths of history … also all the accumulated culture of the past five to ten thousand years" (Winnicott 1986, 36). According to Winnicott, the artist has an urgent need to communicate and at the same time to hide. Healthy people generally communicate and enjoy communicating, but it is also true that each individual is an isolated, permanently uncommunicating, permanently unknown, in fact unfound subject (187). Concerning the core of the self, Winnicott (1971) writes: "It is here that silence is equated with communication, stillness with movement … it is, like the music of the spheres, absolutely personal. It belongs to being alive. … Hidden away somewhere there exists a secret life that is satisfactory because of its being creative or original to that human being" (68). "Whatever definition of creativity we arrive at, it must include the idea that life is worth living or not, according to whether creativity is or is not a part of an individual person's living experience" (Winnicott 1970, 39).

Winnicott shows the importance of an intermediate area of experience, "to which inner reality and external life both contribute. … It shall exist as a resting-place for the individual engaged in the perpetual human task of keeping inner and outer reality separated yet interrelated," a potential space for play that bridges subjectivity and objectivity. "This intermediate area of experience, unchallenged in respect of its belonging to inner or external (shared) reality, constitutes the greater part of the infant's experience, and throughout life is retained in the intense experiencing that belongs to the arts and to religion and to imaginative living, and to creative scientific work" (Winnicott 1971, 14). The sense of beauty lies in the potential space, this intermediate area of longing where we dream of an ideal self and ideal world; this represents our creative engagement between the self and the world and over time deepens our perception and sensation of beauty.

142 Circa 335 BC, from two books—on tragedy and on comedy—probably only the tragedy has survived.

143 As the Swiss author and playwright Friedrich Dürrenmatt pointedly remarked, "my freedom as an artist is that I can play with this world."

Repetition compulsion and retrospective attribution

Unpleasant thoughts and fantasies for which no solution has been found (e.g., infantile traumatic events) are stored in our implicit memory[144] and are unconsciously compulsively repeated through action, for instance, through nonverbal expression, which in psychoanalytic therapy has to be relived, felt, and worked through, a process that demands time. Earliest experiences are not stored in the form of retrievable memories. The missing engrams are often only reconstructed, sometimes starting from recurrent "acting." Unassimilated past affective experiences are brought into the present, and the compulsion to repeat them represents the urge to seek re-transcription of a memory in a new context and within a meaningful relationship.

The new context (i.e., the analytic setting) permits and contains regressive as well as progressive movements, that is, growth; there is a simultaneous communication between the symbolic actualization of early experienced relations and more advanced representations of the patient. This setting in psychoanalytic processes allows the analyst to observe multiple levels of reality (Modell 1989). Transitional states from unrepresented to represented experiences underscore the dynamic and changing nature of the setting and of psychoanalysis itself.

For patients with traumatic experiences in their early childhood, the therapist needs to be attentive to the nonverbal expression of emotions emerging in the transference relationship, as the events of these affects, stored in implicit memory, can neither be recalled nor verbalized. The patient needs to hear the therapist's affective resonance and understanding of those early childhood demands, wishes, deprivations, and distress. The therapist has to name the affective atmosphere, sensed in the transference. The often very intense and confused emotions of the patient have then to be verbally differentiated in various nuances by the therapist, so that the patient can perceive and consciously experience the feelings and qualify them with words, for example, fear, anger, sadness, or pain. Fantasies and images related to the patients' feelings emerge, and associations and memories linked to these emotions are then revealed by the patient. The feelings of (repeated) traumatic experiences need to be extensively expressed, again and again and over a long period of time to allow the patient to gradually distinguish the various emotions; therefore, therapists have to be reliable in their emotional attitude and attentive to the nonverbal multiple manifestations of a patient. Some patients may eventually remember traumatic events; others will have no memories at all. What is important for the psychotherapeutic process is the expression of the remembered feelings and their understanding in connecting early experiences and actual relationships.

[144] What we have learned and understood how to deal with is stored in implicit nondeclarative memory, is automatized, and is not retrievable. Declarative memory contains thoughts and fantasies that can be retrieved, worked on, and a solution found, before being stored in implicit memory and automatized.

Freud (1887–1904) wrote to Fliess: "I am working on the assumption that our psychic mechanism has come into being by processes of stratification: the material present in the form of memory traces being subjected from time to time to a rearrangement in accordance with fresh circumstances—to a retranscription" (207).[145] The associations of affective intra- and interpersonal, as well as bodily internal and interactive earlier experiences lead to the reawakening of these lived experiences and enable retroactive (*nachträglich*) re-elaboration and working-through in the analytic encounter. Emotionally meaningful metaphors and a respectful, emotionally engaged dialog help the patient to find a conscious self-awareness of the lived experience.

Mutual and mutative shared experiences are called "now moments" by Stern (2004), "sacred moments" by Winnicott (1971), and "implicit relational knowledge" (Stern 1989, BCPSG 2010). "Implicit relational knowing and meaning" play a key role in the intersubjective field and the reorganization of affective implicit experiences. The mutual implicit relationship, in which patient and therapist share intersubjective unconscious knowledge and understanding, often an experience of surprise, favors emotional changes and a (re)-organization of the patient's relationship with him- or herself and others (Stern et al. 1998). His or her past is carried forward into the present at the stage of lived experiences. It lies then in the analyst's ability to record, understand, and then verbalize the meaning of the lived emotional expressions in the intersubjective relationship—the primary or primitive emotions that are evoked in the analyst—and finally to connect the symbolic signification to the patient's past.

The psychoanalytic process is based on an intersubjective relationship-reality, involving the creation of a relational space in which latent development resources and resilience perspectives of a patient and mutual expectations of the patient and therapist are recorded. New functional possibilities and opportunities for more suitable integrations are explored and a more profound understanding of a commonly shared narrative is elaborated. The aim of the psychoanalytic process is directed toward working out new scope, open space and freedom, creation of alternatives, and more suitable forms of coping with life events (Bürgin and Steck 2013). Psychoanalytic therapy is associated with a time to remember, a time of thoughtfulness for comprehension. The need to understand creates a deep introspection, reverie, and contemplation. A therapeutic session allows time to stand still, maintains a present, and enables the immersion in memories of the past and involvement into the future.

[145] Childhood memories of the first years of life are modified or constructed at later developmental periods by the process of *Nachträglichkeit*, that is, by means of "retrospective attribution" (Modell 2006, 36). Events and intrapsychic experiences of the past, which the small child was not able to accommodate, only later find meaning and interpretation.

Trans- or intergenerational transmission of trauma

Individual psychotherapy must never lead to re-traumatization or pathological grief. The therapeutic process of a patient with a history of a personal trauma in early childhood may in certain cases reveal a transgenerationally transmitted nonintegrated traumatic experience of a parent. Through identification with the associated painful parental emotions, the patient—as a child—unconsciously assumed intrapsychic, transgenerational conflict representations. This revelation renders the therapeutic process particularly complex and is often linked with the patient's great fear of a personal breakdown. Psychic elaboration may be extremely painful due to the necessity of the multi-layered working through of the traumatic experiences—their mingling and condensation—and due to the different and changing type of the transference-relation. While phantasms and affects of a personal trauma can eventually be linked with personal memories and the life story of a patient, the emotions inherited from a parent are experienced as alienating and frightening and cannot be integrated into the personal history. Only through retroactive re-elaboration and working-through in the analytic encounter can unconscious identification with past destinies and life stories be tentatively grasped and comprehended; their effects in the present remain cryptic and confused. In transference and countertransference relationships, the main difficulty is to understand and assign emotions, bodily manifestations, associations, and memories of both personal and transgenerational traumas. For these patients and for the therapeutic working-through, the serious challenge is the fact that their phantasms, feelings, and ideas of the transgenerational transmitted trauma of their parents are not linked to their individual memories and emotions. Patients repeatedly experience recurring feelings of emptiness, an irretrievable and hard-to-bear absence of the personal life story of their parents.

Psychoanalytic understanding of creativity in dreams

Dream narratives allow images to be connected with emotions and the search for meaning. According to Freud, dreams are the royal road to the unconscious; they are probably the best tools for analytic work with patients that experienced early trauma. The often overwhelming affects and emotions in dreams of experienced events that cannot be remembered, for which no words can be found by the patient, evoke—in the intersubjective relationship and in transference/counter-transference—emotions, thoughts, and images in the analyst. It is through the shared emotional investment between patient and therapist that these dreams find symbolic representation, meaning, and reconstruction in the analytic process and allow the patient to retrieve lost parts of his self and his livelihood.

Johan August Strindberg (1849–1912) was a Swedish playwright, novelist, poet, essayist, and painter. In the preface of his *A Dream Play* (1902) he notes:

> The disconnected but apparently logical form of a dream. Everything can happen; everything is possible and likely. The characters split, double, multiply, evaporate, condense, dissolve and merge. But one consciousness rules them all: the dreamer's; for him there are no secrets, no inconsistencies, no scruples, and no laws. He does not judge or acquit, he merely relates; and because a dream is usually painful rather than pleasant, a tone of melancholy and compassion for all living creatures permeates the rambling narrative.

Strindberg called the play "the child of my greatest pain." He wrote the play after an extremely tormented period in his life, on which he commented: "I feel like a deaf-mute, as I cannot speak and am not permitted to write; sometimes I stand in the middle of my room that seems like a prison cell, and then I want to scream so that walls and ceilings would fly apart, and I have so much to scream about, and therefore I remain silent" (Lagercrantz 1984, 57).

In *The Interpretation of Dreams* (1900–1901, 509) Freud describes a patient's dream: A father had been watching beside his child's sickbed for days and nights on end. After the child had died, he went into the next room to lie down, but left the door open so that he could see from his bedroom into the room in which his child's body was laid out, with tall candles standing round it. An old man had been engaged to keep watch over the body; he sat beside it murmuring prayers. After a few hours' sleep, the father had a dream that his child was standing beside his bed, caught him by the arm, and whispered to him reproachfully: "Father, don't you see I'm burning?" He woke up, noticed a bright glare of light from the next room, hurried into it and found that the old watchman had dropped off to sleep and that the wrappings and one of the arms of his beloved child's dead body had been burned by a lighted candle that had fallen on them.

This dream, explains Freud, contains the fulfillment of a wish, namely the wish of the father that his child is still alive. The father does not acknowledge the external reality, that is, the death of his child, as he is unable to face the truth, refusing to be fully aware of it. The dream can be considered as a nightmare from which the father awakens frightfully. Does the nightmare demonstrate a traumatic repetition? Through the child's reproachful words "Don't you see I'm burning?" the father seems to admit his failure at preventing his child's death. Does the dream represent the father's survival guilt? His life will be forever linked with the witnessing of his child's death. What tremendous emotional burden may lie behind the child's words, spoken in a reproachful tone? Is the "burning" an allusion to the high fever caused by the illness the child suffered? Can the words "Don't you see" be understood as the father's denial of his child's death and belong to the father's grief, the beginning of a mourning process?

Freud (1929) in a letter to Binswanger writes: "One knows that the acute mourning after such a loss will run its course, but one will remain unconsoled and never find a substitute. Everything that takes its place, even if it should fill that place entirely, remains something else. And actually, it's good that way. It is the only way to continue the love, which after all one does not want to give up" (386).

Dreams and the free associations[146] of dreams are means for gaining access to the unconscious; dreams are generated during sleep without the control of the prefrontal lobes, while instinctual, limbic system functions are at work. They allow access to thoughts or fantasies subjectively forbidden, as considered, for example, too dangerously violent, shameful, guilt-laden, or criminal. A psychoanalytic therapy, which may consist mainly of telling and associating to dreams, indicates that the patient strives for self-knowledge but only permits this gain as a means of staying in touch with nonawareness. The following statement: "I cannot be made responsible for what I am dreaming!" demonstrates this defense mechanism. For Freud, the unconscious is what is unrepresentable: feelings, thoughts, urges, memories outside of conscious awareness. Implicit memories are memories of affects and emotions, which are felt, even intensively, for instance, in critical or traumatic life events; events that cannot be consciously remembered. When the prefrontal lobe's focused attention is given up, more implicit memories are at work, allowing creativity.

The first child analysis

In 1909 Freud published *The Analysis of a Phobia in a Five-Year-Old Boy*, demonstrating his theory of the oedipal complex. Freud's interpretations focus on the boy's intense love for his mother and hatred for his father and was the first analysis of a child that Freud called "Little Hans." Freud analyzed the child's symptoms (a horse phobia) with his father, Max Graf, who furnished Freud with notes and dreams of his son Herbert.

As Freud reports, for Little Hans the sound experience creates something uncanny, giving rise to anxiety and a kind of derealization. His exploration of noises can be understood as a wish to understand his own bodily functions and those of others on the two fundamental sensory modes: the mode of seeing, which corresponds to the visual drive, and the mode of hearing, which corresponds to auditory activity.

Max Graf (1873–1958) was a professor at the Academy for Music and the Performing Arts in Vienna, a music critic and author, and a member of Freud's Wednesday night study group. He knew Freud through his wife, who had been a patient of Freud. In

[146] Free association is the expression of the content of consciousness without censorship as an aid in gaining access to unconscious processes. Freud used free association to help his patients discover unconscious thoughts and feelings that had been repressed or ignored.

Freud's Wednesday circle, Max Graf proposed to examine artworks such as literature according to the concept he called "applied analysis"; the analyst was to look at repetitions in a piece of literary work, thus enabling him to find and interpret the author's unconscious fantasies. "The analysis of that fantasy would therefore be performed in the same way through which a clinical psychoanalyst would analyze a dream or a slip, taking into account, according to Graf's protocol, information obtained from the artist's work and from various bibliographical sources" (Padavona and Darribab 2016, 111).

Graf had already spoken about his idea of "applied analysis" at a conference called Creative Writers and Day-Dreaming (1908). Freud approved of Graf's concept, which probably influenced his writings on several texts, inter alia the one on Leonardo da Vinci. Freud states: "As today we have excellent methods in the psychoanalysis techniques, which help us surface these hidden elements, we may attempt to fill the gap there is in the history of Leonardo's life by analyzing his childhood fantasy" (Freud 1910, 79).

Max Graf wrote in the preface to his article "Richard Wagner's *Flying Dutchman*" (1910):

> With this work I want to record the memory, in which sense the conceited little society, which gathered weekly during several years in the hospitable home of Professor Freud, dealt with psychological problems. In front of this circle of friends who attempted with joint work to test the ideas of Freud in a variety of fields, I held a talk about Richard Wagner's *Flying Dutchman,* which has become the point of departure, from where I advanced to the present work. Because the thoughts that I develop here are the result of an uninterrupted exchange of views with Professor Freud and the many suggestions that I have received in discussions in his house slowly germinated and the present writing is the fruit of a multi-year exchange of ideas. It would be impossible for me to differentiate in this work what ideas spontaneously rose in me, what I think I owe to the leadership by Professor Freud, what to the criticism of individual colleagues. So, let this study be dedicated in memory to the old circle of friends to which it owes its origin, to the lively hours of common spiritual pursuit.[147]

In 1922 Freud added to *The Analysis of a Phobia in a Five Year Old Boy* the following note:

> A few months ago—in the spring of 1922—a young man introduced himself to me and informed me that he was the "Little Hans" whose infantile neurosis had been the subject of the paper which I published in 1909. I was

[147] In 1942 the paper "Reminiscences of Professor Sigmund Freud" by Max Graf was published in *The Psychoanalytic Quarterly*.

> very glad to see him again, for about two years after the end of his analysis I had lost sight of him and had heard nothing of him for more than ten years. The publication of this first analysis of a child had caused a great stir and even greater indignation, and a most evil future had been foretold for the poor little boy, because he had been "robbed of his innocence" at such a tender age and had been made the victim of a psychoanalysis. But none of these apprehensions had come true. Little Hans was now a strapping youth of nineteen. He declared that he was perfectly well and suffered from no troubles or inhibitions (Freud 1909, 147).

Herbert Graf (1903–1973) worked as an opera director in different cities in Austria and Germany, and then emigrated in 1936 to the United States, where he became stage director at New York's Metropolitan Opera in 1936. He returned to Europe, where he directed operas at London's Royal Opera House and Covent Garden, and later at the Zurich Opera and Geneva's Grand Théâtre in Switzerland. Herbert Graf wrote several books about opera.[148]

Herbert Graf referred to his discovery that he was "Little Hans" and his meeting with Freud in an interview in German in 1959:

> The strange thing is this: I was not aware of anything (regarding the case history) which ever happened to me until my parents were divorced when I was about sixteen or seventeen, when I had to take care of the moving of the library of my father from my mother's home to what later was his home. I was interested in psychology and so forth at that time, but it was the first time that this particular analysis, which concerned me, fell into my hands. And I saw it, I read it, and, of course, my name is not the real name, but the names of my aunt and other persons in it are correct names; for instance, I have an aunt, the sister of my mother, who is called Maritschi, which is a very unusual name, and this name was in it in the correct way. And in reading this I realized that the whole thing had to do with me. And I went to my father who, of course, knew a lot about these things which I didn't, and I asked: What is this? It obviously concerns me?! My father said: Yes, this is so, and he told me the entire story of this analysis, which went through his hands actually. As I understand it, I had not seen Freud except in the beginning once and the end once, when I was five years old. So, I asked him whether it was true. And he said, yes, it is all true. And then we discussed it. I said I would like to meet Professor Freud now (Wakefield 2007, 185).

[148] *The Opera and its Future in America*, W. W. Norton, New York, 1941; *Opera for the People*, University of Minnesota Press, Minneapolis, 1951; and *Producing Opera for America*, Atlantis Books, Zurich and New York, 1961.

The analysis of Samuel Beckett

Samuel Beckett (1906–1989), born in Dublin, Ireland, was a novelist, playwright, and poet with an Anglo-Irish background. Beckett (1937) promoted a "Literature of the unword." He received the Nobel Prize in Literature in 1969 "for his writing, which—in new forms for the novel and drama—in the destitution of modern man acquires its elevation." He did not accept the prize in person, thus apparently avoiding a speech at the ceremony.

According to his biographer James Knowlson (1996), Beckett slept as a small boy with a night-light and his dearest teddy bear, or with Frank, his brother who was four years his elder. At night he heard intensely frightening sounds, which he remembered all his life (17). As a boy, he was already prone to suffering multiple accidents, for example, by throwing himself from the tops of trees, burning his face, or while diving, behaviors that were considered potentially suicidal. Beckett's father died when he was twenty-seven years old. "I will never have anyone like him," he said and remembered the last words his father had addressed to him: "Fight fight fight" (19–20).

During this time, Beckett contacted Wilfred Bion, who was then a trainee analyst at the Tavistock Institute in London; Becket was his first analysis under supervision.[149] Dr. Geoffrey Thompson, a physician and friend, considered Beckett's symptoms to be of psychosomatic origin and convinced him to consult Bion. Beckett suffered from "a bursting, apparently arrhythmic heart, night sweats, shudders, panic, breathlessness, and, at its most severe, total paralysis" (176). He began psychoanalysis early in 1934 and stayed in therapy for over two years.

In an interview in 1989 with James Knowlson, a friend of Beckett for over twenty years, Beckett recalled the sessions as follows:

> I used to lie on the couch and try to go back in my past. I think it probably did help. I think it helped me perhaps to control the panic. I certainly came up with some extraordinary memories of being in the womb. Intrauterine memories. I remember feeling trapped, of being imprisoned and unable to escape, of crying to be let out but no one could hear, no one was listening. I remember being in pain but being unable to do anything about it. … I think it all helped me to understand a bit better what I was doing and what I was feeling (177).

Becket said of Knowlson: "The one who knows my work best." The key to understanding Beckett, as stated by Dr. Geoffrey Thompson, was to be found in his relationship with his mother (178).

[149] Bion himself was unaware that his presence had exerted such an extensive influence: "I don't think I did him much good, but I probably didn't do him much harm either," he told his wife (letter from Francesca Bion 1999).

Beckett discovered that his symptoms were linked to a "diseased condition that began in a time which I could not remember" (180). He understood that his physical symptoms were caused by his isolation from others, as well as his superiority-feelings and his "morbid, obsessive immersion in self" (180).

In 1934 Beckett interrupted his therapy for one month and stayed at his mother's house. He suffered from acute abdominal pains for which no organic etiology could be found. His fears, panic, and anxiety at night were still at the age of thirty-eight so intense that he slept with Frank, his older brother. To MacGreevy he wrote: "I am obliged to accept the whole panic as psychoneurotic—which leaves me in a hurry to get back and go on" (186). After seven months of therapy with Bion, he felt that it helped him somehow. "Will the demon … disable me any the less with sweats and shudders and panics and rages and rigors and heart bursting because my motives are unselfish. … Is there some way of devoting pain and monstrosity and incapacitation to the service of a deserving cause? Is one to insist on a crucifixion for which there is no demand? (181).

The following lines can be found in the notes Beckett made at the time he was undergoing analysis and reading psychoanalytic literature: "Anxiety of a child left alone in a dark room due to his unconscious being reminded of intrauterine situation, terminated by frightening severance from mother." These notes seem to result from his reading of Otto Rank's text *The Traumatic Experience of Birth* (178).

Beckett's symbiotic relationship with his mother—of whom he wrote in a letter "Mother's conscientious cafard" (185)—influenced him to leave Ireland for France. "I am what her savage loving has made me, and it is good that one of us should accept that finally" (273). As Knowlson writes:

> He was profoundly affected by what he described as the "terrible moral and physical distress" that she [his mother] clearly experienced whenever she surfaced from her state of profound lethargy. He sat watching over her for an entire week, leaving the Nursing Home only when it was absolutely necessary in order to eat or, when he could no longer bear to watch her suffer, to walk disconsolately alone along the towpath of the Grand Canal. Sitting by her bedside, he longed earnestly, yet compassionately that it would soon be "all over and done with, at last." In a letter, he wrote: "My mother's life continues its sad decline. It is like the decrescendo of a train I used to listen to at Ussy,[150] interminable, starting up again just when one thinks it is over and silence restored forever (382).

[150] Ussy-sur-Marne, France.

In his subjective lived experience Beckett felt abandoned by his mother; his writings *First Love*,[151] *From An Abandoned Work*,[152] and *The Unnamable* are witnesses to his infinite loneliness and feelings of not existing: "Where I am there is no one but me who is not" (Beckett 1958, 94[153]). In *The Unnamable*, which according to Knowlson is the most deeply personal book Beckett ever wrote, he seems to describe the symptoms of his own suffering: "I have to puke my heart out too, spew it up whole along with the rest of the vomit, it's then at last I'll look as if I mean what I'm saying, it won't be just idle words. Well, don't lose hope, keep your mouth open and your stomach turned, perhaps you'll come out with it one of these days" (Beckett 1959, 338).

Knowlson describes Beckett as possessing "almost certainly … a photographic memory" (220). He writes of his "remarkable ability to draw on his knowledge of one artistic medium and see its possibilities for transformation and use in another" (Knowlson 2003, 53–54.) "He writes paintings," observed Billie Whitelaw, actress and lifelong collaborator of Beckett (Cohn 1980, 31). Oppenheim (2000, 771) compared Beckett to a painter.

Didier Anzieu, in his biography of Beckett (2004), writes of the play *Waiting for Godot*: "The brilliance of laughter provoked in the reader, the spectator, makes tolerable the unveiling of the nothingness that occupies the heart of our being" (np).

In Act I of *Waiting for Godot* (1952), the question "What am I to tell Mr. Godot, Sir?" is answered by: "Tell him … (he hesitates) … tell him you saw us"…; in Act II: "Tell him … (he hesitates) … tell him you saw me and that … (he hesitates) … that you saw me" (34, 59).

Beckett's tendencies to the visual representation or even the enacting of an absent object in ekphrastic[154] forms lay at the source of his creativity. His obsessive preoccupation with seeing and being seen is represented in verbal forms in Beckett's creative writing. "Is anyone looking at me? Is anyone bothering about me at all?" (the woman) and "Am I as much as … being seen?" (the man) say two characters in Beckett's *Play* (1963,154–157). In *Endgame* (1957), blind Hamm, one of the two main figures, longs intensively to be seen and mirrored, which finally his three-legged black toy dog fulfills: "His hand on the dog's head he asks: 'Is he gazing at me?' and receives a yes answer. 'As if he were asking me to take him for a walk?'" And then: "Leave him like that, standing there imploring me" (41).

"More and more my language appears to me like a veil which one has to tear apart in order to get to those things (or the nothingness) lying behind it. … To drill one hole after another into it until that which lurks behind, be it something or nothing, starts

[151] A short story written in French in 1946.

[152] This "meditation for radio" by Samuel Beckett was first broadcast on BBC Radio 3's *Third Programme* on Saturday, December 14, 1957.

[153] *Sans* in French, translated in English by nothingness.

[154] Ekphrasis or ecphrasis stands for the description of a work of art produced as a rhetorical exercise, often used in the adjectival form ekphrastic. A vivid, often dramatic, verbal description of a visual work of art, either real or imagined.

seeping through—I cannot imagine a higher goal for today's writer" (Beckett 1937, in Fehsenfeld and Overbeck 2008, 518).

"Talking of speaking ... what if I went silent? ... The tears stream down my cheeks from my unblinking eyes. What makes me weep so? ... Perhaps it is liquified brain" (Beckett 1959, 309). "How, in such conditions, can I write, to consider only the manual aspect of that bitter folly? I don't know. I could know. But I shall not know. Not this time. It is I who write, who cannot raise my hand from my knee. It is I who think, just enough to write, whose head is far" (303).

Beckett's references to silence and the unnamable suggest his difficulty with evocative memory and indicates a deficiency during infancy of sensitive receptiveness by his caregivers. The quality of the early emotional relationship between infant and mother and the creation of mental representations by internalization is of crucial importance as discussed previously. The failing of these processes leads to a void and impairs the perception and understanding of feelings, beliefs, and behaviors of oneself and of others.

Beckett's drama figures suffer from psychic and somatic disturbances. They lack a true sense of identity and an emotionally significant relatedness to their surroundings. They are presented with disfigured body-images and seem to reflect Beckett's own psychosomatic symptoms.

Didier Anzieu suggests that Becket fulfilled a kind of self-analysis in his Trilogy (the novels *Molloy, Malone Dies*, and *the Unnamable*) in a process of *Nachträglichkeit*, that is, of retrospective attribution: "The originality of Beckett's narrative writing derives from the attempt (unacknowledged and probably unconscious) to transpose into writing the route, rhythm, style, form and movement of a psychoanalytic process in the course of its long series of successive sessions, with all the recoils, repetitions, resistances, denials, breaks and digressions that are the conditions of any progression" (Anzieu 1983, 80). At the same time, these writings represent a process for discovering or knowing himself by letting others speak.

Psychoanalysts and their creative expression of personal experiences

Didier Anzieu (1923–1999) was a French psychoanalyst and the founder—together with his wife Annie Anzieu and Florence Guignard—of the European Society for Child and Adolescent Psychoanalysis[155] in 1994. His life and work has been shaped by "the conjunction of his personal history, his psychoanalytic history, and the history of the French psychoanalytic movement."[156]

[155] SEPEA Société Européenne pour la Psychanalyse de l'Enfant et de l'Adolescent.

[156] *Dictionnaire international de la psychanalyse*, entry: Anzieu, Didier, article by René Kaës, Hachette Littératures, Paris, 2005.

At the age of sixty, Anzieu (1986) said: "I might put it this way—it sounds banal, but in my case, it seems true: I became a psychoanalyst to care for my mother. Not so much to care for her in reality, even though I did succeed in helping her, in the last quarter of her life, to find a relatively happy, balanced life. What I mean is, to care for my mother in myself and other people. To care, in other people, for this threatening and threatened mother" (20).

Marguerite Pantaine, Didier Anzieu's mother, was born in 1892. Her own mother Jeanne had endured two traumatic life events before her birth: she had lost Marguerite's elder sister, also named Marguerite, who was burned alive at the age of five; then she gave birth to a stillborn child. One and a half years after this second loss, Anzieu's mother was born.

Marguerite Anzieu Pantaine's first pregnancy in 1921 ended with the loss of a daughter who died by cord strangulation. Two years later Didier Anzieu was born, but only fifteen months after her son's birth, Anzieu's mother had to be hospitalized. In 1931 she was arrested for attacking an actress with a knife. Lacan[157] wrote his doctoral thesis on her (by using her case history) under the pseudonym of "Aimée."

In *Une peau pour les pensées* (1986b, 1990), Anzieu speaks of his mother:

> [She] was the third child in the family, the third or fourth … That's the problem. Before her, in fact, three daughters were born. The family lived in a large stone house close to the stable and the fields. The main room was heated by a large fireplace filled with big burning logs, where they cooked, and there were benches in it that you could sit on. This happened before my mother was born. It was a feast day. Marguerite, the youngest of the three daughters, had an organdie dress on, ready to go to church. She'd been left for a moment in the charge of the eldest girl, the one who was to become my godmother. The child was lightly dressed, it was cold, she went up to the fire to warm herself … and was burnt alive. It was a dreadful shock for her parents and her two sisters. So my mother was conceived as a replacement for the dead child. And since she was another girl, they gave her the same name, Marguerite. The living dead, in a way. … It's no coincidence that my mother spent her life finding ways to escape from the flames of hell. … It was a way of accepting her fate, a tragic fate. Why was she depressed? Because of her sensitive character. It made her unable to deal with my birth, which brought back the terrible memory of the stillborn baby. And why this sensitivity? I think it was due to the circumstances of her own birth. My mother only spoke openly of this once. But I knew it as a family legend. I think her depression goes back to this untenable position. She had put it off after the birth of her little girl who was stillborn, which seemed an implacable repetition of fate.

[157] Jacques Lacan was a French psychoanalyst and psychiatrist.

> And then my birth, which was successful, brought back that intolerable threat (19–20).

The last sentence in *Une peau pour la pensée* reads: "Love shows intelligence when it helps to build in the child, the friend, or the companion a flexible and firm envelope that delimits and unifies—a bark for the trunk, oxygen for the leaves, a living skin for his thoughts."

Anzieu (1981) distinguishes "creativity, a set of predispositions of character," from "creation," which is the invention or composition of a creative work. Dream work, bereavement work, creative work all have in common the fact that they constitute phases of a crisis: as in any crisis, there is an internal upheaval, a questioning of the acquired structures, a regression to sources unused, followed by the hasty invention of a new equilibrium and the creative surpassing. In creative work, negative and destructive sides are inseparably linked to positive and creative ones. The overabundance of a writer's representations and drives initiates the creative process, which has a healing effect on narcissistic injuries.

Human subjectivity—according to Anzieu—is at once psychic and somatic, and therefore mind and body are produced by both and productive of one another. Inside and outside are mutually constitutive, that is, body and mind are relational, as are self and other, nature and culture. Anzieu's work demonstrates that there are limits to human subjectivity. Unlike those who emphasize fluidity, instability, and malleability in their approaches to subjectivity, Anzieu emphasizes that containment, continuity, and integration, that is, a secure experience of a baby's own skin, are essential for the subject to survive and indeed flourish, for developmental processes such as individuation, and finally individuality. The ability to consider human subjectivity in its broadest sense requires the enduring and coping with experiences of pain and suffering (Lafrance 2013).

Anzieu (1986) is the author of *Freud's Self-Analysis*, a fifteen year-long investigation into Freud's creative process that refers to Freud's childhood memories, an analysis of his dreams and letters to Fliess, and more. The creative genius is one of Anzieu's preoccupations, and he states that the analytic session represents a privileged possibility to observe others think and to watch oneself think. Central to Anzieu's ever-present preoccupation in his numerous works and publications was the question of how the analytical way of thinking can liberate obstructions, barriers, impediments of thoughts into enjoyable thinking? This preoccupation is always the subject of his conceptualization of the ego-skin, his research on groups (for example, analytic psychodrama group therapy), and of artistic creativity.

Jean-Bertrand Pontalis (1924–2013) was one of France's pre-eminent psychoanalysts and co-author of the classic *The Language of Psychoanalysis*. He was a member of the editorial committee of *Les Temps Modernes*.

His autobiography *Love of Beginnings* (1993)[158] emphasizes so-called holes in discourse, where the process of evading schemes and ways of thinking opens new beginnings: "When words fail, it is because, without realizing it, one is about to touch a different earth" (81). It is a lyrical meditation on his own life, considered a masterpiece of autobiography.

Jean-Bertrand Pontalis lost his father at the age of nine. The adults in his family believed that he was too young to understand, which meant that the young Pontalis was left with the certitude that he was the only one who truly "understood." He wanted to be the only one to experience *this* death secretly. Thus, his idea that there was only an intimate, constant, silent relation with death was asserted. The only picture of himself and his father was taken three days before the death of his father; it shows the father laying his arm on his son's shoulder. This photograph, held in a frame, stood on Pontalis's writing table and represented for him a "whole time," "the frame of his life": father and son, holding each other and relying on each other, invulnerable together. Young Pontalis remained silent: the silence of death to bring the dead to life. "I saved a father from oblivion; I saved a son from abandonment. … So as not to mourn my father, I will always remain more or less in grieving language. … Everything that happened in my life later on, is surely related to this initial event" (Pontalis 1993, 34). His multiple publications and his activities were meant to compensate for the loss of his father.

"Since life is so fragile—my father died without notice following an acute appendicitis—there was certainly something infinitely less fragile: that is the bond with the one I had lost; later this became a relation with absence, with what does not occupy directly the field of vision, with the indicible, inexpressible. Occupied, possessed, overwhelmed by an absence, everything I could imagine and was not present, gained for me some sort of eternity" (86).

"I am especially attached to dreams (or dreams are very attached to me). In our nightlife, in our dreams, we are close to those who are often far away. We may even be close to those we have loved or hated, who have disappeared, either they are dead, or one has lost sight of them. They get closer to us in a more intense presence, sometimes more vividly than in everyday life, in what is called reality" (143). "I have always been interested in the in-between and the poorly defined places. What Freud called the 'intermediate realm,' like the unconscious, the dreams."[159]

Pontalis—many years after the death of his dog Oreste—continued to speak to his dog in his dreams, where the dog always replied, "I don't believe you." Pontalis only later understood the meaning of his dog's answer. The name Oreste is the phonetic rendering of "O reste" in French, meaning: Oh, stay with me, do not forsake me. Pontalis's father used to call his sons "dogs," when inviting them for a ride in his car—a demonstration of affection according to Pontalis. He himself—as Pontalis tells

158 *L'amour des commencements*, Gallimard, Paris, 1986.

159 Interview with J.-B. Pontalis by Pascale Frey, *L'Express*, March 1, 2000.

the story—should have shown more affection to his dog; then Oreste might not have replied "I don't believe you."

In his book *Windows*,[160] there are stories emanating from phrases Pontalis heard or images he saw; he spent hours in front of a window while writing. In this book he quotes Rilke's poem "Window":

> Window, you, oh measure of waiting,
> so many times filled,
> when a life pours and gets impatient
> to another life.
> You who separate and who attract,
> changing like the sea,
> ice, suddenly, where our figure is reflected
> mingled with what we see through;
> sample of a compromised freedom
> by the presence of the spell;
> taken by which among us is equalized
> the big one too much outside.
> Poetry seems to have the power to maintain the present, bringing time to
> a standstill.

[160] *Fenêtres*, Gallimard, Paris, 2000.

EPILOGUE

Leonardo da Vinci knew that art was a science and that science was an art.
Walter Isaacson[161]

Leonardo da Vinci (1452–1519)

There are some human beings who are endowed with exceptional intellectual and creative skills, regarded as geniuses, and blessed with scientific and artistic creativity. This is the case for Leonardo da Vinci, the universal artist, who was celebrated recently on the occasion of the 500th anniversary of his birthday. "What made Leonardo a genius … was creativity, the ability to apply imagination to intellect. His facility for combining observation with fantasy. … Leonardo's genius … was its universal nature" (Isaacson 2017, 518). "[There was] none who was as creative in so many different fields. … One, who sought to understand all of creation, including how we fit into it" (519).

Leonardo da Vinci was born out of wedlock. After his birth, his mother Caterina married and had four daughters and one son to her husband Accattabriga. As a widow, she wished to live with Leonardo and joined him at the age of about sixty, but died apparently soon after her arrival.

161 Isaacson (2017).

Leonardo's father Piero da Vinci, a notary, never married Caterina and never legitimated his son; he had four wives and in all, nine other sons and two daughters. He died in 1504, at the age of seventy-eight, and left Leonardo without any inheritance.

In the 1480s Leonardo wrote a letter to Ludovico Maria Sforza, Duke of Milan, presenting his skills and offering to work for him. In this letter, Leonardo describes himself as an engineer and includes a list of detailed military projects. Only at the end of his letter does he state: "In time of peace I believe I can give as complete satisfaction as any other in the field of architecture, and the construction of both public and private buildings, and in conducting water from one place to another. Also, I can execute sculptures in marble, bronze, and clay. Likewise, in painting, I can do everything possible" (95). Leonardo served the Duke for sixteen years; it was also the Duke who commissioned the painting *The Last Supper.*

In 1507 at the age of fifty-five, Leonardo adopted Franceso Melzi, an aspiring young artist who was then fourteen years old. Leonardo became his legal guardian and adoptive father, as well as his teacher and employer; Francesco stayed at his side for the rest of his life.

Leonardo was extremely sensitive, was fascinated by nature, and loved animals. This led him to write that "nature has given sensibility to pain to living organisms that have the power of movement, in order to preserve those parts which might be destroyed by movement" (131). "Pleasure and pain are represented as twins, because there is never one without the other" (138). "He had an uncanny ability to convey movements—of the body and the mind" (518).

Leonardo studied the anatomy of the human body and developed a profound knowledge of human physiology. His studies on the human fetus are remarkable. He wrote on his anatomical drawing of a human fetus: "If it breathed it would drown, and breathing is not necessary because it is nourished by the life and food of the mother" and added "one and the same soul governs these two bodies and one and the same soul nourishes both" (422).

Dying, Leonardo lamented having "offended against God and men by failing to practice his art as he should have done" (533).

The *Mona Lisa* "became more than a portrait of an individual. It became universal, a distillation of his universal wisdom about outward manifestations of our inner lives and about the connection between ourselves and our world" (494).

His portrait of the *Mona Lisa* is considered one of his greatest achievements and exemplifies Leonardo's genius in depicting the subtleties of facial emotions, her almost magical gaze and mysterious smile. Leonardo worked on the painting for more than a decade, perfecting it over the years until his death. At the time when he was working on Lisa's smile, he was studying anatomy, dissecting muscles, and nerves, trying to understand the origin of facial movements. As the British art historian Kenneth Clark remarked: "The science, the pictorial skill, the obsession with nature, the psychological insight is all there and so perfectly balanced" (477).

ACKNOWLEDGMENTS

The present book stems from Barbara Steck's passion for art and her great interest in the journeys of artists. Andreas Steck was exposed at a young age to the art brut movement through his father Hans Steck, who discovered Aloïse, one of the most well-known art brut artists. *Creativity and Art* derives from the many encounters with colleagues, scientists, and friends who share a common fascination with the unique lived experience of artists and the inner nature of creativity.

We are appreciative to all artists, whose quotes, texts, and remarks we use to illustrate their beliefs, struggles, pains, and joys. We hope that we are faithful to their message and the rendering is accurate. We acknowledge that translation is a complicated task: it is easier to return the content of a text; it is rather more difficult to represent its atmosphere, its musicality.

In the chapters 2, 3, 5, 9, 12, and 19 we have taken some previously published material from *Brain and Mind.* We are very thankful to Lucas Giossi and Marc Bachmann at EPFL Press for their personal commitment and support for this project. We are grateful to Jo Nicoud-Garden for English language editing and Kim Nanette for the book design. We express our appreciation to Eric Bernardi for his professional drawing of the figures. We thank the *Association Art et Médecine* (www.art-medecine.ch) for their financial support.

ABOUT THE AUTHORS

Andreas Steck is a professor emeritus of Neurology at the University of Basel. He trained in neurology in the USA and Switzerland. Nationally and internationally, he has committed himself to the field of neurology for decades. He was a president of the Swiss Neurological Society and a founding member and president of the European Neurological Society. His research interests are directed at a better understanding and treatment of neurological disorders. He is the author of numerous publications in scientific journals and is an editor of the Swiss Archives of Neurology, Psychiatry and Psychotherapy. He co-authored with his wife Barbara, Brain and Mind, a book exploring how the brain works.

Barbara Steck is a lecturer emeritus in Child and Adolescent Psychiatry and Psychotherapy of the University of Basel. She trained in psychoanalysis and family therapy and worked many years in the child and adolescent psychiatric departments of the Universities of Lausanne and Basel and in private practice. Her longtime interest in the fields of adoption, traumatization, grief, and families with ill parents, as well as individual psychotherapy and group psychodrama lead to numerous publications. She is author or co-author of books on adoption, psychosomatics, indication for psychotherapy of children and adolescents, with her husband Andreas on brain and mind and is still active as a psychoanalytic therapist and supervisor.

INDEX

BIBLIOGRAPHY

Aarvik, E. (1986): The Nobel Peace Prize. Sweden.

Abella, A. (2010): Contemporary Art and Hanna Segal's Thinking on Aesthetics. Int J Psychoanal 91:163–181.

Abraham, K. (1911): Giovanni Segantini ein psychoanalytischer Versuch. Schriften zur angewandten Seelenkunde. Heft 11. Vienna.

Abraham, N., and Rand N. (1978): The Phantom of Hamlet or the Sixth Act: Abraham, N., and Torok, M. (1987): L'écorce et le noyau. Flammarion. Paris.

Preceded by the Intermission of Truth. The Johns Hopkins University Press. Baltimore.

Abrams, D. (1993): Freud and Max Graf: On the Psychoanalysis of Music. In: Psychoanalytic Explorations of Music, (eds) S. Feder, R. Karmel and G. Pollock. Int. Univ. Press. Madison, CT.

Alford, C. F. (2012): Hanna Segal—A Memorial Appreciation. Psychoanalysis, Culture and Society 17, 317–324.

Amaducci, L., Grassia, E., and Boller, F. (2002): Maurice Ravel and Right-hemisphere Musical Creativity: Influence of Disease on his Last Musical Works? European J Neurol. 9.

Amenta, C. (2005): The Opening of the Mahler Ninth Symphony and the Bernstein "Heart-beat" Hypothesis. Naturlaut 4: 17–18.

Anderson, M. (1997): Carl Linnaeus: Father of Classification. Enslow Publishers, Springfield, NJ.

Andrade, V.M. (2005): Affect and the Therapeutic Action of Psychoanalysis. Int J Psychoanal. 86: 677–97.

Andreasen, N. (2005): The Creating Brain: The Neuroscience of Genius. Dana Press. New York.

Anzieu, D. (1974): Le moi-peau. Nouvelle Revue de Psychanalyse, 9, Le dedans et le dehors. Gallimard. Paris.

Anzieu, D. (1976): L'enveloppe sonore du Soi. Nouvelle Revue de Psychanalyse, 13, Narcisses. Gallimard. Paris.

Anzieu, D. (1979): The Sound Image of the Self. Int Rev Psychoanal 6:23–36.

Anzieu, D. (1981): Le corps de l'oeuvre. Gallimard. Paris.

Anzieu, D. (1983): Un Soi disjoint, une voix liante: l'écriture narrative de Samuel Beckett. Nouvelle revue de psychanalyse, 28, 71–85. Translation by Steven Connor.

Anzieu, D. (1986): The Self-analysis of Freud and the Discovery of Psychoanalysis. Hogarth Press and the Institute of Psychoanalysis. London.

Anzieu, D. (1986b): Une peau pour les pensées. Entretiens avec Gilbert Tarrab. Clancier-Guenaud. Paris.

Anzieu, D. (1987): Les signifiants formels et le moi-peau. In: Anzieu, D., (ed.) Les enveloppes psychiques, 1–22. Dunod. Paris.
Anzieu, D. (1989): The Skin Ego. Yale University Press. New Haven.
Anzieu, D. (1992): Beckett et le Psychanalyste. L'Aire. Archimbaud. Paris.
Anzieu, D., and Tarrab, G. (eds) (1990): A Skin for Thought: Interviews with Gilbert Tarrab on Psychology and Psychoanalysis. Karnac Books. London.
Apollinaire, G. (1950): The Cubist Painter's Aesthetic Meditations. Editions Pierre Cailler. Geneva.
Appelfeld, A. (2004): The Story of a Life. Schocken Books. New York. Translated from Hebrew by Aloma Halter.
Aristotle (2001): The Basic Works of Aristotle. McKeon R. (Ed.). Modern Library. New York.
Asafyev, B. V. (2008): The Operas of Tchaikovsky in Symphonic Etudes. Portraits of Russian Operas and Ballets. Scarecrow Press. Lanham, Maryland.
Baars, B. J. (1988): A Cognitive Theory of Consciousness. University Press. Cambridge.
Bakewell, S. (2016): At the Existentialist Café. Chatto and Windus. London.
Ball, M. J., Fisman, M., and Hachinski, V. A. (1985): New Definition of Alzheimer's Disease: A Hippocampal Dementia. Lancet. 1,14.
Baralea, F., and Minazzi, V. (2008): Off the Beaten Track: Freud, Sound, and Music. Statement of a Problem and Some Historico-critical Notes. Int J Psychoanal 89:937–957.
Barlow, H. B. (1981): The Ferrier Lecture 1980. Critical Limiting Factors in the Design of the Eye and Visual Cortex. Proc R Soc Lond, 212,1.
Barrett, D. (2001): The Committee of Sleep: How Artists, Scientists, and Athletes Use Their Dreams for Creative Problem Solving—and How You Can Too. Crown Books Random House. New York.
Barthes, R. (1982): L'Obvie et lobtus. Seuil. Paris.
Baumann, D. (1997): The Reception of Adolf Wölfli's Work (1921–1996). In: Adolf Wölfli. Draftsman, Writer, Poet, Composer, (ed.) Spoerri E. et al. Cornell University Press. Ithaca.
BCPSG (The Boston Process Change Study Group) (2010): Change in Psychotherapy: A Unifying Paradigm, Norton Professional Books. W. W. Norton. New York.
Beckett, S. (1937): Letter to Axel Kaun. Disjecta: Miscellaneous Writings and a Dramatic Fragment. Calder Publication 2001. London.
Beckett, S. (1956): Waiting for Godot. Faber and Faber. London.
Beckett, S. (1957): Endgame. A Play in One Act. Faber and Faber. London.
Beckett, S. (1958): The Unnamable. Grove Press. New York.
Beckett, S. (1959): Molloy, Malone Dies, The Unnamable. John Calder. London.
Beckett, S. (1963): Play. A Play in One Act. Faber and Faber. London.
Bell, A. O., and McNeillie, A. (eds) (1980): The Diary of Virginia Woolf. Volume III: 1925–1930. Hogarth. London.
Bell, D. L. (2015): Reason and Passion: A Tribute to Hanna Segal. Int J Psychoanal 96:177–200.
Berberian, M. (2003): Communal Rebuilding after Destruction: The World Trade Center Children's Mural Project. Psychoanalytic Social Work 10 (1): 27–4.
Berthoz, A,. and Debru, C. (2015): Anticipation et prédiction. Odile Jacob. Paris.
Bigsby, C. (2008): Arthur Miller. Harvard University Press. Cambridge, MA.
Bion, W. R. (1962): Learning from Experience. Heinemann. London.
Bion, W. R. (1970): Attention and Interpretation. Karnac. London.
Bjornstad, K. (1995): Edvard Munch. Die Geschichte seines Lebens. Insel Verlag, Frankfurt am Main and Leipzig.
Blood, A. J., and Zatorre R. J. (2001): Intensely Pleasurable Responses to Music Correlate with Activity in Brain Regions Implicated in Reward and Emotion. Proc Natl Acad Sci USA. 98(20):11818–23.
Boissière, A. (2018): Le mouvement à l'œuvre. Editions Mimésis, Sesto San Giovanni, MI.
Bollas, C. (1978): The Aesthetic Moment and the Search for Transformation. Annual of Psychoanalysis, 6 (1978), 385-94.

Bollas, C. (1979): The Transformational Object. Int. J. Psychoanal 60:97–107

Bollas, C. (1982): On the Relation to the Self as an Object. Int. J. Psychoanal 63:347–359.

Bollas, C. (1987): The Shadow of the Object: Psychoanalysis of the Unthought Known. Free Association. London.

Bray, S., Shimojo, S., and O'Doherty, J. P. (2010): Human Medial Orbitofrontal Cortex Is Recruited During Experience of Imagined and Real Rewards. J Neurophysiol 103, 2506.

Breuer, J., and Freud, S. (1895): Studien über Hysterie. G.W. Bd. 1.

Briggs, J. (2006): Virginia Woolf: An Inner Life. A Harvest Book, Harcourt Inc. London.

Brodt, S., Gais, S., Beck, J., et al. (2018): Fast Track to the Neocortex: A Memory Engram in the Posterior Parietal Cortex. Science. 362, 1045.

Brown, A. (2016): Interview 30 July 2016 11.00 BST.

Bürgin, D., and Steck, B. (2013): Indikation psychoanalytischer Psychotherapie bei Kindern und Jugendlichen. Diagnostisch-therapeutisches Vorgehen und Fallbeispiele. Klett-Cotta. Stuttgart.

Buk, A. (2009): The Mirror Neuron System and Embodied Simulation: Clinical Implications for Art Therapists Working with Trauma Survivors. The Arts in Psychotherapy 36.

Camus, A. (1994): Le Premier homme. Gallimard. Paris.

Carota, A., Iaria, G., Berney, A., et al. (2005): Understanding Van Gogh's Night: Bipolar Disorder. In: Bogousslavsky J. and Boller F. (eds): Neurological Disorders in Famous Artists. Front Neurol Neurosci.19,121, Karger. Basel.

Carr, E. H. (2016): Dostoevsky 1821–1881. Routledge, Abingdon-on-Thames.

Carta, S. (2009): Music in Dreams and the Emergence of the Self. J Anal Psychol. 54(1):85–102.

Castoriadis-Aulagnier, P. (2001): The Violence of Interpretation: From Pictogram to Statement. Brunner/Routledge. Hove, U.K. and Philadelphia. Translated by Alan Sheridan.

Chanda, M. L., and Levitin, D. J. (2013): The Neurochemistry of Music. Trends Cogn Sci. 17(4):179–93.

Changeux, J. P. (1994): Raison et plaisir. Odile Jacob. Paris.

Changeux, J. P. (1997): Neuronal Man: The Biology of Mind. Princeton University Press. Princeton.

Changeux, J. P. (2008): Du Vrai, Du Beau, Du Bien, une nouvelle approche neuronale. Odile Jacob. Paris.

Chaplin, C. (1964): My Autobiography. Simon and Schuster. New York.

Cheng, F. (2008): Cinq méditations sur la beauté. Albin Michel. Paris.

Cheshire, N. M. (1996): The Empire of the Ear: Freud's Problem with Music. Int. J. Psycho-Anal., 77, 1127–1168.

Chomsky, N. (2000): The Architecture of Language. University Press. Oxford.

Christian, C. (2007): Sibling Loss, Guilt, and Reparation: A Case Study. Int J Psychoanal 88:41–54.

Claudel, C. (2014): Correspondances. Edition Gallimard. Paris

Cohen, D. (2006): Life Is with Others, Selected Writings on Child Psychiatry. Yale University. New Haven.

Cohn, R. (1980): Just Play: Beckett's Theater. Princeton University Press. Princeton.

Cole, M., and Wertsch, J. W. (1996): Beyond the Individual-social Antinomy in Discussions of Piaget and Vygotsky. Hum. Dev. 39, 250.

Constantinescu, A. O., O'Reilly, J. X., and Behrens, T. E. J. (2016): Organizing Conceptual Knowledge in Humans with a Gridlike Code. Science, 352:1464.

Cordulack, S. W. (2002): Edvard Munch and the Physiology of Symbolism. Manuscript 1891. Madison, NJ.

Coulter, H. (2016): Pictures on My Analyst's Walls: Reflections on the Art of Käthe Kollwitz, the Nazis, and the Art of Psychoanalysis. British Journal of Psychotherapy 32, 4: 475–490.

Craig, A. D. (2009): How Do You Feel Now? The Anterior Insula and Human Awareness. Nat Rev Neurosci. 10, 59.

Crick, F. (1995): The Astonishing Hypothesis: The scientific Search for the Soul. Simon and Schuster. New York.

Dali, S., and Ballard, J. G. (2007): Diary of a Genius. Solar Books. Chicago.

Dalla Bella, S., Białuńska, A., and Sowiński, J. (2013): Why Movement Is Captured by Music, but Less by Speech: Role of Temporal Regularity. PLoS One. 2013 2;8(8):e71945.

Damasio, A. (1994): Descartes' Error: Emotion, Reason, and the Human Brain. Putnam Publishing. New York.

Damasio, A. (1999): The Feeling of What Happens: Body and Emotion in the Making of Consciousness. Harcourt Brace. New York.

Damasio, A. (2018): The Strange Order of Things. Pantheon Books. New York.

Darwin, C. (1860): On the Origin of Species, by Means of Natural Selection. D. Appleton and Company. New York.

Darwin, C. (1872): The Expression of the Emotions in Man and Animals. John Murray. London.

Davies, N., and Eagle, G. (2013): Conceptualizing the Paternal Function: Maleness, Masculinity or Thirdness? Contemporary Psychotherapy, 49(4), 559–585.

De Haan, E. H., and Cowey, A. (2011): On the Usefulness of "What" and "Where" Dehaene, S., Changeux, J. P., Naccache, L., et al. (2006): Conscious, Preconscious, and Subliminal Processing: A Testable Taxonomy. Trends Cogn Sci.10, 204.

Pathways in Vision. Trends Cogn Sci. 15, 460.

Deknatel, F. B. (1950): Edvard Munch. Institute of Contemporary Art;

Chanticleer Press Exhibition.

De La Grange, H. L. (1973): Mahler. Doubleday. New York.

Delay, J., and Volmat, R. (1956): Expressions plastiques de la folie. Médecine de France. Paris.

De Montaigne, M. (1910) : Essays of Montaigne, vol. 1, revised by William Carew Hazlett. Edwin C. Hill. New York. Translated by Charles Cotton.

De Saint-Exupéry, A. (1946): Le petit prince. Folio Junior. Gallimard. Paris.

DeSalvo, L. (1989): Virginia Woolf: The Impact of Childhood Sexual Abuse on Her Life and Work. Ballantine Books. New York.

Descartes, R. (1644/1911): The Principles of Philosophy. Cambridge University Press. Translated by E. Haldane and G. Ross.

Dimitrijevic, A. (2014): Gustav Mahler: A Life in Crisis by Stuart Feder (2004): A Review Essay. Yale University Press. New Haven.

Dirks, J., and Gibson, E. (1977): Infants' Perception of Similarity between Live People and their Photographs. Child Dev. 48, 124.

Dolensek, N., Gehrlach, D. A., Klein, A. S., et al. (2020): Facial Expressions of Emotion States and their Neuronal Correlates in Mice. Science, 368, 89.

Domin, H. (1968): Wozu Lyrik heute. Dichtung und Leser in der gesteuerten Gesellschaft. Fischer Verlag. Frankfurt.

Domin, H. (1978): Römerbergrede. In: Gesammelte Essays.

Domin, H. (1987): Gesammelte Gedichte. Fischer Verlag. Frankfurt.

Domin, H. (1987b): Interview with Adelbert Reif. In: Gesammelte Autobiographische Schriften.

Domin, H. (1992): Gesammelte Autobiographische Schriften. Fischer Verlag. Frankfurt.

Domin, H. (1993): Gesammelte Essays: Heimat in der Sprache. Fischer Verlag. Frankfurt.

Dürrenmatt, F. (1998) Werkausgabe, 36,94. Diogenes. Zurich

Edelman, G. M., and Tononi, G. (2000): A Universe of Consciousness: How Matter Becomes Imagination. Basic Books. New York.

Edelstein, M. (2000): Sans Souci, l'Art d'Aloïse. Arte. France.

Ehrenfeld, T. (1983): Why Executives Collect. Fortune, January 11.

Ehrenzweig, A. (1953): The Psychoanalysis of Artistic Vision and Hearing. George Braziller. New York.

Eichenbaum, H. (2015): The Hippocampus as a Cognitive Map of Social Space. Neuron, 87:9.

Ekman, P., Friesen, W., and Ellsworth, P. (1972): Emotion in the Human Face: Guidelines for Research and an Integration of Findings. Pergamon Press. New York.

Eliot, T. S. (1909–1950): The Complete Poems and Plays 1909–1950. Harcourt Brace and Company. New York.

Eliot, T. S. (1919): Tradition and Individual Talent. In: Selected Essays 1960. Harcourt, Brace and World. New York.

Eliot, T. S. (1936): Four Quartets. In: Collected Poems 1909–1935.
Erel-Brodsky, H. (2016): I'm All Ears—Thoughts on Psychoanalysis: The Musical Reverie. Contemporary Psychoanalysis Vol. 52, No. 4: 578–601.
Esman, A. H. (2004): Adolf Wölfli, 1864–1930. Am J Psychiatry 161,9.
Esman, A. H. (2004b): Ernst Kris and the art of the mentally ill. Int J Psychoanal. 85, 923.
Etchegoyen, L. (2004): Language and Affects in the Analytic Practice. Int J Psychoanal. 85(Pt 6): 1479–83.
Etkin, A., Büchel, C., and Gross, J. J. (2015): The Neural Bases of Emotion Regulation. Nat Rev Neurosci. 16,693.
Etkin, A., Klemenhagen, K. C., Dudman, J. T., et al. (2004): Individual Differences in Trait Anxiety Predict the Response of the Basolateral Amygdala to Unconsciously Processed Fearful Faces. Neuron. 44,1043.
Fairbairn, W. R. D. (1938): The Ultimate Basis of Aesthetic Experience. Br J Psychol 29:167–81.
Feder, S. (2004): Gustav Mahler: A Life in Crisis. New Haven: Yale University Press. In: Dimitrijevic A. (2014).
Fehsenfeld, M. D., and Overbeck, L. M. (2008): The Letters of Samuel Beckett. Vol. 1, 1929–1940. Cambridge University Press. Cambridge.
Ferenczi, S. (1955): The Confusion of Tongues between Adults and the Child. In: Final Contributions to the Problems and Methods of Psychoanalysis, (ed.) Michael Balint. Hogarth. London.
Ferenczi, S. (1955b): Aphoristic Remarks on the Theme of Being Dead—Being a Woman. In: M. Balint (ed.), Final Contributions to the Problems and Methods of Psychoanalysis. Basic Books. New York.
Ferreri, L., Mas-Herrerod, E., and Zatorre, R. J. (2019): Dopamine Modulates the Reward Experiences Elicited by Music Proc Natl Acad Sci USA.116, 3793.
Ffytche, M. (2012): "Night of the Unexpected: A Critique of the "Uncanny" and its Apotheosis within Cultural and Social Theory. New Formations: a Journal of Culture, Theory, Politics, 75 (1). 63–81.
Fischer, G., and Riedesser, P. (1999): Lehrbuch der Psychotraumatologie. Reinhardt Verlag. München Basel.
Fischer, J. (2018): Psychoanalytikerin trifft Marina Abramovic. Scheidegger und Spiess AG. Zurich.
Fisher, R. (1930): The Genetical Theory of Natural Selection. Clarendon Press.
London.
Fisher, S., and Ridley, M. (2013): Culture, Genes, and the Human Revolution. Science, 340:929.
Fiske, S. T., Cuddy, A. J., and Glick, P. (2007): Universal Dimensions of Social Cognition: Warmth and Competence. Trends Cogn Sci. 11,77.
Fivaz, R. (1989): L'ordre et la volupté. Presses polytechniques romandes. Lausanne, Suisse.
Fivaz-Depeursinge, E. and Corboz-Warnery, A. (1999): The Primary Triangle. Basic Behavioral Science. New York.
Forel, J. (1953): Aloyse ou la peinture magique d'une schizophrène. Imprimerie Jaunin. Lausanne, Suisse.
Forel, J., and MacGregor, J. (2014): Reminiscences, Jacqueline Marie Porret-Forel, Raw Vision; 83.
Foster, H. (ed.) (1983): Anti-aesthetic: Essays on Postmodern Culture. Bay Press. Toronto.
Fowles, J. (1963): The Collector. Little, Brown and Company, Boston.
Fraiberger, S. P., Sinatra, R., Resch, M., et al. (2019): Quantifying Success and Reputation in Art. Science 362, 825.
Freud, A. (1965): Normality and Pathology in Childhood. New York: International University Press.
Freud, E. L. (1961): Letters of Sigmund Freud 1873–1939, 1-478. The Hogarth Press. London.
Freud, S. (1887–1904): In the Complete Letters of Sigmund Freud to Wilhelm Freud, S. (1890–1939): Gesammelte Werke online
Fliess. (ed.) J. M. Masson. Harvard University Press. Cambridge, Mass.
Freud, S. (1900–1901): The Interpretation of Dreams. Vol. IV- V. Hogarth Press. London.
Freud, S. (1901): Psychopathology of Everyday Life. SE, Hogarth Press. London.
Freud, S. (1905): Psychopathic Characters on the Stage. SE 7, 303–10. Hogarth Press. London.
Freud, S. (1907): Delusions and Dreams in Jensen's Gradiva. SE 9, p. 3–95. Hogarth Press. London.
Freud, S. (1908): Creative Writers and Daydreaming. SE 9, p. 141–54. Hogarth Press. London.

Freud, S. (1908b): Civilized Sexual Morality and Modern Nervous Illness in the Journal Sexual-Probleme.
Freud, S. (1909): Analysis of a Phobia in a Five-Year-Old Boy. SE 10: 1-150. Hogarth Press. London.
Freud, S. (1909–1939): Das entwicklungsgeschichtliche Interesse an der Psychoanalyse. Ges. Werke, Bd. VIII. Frankfurt/M. Fischer.
Freud, S. (1910): Leonardo da Vinci and A Memory of His Childhood. Norton. New York.
Freud, S. (1911): Formulations on the Two Principles of Mental Functioning. SE 12, p. 213–26. Hogarth Press. London.
Freud, S. (1912): The Dynamics of Transference, vol. XII. Hogarth Press; p. 97–108. London.
Freud, S. (1913): The Claims of Psychoanalysis to Scientific Interest. SE 13, p. 164–90. Hogarth Press. London.
Freud, S. (1914): The Moses of Michelangelo. SE 13, p. 211–238. Hogarth Press. London.
Freud, S. (1915): On Transience. SE, 14, 305-308. Hogarth Press. London.
Freud, S. (1919): The Uncanny. SE 17, p. 217–56. Hogarth Press. London.
Freud, S. (1920): Beyond the Pleasure Principle. S.E. 18. Hogarth Press. London.
Freud, S. (1924): A Short Account of Psychoanalysis. SE 19., p. 191–212.
Freud, S. (1925): The Resistances to Psychoanalysis. Standard Edition, Vol. 19.
Hogarth Press. London.
Freud, S. (1927): The Future of an Illusion. SE 21, p. 3–56. Hogarth Press. London.
Freud, S. (1929): Letter to Binswanger. Letter 239. In: Freud, E. L., (ed.) (1960): The Letters of Sigmund Freud 1873–1939. Basic Books. New York.
Freud, S. (1930): Civilization and its Discontents. SE 21, 59–145. Hogarth Press. London.
Freud, S. (1936): Letter to M. Bonaparte, 06.12.36. In: Freud, E. L., (ed.) (1960): The Letters of Sigmund Freud, 1873–1939. Basic Books. New York.
Galilei, V. (1581): Dialogo della musica antica e della moderna. in Source Reading in Music History (1950) (ed.) O. Strunk. Norton. New York.
Gary, R. (1962): Promise at Dawn. Penguin Modern Classics. London.
Gary, R. (1977): The Life Before Us. New Directions Books. New York. Translated by R. Manheim.
Gibran, K. (1923): The Prophet. Knopf. New York.
Glocker, M. L., Langleben, D. D., Ruparel, K., et al. (2009): Baby Schema in Infant Faces Induces Cuteness Perception and Motivation for Caretaking in Adults. Ethology. 115,257.
Goethe, J. W. (1811–1833): From My Life: Poetry and Truth. Harrison and Co. Printers. London.
Goldman, C. (2007): Camus, Sartre, Gary et les enfants surdoués: absence paternelle, depression maternelle et symbolisation, Le Carnet PSY.1. 114.
Gombrich, E. H. (1995): The Story of Art. Phaidon Press. New York.
Gomez, J., Barnett, M. A., Natu, V., et al. (2017): Microstructural Proliferation in Human Cortex Is Coupled with the Development of Face Processing. Science. 355,68.
Gonzalez, W. G., Zhang, H., and Harutyunyan, A. (2019): Persistence of Neuronal Representations through Time and Damage in the Hippocampus. Science. 365,821.
Goodale, M. A., and Milner, A. D. (1992): Separate Visual Pathways for Perception and Action. Trends Neurosci. 15, 20.
Goulding, P. G. (1992) : Classical Music: The 50 Greatest Composers and Their 1,000 Greatest Works. Random House Publishing Group.
Graf, M. (1942): Reminiscences of Professor Sigmund Freud. Psychoanalytic
Quarterly, 11:465–76.
Green, A. (1997): The Dead Mother in Private Madness. Karnac. London.
Greenacre, P. (1957): The Childhood of the Artist. The Psychoanalytic Study of the Child, 12:47–72. International Universities Press. New York.
Greenacre, P. (1962): Discussion and Comments on the Psychology of Creativity. Journal of The American Academy of Child Psychiatry. 1,1: 129–137.

Guyotat, J. (1980): Mort/naissance et filiation. Etudes de psychopathologie sur le lien de filiation. Masson. Paris.

Hagman, G. (2000): The Creative Process. In: How Responsive Should We Be? Progress in Self Psychology, (ed.) A. Goldberg. The Analytic Press. Hillsdale, NJ.

Hagman, G. (2002): The Sense of Beauty. Int. J. Psychoanal. 83, 661.

Hagman, G. (2005): in Aesthetic Experience: Beauty, Creativity, and the Search for the Ideal. Rodopi. Amsterdam New York.

Hagman, G. (2008): The Creative Analyst: How Art Can Inform Clinical Practice, International Journal of Psychoanalytic Self Psychology, 4:1, 40–58.

Has-Ellison, J. T. (2006): Review of Gustav Mahler. Canadian Journal of History, 95.

Haxby, J. V., Hoffman, E. A., Gobbini, M. I. (2000): The Distributed Human Neural System for Face Perception. Trends Cogn Sci.4,223.

Heard, E., and Martienssen, R. A. (2014): Transgenerational Epigenetic Inheritance: Myths and Mechanisms. Cell, 157:95.

Heidegger, M. (1959): The Ode on Man in Sophocles Antigone, from an Introduction to Metaphysics. Yale University Press. New Haven, CT.

Heidegger, M. (1996): Hölderlin's Hymn "The Ister." Indiana University Press. Bloomington, Indiana.

Heinrich, D., and Förster, E. (1997): The Course of Remembrance and Other Essays on Hölderlin. Stanford University Press, Redwood City, CA.

Henke, K. (2010): A Model for Memory Systems Based on Processing Modes Rather than Consciousness. Nat Rev Neurosci.11(7):523.

Hickok, G., and Poeppel, D. (2004): Dorsal and Ventral Streams: A Framework for Understanding Aspects of the Functional Anatomy of Language. Cognition. 92,67.

Hirsch, M. (1999): Psychodynamik und Identitätsschicksal des Ersatzkindes. In: Sohni H. (Ed.): Geschwisterlichkeit—Horizontale Beziehungen in Psychotherapie und Gesellschaft. Göttingen.

Hirsh, D. (2018): Unconscious Pacts and the Bisexuality of the Countertransference in the Psychoanalytic Process. In: Psychic Bisexuality: A British–French Dialogue, (ed.) R. J. Perelberg. Routledge. London.

Ho, B. C., Andreasen, N. C., Nopoulos, P., et al. (2003): Progressive Structural Brain Abnormalities and their Relationship to Clinical Outcome: A Longitudinal Magnetic Resonance Imaging Study Early in Schizophrenia. Arch Gen Psychiatry. 606,585.

Hölderlin, F. (1797) : Hyperion oder der Eremit in Griechenland. Erster Band. Tübingen. S. 94–96.

Hoffmann, E. T. A. (1813): Konzertberichte. LaaberVerlag. Laaber 1987, 252–265.

Holm-Hadulla, R. M. (2003): Psychoanalysis as a Creative Shaping Process. Int J Psychoanal. 84:1203–1220.

Hubel, D. H., and Wiesel, T. N. (1968): Receptive Fields and Functional Architecture of Monkey Striate Cortex. J Physiol. 195, 215.

Hugo, V. (1886): William Shakespeare. A. C. McClurg. Chicago.

Hyland, D. A. (2004): Questioning Platonism. Continental interpretations of Plato. State University of New York Press. Albany. New York.

Isaacson, W. (2017): Leonardo da Vinci. The Biography. Simon and Schuster. London, New York.

Ishizu, T., and Zeki, S. (2011): Toward A Brain-Based Theory of Beauty. PLoS ONE 6. e21852.

Jacob, F. (1988): The Statue Within: An Autobiography. Basic Books. New York.

Jacob, F. (2001): Of Flies, Mice, and Men. Harvard University Press. Cambridge, MA.

Janusz Rybakowski, J., Klonowska, P., Patrzała, A., et al. (2008): Psychopathology and Creativity. Arch. Psychiatry Psychother. 1, 37.

Jasanoff, A. (2018): The Biological Mind. Basic Books. New York.

Jentsch, E. (1904 and 1911): Notes How Uncanny Effects Are Readily Produced in Music. Musik und Nerven, vol. 2:56–7.

Jeste, S. S. (2011): The Neurology of Autism Spectrum Disorders. Curr Opin Neurol,24,132.

Jiang, J., Rickson, D., Jiang, C. (2016): The Mechanism of Music for Reducing Psychological Stress, The Arts in Psychotherapy 48, 62–68.

Jiménez, J. P. (2006): After Pluralism: Towards a New, Integrated Psychoanalytic Paradigm. Int J Psychoanal. 87(Pt 6):1487–507.

Jones, E. (1955): Sigmund Freud. Life and Work. Vol. II: Years of Maturity 1901–1919. Hogarth Press. London.

Josselyn, S. A., and Tonegawa, S. (2020): Memory Engrams: Recalling the Past and Imagining the Future. Science.367, eaaw4325.

Jurist, E. I. (2006): Art and Emotion in Psychoanalysis. Int J Psychoanal 87:1315–34.

Kaelberer, M. M., Buchanan, K. L., Klein, M. E., et al. (2018): A Gut-Brain Neural Circuit for Nutrient Sensory Transduction. Science,361:1219 eaat5236.

Kaas, J. A.(1989): Why Does the Brain Have So Many Visual Areas? J Cogn Neurosci. 1(2):121.

Kahr, B. (1996): D.W. Winnicott: A Biographical Portrait. Karnac. London.

Kandel, E. R. (2012): The Age of Insight: The Quest to Understand the Unconscious in Art, Mind, and Brain, from Vienna 1900 to the Present. Random House. New York.

Kandel, E.R. (2018): The Disordered Mind. Robinson. London.

Kappas, A. (2006): Appraisals Are Direct, Immediate, Intuitive, and Unwitting … and Some Are Reflective. Cogn Emot. 20: 952.

Kertesz, I. (2004): Kaddish for an Unborn Child. Vintage. New York.

Kjetsaa, G. (1989): Fyodor Dostoyevsky: A Writer's Life. Fawcett. Columbine Minnesota.

Kim, D. Y., and Camilleri, M. (2000): Serotonin: A Mediator of the Brain-Gut Connection. Am J Gastroenterol, 95:2698.

Kleinschmidt, A., Büchel, C., Zeki, S., et al. (1998): Human Brain Activity During Spontaneously Reversing Perception of Ambiguous Figures. Proc Biol Sci. 265,2427.

Knowlson, J. (1996): Damned to Fame: The Life of Samuel Beckett. Bloomsbury. London.

Knowlson, J. (2003): Images of Beckett. Cambridge University Press. Cambridge.

Kohon, G. (2016): Reflections on the Aesthetic Experience: Psychoanalysis and the Uncanny. Routledge. London.

Kohut, H. (1986): Forms and Transformations of Narcissism. In: Essential Papers on Narcissism, (ed.) Andrew P. Morrison. NYU Press. New York.

Kollwitz, K., and Kollwitz, H. (ed.) (1968): Ich sah die Welt mit liebevollen Blicken—Käthe Kollwitz: Ein Leben in Selbstzeugnissen. Herausgegeben von Hans Kollwitz. Fackelträger Verlag. Hannover.

Kraus, B. J., Brandon, M. P., Robinson, R. J., et al. (2015): Running in Place, Grid Cells Integrate Elapsed Time, and Distance Run. Neuron. 88: 578.

Kris, E. (1952): Psychoanalytic Explorations in Art. Int. Univ. Press. New York.

Lafrance, M. (2013): From the Skin Ego to the Psychic Envelope: An Introduction to the Work of Didier Anzieu. Centre for Sensory studies. University of Montreal. Quebec Canada.

Lagercrantz, O. (1984): August Strindberg. Farrar Straus Giroux. New York. Translated by Anselm Hollo.

Lambert, S. (2016): Avant Godot. Arléa. Paris.

Laplanche, J. (1999): Essays on Otherness. Routledge. London.

Laplanche, J., and Pontalis, J. B. (1973): The Language of Psychoanalysis. W. W. Norton. New York. Translated by Donald Nicholson-Smith.

Le Clézio, J. M. G. (2004): L'Africain Traits et portraits. Mercure de France. Paris.

Le Clézio, J. M. G. (2008): The Nobel Foundation.

Le Clézio, J. M. G. (2020): L'enfant et la guerre. Gallimard. Paris.

Le Doux, J. E. (2000): Emotions Circuits in the Brain. Annu. Rev. Neurosci. 23:155.

Loewald, H. (1988): Sublimation. Yale University Press. New Haven.

Lombroso, C. (1895): Genio e Follia. Bocca. Torino, Italy.

Mächtlinger, V. (2002): Das Skandalon der ersten Kinderanalyse—die Eltern des kleinen Hans. In: Sigmund Freud (2000): Analyse der Phobie eines fünfjährigen Knaben. Fischer Verlag. Frankfurt am Main.

Mahler, G. (1946): Memories and Letters. John Murray. London.

Mahler, G. (1982): Gustav Mahler: Briefe 1879–1911. Blaukopf, H. (ed.) Revised and enlarged edition. Publications of the Gustav Mahler Society. Vienna.

Maiello, S. (2001): Prenatal Trauma and Autism. J Child Psychother. 27(2):107–24.
Mancia, M. (2006): Implicit Memory and Early Unrepressed Unconscious: Their Role in the Therapeutic Process (How the Neurosciences Can Contribute to Psychoanalysis). Int J Psychoanal. 87(Pt 1):83–103.
Marshel, J. H., Kim, Y. S., Machado, T. A., et al. (2019): Cortical Layer-specific Critical Dynamics Triggering Perception. Science.365, eaaw5202.
Mary, A., Dayan, J., and Leone, G. (2020): Resilience after Trauma: The Role of Memory Suppression. Science 367, 756.
Mathon, B. (2011): histoire.ontheway.
Matte-Blanco, I. (1988): Thinking, Feeling, and Being: Clinical Reflections on the Fundamental Antinomy of Human Beings and World. Routledge. London. New Library of Psychoanalysis, vol. 5. In: Jiménez J.P. (2006).
Mayer, S. (2009): Interview with Per Olov Enquist. Die Zeit, March 12, 2009, Nr. 12.
Miller, W. L. (2018): The Hypothalamic-Pituitary-Adrenal Axis: A Brief History. Horm Res Paediatr,89,212.
Milner, A. D., and Goodale, M. A. (2008): Two Visual Systems Reviewed. Neuropsychologia. 46,774.
Minturn, K. (2004): Dubuffet, Lévi-Strauss, and the Idea of Art Brut: Anthropology and Aesthetics. 46, 247.
Misteli, D. (2014): Gegen den Zerfall arbeiten taktile Realität in einem Spätwerk Vincent van Goghs. ALL-OVER #7.
Mitchell, D. (1958): Mahler and Freud. This essay was originally published in Chord and Discord 2(8): 63–68.
Modell, A. H. (1989): The Psychoanalytic Setting as a Container of Multiple Levels of Reality: A Perspective on the Theory of Psychoanalytic Treatment, Psychoanalytic Inquiry, 9:1, 67–87.
Modell, A. H. (2006): Imagination and the Meaningful Brain. MIT Press. Cambridge.
Morgenthaler, W. (1921): Ein Geisteskranker als Künstler (Adolf Wölfli). Bern 1921. Madness and Art. (1900). Esman A. H. (ed.). University of Nebraska Press, Lincoln, Nebraska. Translated by A. H. Esman.
Morgenthaler, W. (1964): Adolf Wölfli. Collection de l'Art Brut, fascicule 2, Paris. Translation by Henri-Pol Bouché.
Moro, M. R. (1989): L'enfant exposé. La pensée sauvage. Grenoble.
Morrison, T. (1987): Beloved. Knopf. New York.
Morrison, T. (2017): The Origin of Others. The Charles Eliot Norton Lectures. Harvard University Press. Cambridge, MA.
Morrison, T. (2019): The Source of Self-regard. Knopf. New York.
Moser, E., Kropff, E., and Britt Moser, M. (2008): Place Cells, Grid Cells, and the Brain's Spatial Representation System. Annu. Rev. Neurosci. 31:69.
Moutoussis, K., and Zeki, S. A. (1997): Direct Demonstration of Perceptual Asynchrony in Vision. Proc Biol Sci. 264,393.
Munch, E. (2005): The Private Journals of Edvard Munch. We Are Flames Which Pour Out of the Earth. Edvard Munch. Edited and translated by J. Gill Holland.
Musil, R. (1995): The Man without Qualities. Vol. I. Knopf. New York.
Nakata, T., Sandra, E., and Trehubb, S. E. (2004): Infants' Responsiveness to Maternal Speech and Singing. Infant Behav Dev. 27:455–64.
Nalbantian, S. (2008): Neuroaesthetics: Neuroscientific Theory and Illustration from the Arts. Interdiscipl Sci Rev.33,357.
Nathan, T. (2017): Les âmes errantes. Payot. Lausanne, Suisse.
Neihart, M. (1998): Creativity, the Arts, and Madness. Roeper Review. 21:47–50.
Neiman, S. (2008): Moral Clarity. Houghton Mifflin Harcourt, Orlando, FL.
Neisser, U. (1967): Cognitive Psychology. Appleton-Century-Crofts. New York.
Neruda, P. (2004): One Hundred Love Sonnets: XVII and poem 15 from The Essential Neruda: Selected Poems, (ed.) Mark Eisner. City Lights Books. San Francisco, CA.
Nietzsche, F. (1844-1900): In: Twilight of the Idols. (1889) Penguin Classics. London.
Nietzsche, F. (1922): Der Wille zur Macht I—Kapitel 4. Nietzsches Werke Taschen-Ausgabe Band IX.

Nietzsche, F. (1994): Jugendschriften. Hrsg. Hans Joachim Mette. München.
Norman, Y., Yeagle, E. M., Khuvis, S., et al. (2019): Hippocampal Sharp-wave Ripples Linked to Visual Episodic Recollection in Humans. Science. 365, eaax1030.
Novalis (1798/1799): Die Enzyklopädie – Die Philosophischen Wissenschaften.
Noy, P. (1991): How Music Conveys Emotion. In: Psychoanalytic Explorations in Music: Second Series (1993) (eds) S. Feder, R. L. Karmel, and G. H. Pollock. International Universities Press. Madison, WI.
Obama, B. (2004): Dreams from My Father: A Story of Race and Inheritance. Three Rivers Press. New York.
Ogden, T. H. (1995): Analyzing Forms of Aliveness and Deadness of the Transference Countertransference. Int. J. Psychoanal. 76:695709.
Ogden, T. H. (1996): Reconsidering Three Aspects of Psychoanalytic Technique. Int. J. Psychoanal. 77, 883.
Ogden, T.H. (1999): "The Music of What Happens" in Poetry and Psychoanalysis. Int. J. Psychoanal., 80:979994.
Ogden, TH (2014): Fear of Breakdown and the Unlived Life. Int J Psychoanal. 95:205–223.
Oppenheim, L. (2000): The Painted Word: Samuel Beckett's Dialogue with Art. University of Michigan Press. Michigan.
Padavona, C., and Darribab, V. (2016): The Notion of Applied Psychoanalysis in the Early Years of the Psychoanalytic Movement. Psicologia USP, 27, 1, 104–114.
Panksepp, J. (2005): Affective Consciousness: Core Emotional Feelings in Animals and Jumans. Conscious. Cogn. 14: 30.
Panksepp, J. (2011): Cross-Species Affective Neuroscience Decoding of the Primal Affective Experiences of Humans and Related Animals. Plos One, 6, e21236.
Panksepp, J., and Bernatzky, G. (2002): Emotional Sounds and the Brain: The Neuro-Affective Foundations of Musical Appreciation. Behav Processes. 60(2):133–155.
Panksepp, J,. and Trevarthen, C. (2009): The Neuroscience of Emotion in Music. In: Communicative Musicality, (eds) S. Malloch and C. Trevarthen, 105–146. Oxford University Press. Oxford.
Parsons, M. (2014): Living Psychoanalysis: From Theory toEexperience by Michael Parsons Routledge. Hove. UK.
Partanen, E., Kujala, T., Näätänen, R., Liitola, A., Sambeth, A., and Huotilainen, M. (2013): Learning-induced Neural Plasticity of Speech Processing Before Birth. Proc Natl Acad Sci U S A. 110(37):15145–50.
Patel, A. D. (2008): Music, Language, and the Brain. Oxford University Press. Oxford.
Patel, A. D. (2014): Can Nonlinguistic Musical Training Change the Way the Brain Processes Speech? The Expanded OPERA Hypothesis. Hear Res.308:98–108.
Paulson, S., Hustvedt, S., Solms, M., et al. (2017): The Deeper Self: An Expanded View of Consciousness. Ann. N.Y. Acad. Sci. 1406, 46.
Peiri, L. (2012): Collection de l'Art Brut, Lausanne. Skira Flammarion. Paris.
Peretz I. (2006): The nature of music from a biological perspective. Cognition. 100(1):1–32.
Peretz, I., and Coltheart, M. (2003): Modularity of Music Processing. Nat Neurosci. 6(7):688–91.
Pessoa, F. (1998): Fernando Pessoa and Co.: Selected Poems. Grove Press. New York. Translated by Richard Zenith.
Piaget, J. (1953): The Origin of Intelligence in the Child. Routledge and Kegan Paul. London.
Picon, G. (1973): Le travail de Jean Dubuffet. Albert Skira. Geneva.
Pignon, M., and Potin, Y. (2018): 1914-1918. Françoise Dolto, veuve de guerre à sept ans. Gallimard. Paris.
Pontalis, J. B. (1993): Love of Beginnings. Free Association Books. London.
Popova, M. (2015): Turning Trauma into Power: Marina Abramović on How Her Harrowing Childhood Became the Raw Material for Her Art. In: Segal G.Z.: Getting There: A Book of Mentors.
Porret-Forel, J. (1993): Aloïse et le Théatre de l'Univers. Skira. Geneva.
Porret-Forel, J. (2006): Le cloisonné du théâtre. Raw Vision 57.
Porret-Forel, J., and Muzelle, C. (2012): in Aloïse. Le ricochet solaire, 5 Continents Editions. Milan.

Pratt, C. (1952): Music and the Language of Emotion. U.S. Library of Congress. Washington, DC.

Price, M. (2019): Cave Painting Suggests Ancient Origin of Modern Mind. Science, 366:1299.

Prideaux, S. (2007): Edvard Much—Behind the Scream. Yale University Press. New Haven and London.

Prinzhorn, H. (1972): Artistry of the Mentally Ill: A Contribution to the Psychology and Psychopathology of Gestaltung. Springer-Verlag. Vienna New York.

Proust, M. (1981): Remembrance of Things Past. Originally published 1913–1927. Random House. New York. Translated by C. K. Moncrieff and T. Kilmartin.

Prum, R. (2017): The Evolution of Beauty: How Darwin's Forgotten Theory of Mate Choice Shapes the Animal World—and Us. Doubleday. New York.

Quinodoz, J. M. (2008): Listening to Hanna Segal. Routledge. London.

Racamier, P. C. (1999): Le genie des origins. Payot. Lausanne, Suisse.

Rahimi, S. (2013): The Ego, the Ocular, and the Uncanny: Why are Metaphors of Vision Central in Accounts of the Uncanny? Int J Psychoanal 94:453–476.

Reich, W. (1965): Gespräche mit Komponisten. Manesse Verlag Bibliothek der Weltliteratur. Munich.

Reik, T. (1953): The Haunting Melody: Psychoanalytic Experiences in Life and Music. New York: Farrar, Straus and Young. Cited in Alexander Stein (2003): Music, Mourning, and Consolation. JAPA, 52/3, 787–788, 801–802.

Reinhold, A. S., Sanguinetti-Scheck, J. I., Hartmann, K., et al. (2019): Behavioral and Neural Correlates of Hide-and-seek in Rats. Science 365, 1180.

Renfrew, C. (1987): Archeology and Language. The Puzzle of Indo-European Origin. Penguin Books. London.

Ribordy Lambert, F., Lavenex, P., and Banta Lavenex, P. (2015): Improvement of Allocentric Spatial Memory Resolution in Children from 2 to 4 Years of Age. Int. J. Behav. Dev. 39:318.

Rilke, R. M. (1899): Mir zur Feier: Gedichte Insel, Frankfurt (October 1, 2000)

Rilke, R. M. (1902–1926): Selected Letters. (1988). Quartet Books. London. Translated by R. F. C. Hull.

Rilke, R. M. (1920): Die weisse Fürstin. Rilke R.M. (1955-1966): Sämtliche Werke. Band 1–6, Band 1, Wiesbaden, Frankfurt.

Rilke, R. M. (1955–1966): Sämtliche Werke. Band 1–6, Band 1, Wiesbaden und Frankfurt.

Rilke, R. M. (1988): Lektüre für Minuten, Insel Verlag. Frankfurt, Leipzig.

Rilke, R. M. (1989): The Selected Poetry of Rainer Maria Rilke. (ed.) Stephen Mitchell. Vintage International. New York. Translated by Stephen Mitchell.

Rilke, R. M. (1992): Duino's Elegies (1923). Shambhala. Boston, MA. Translated by Stephen Mitchell. Les elegies de Duino, bilingual ed. Garnier-Flammarion. Paris. Translated by Angelloz. In: Sirois (2008).

Rilke, R. M. (1992): New poems/neue Gedichte. Carcanet. Manchester. Translated by S. Cohn.

Rilke, R. M. (1992): In: Sirois 2008, 132–133.

Rilke, R. M., and Kappus, F. X. (1993): Letters to a Young Poet. W. W. Norton and Co. New York.

Rizzuto, A. M. (2003): Psychoanalysis: The Transformation of the Subject by the Spoken Word. Psychoanalytic Quarterly, LXXII.

Rössler, A. (1922): Erinnerungen an Egon Schiele. Verlag Carl Konegen. Vienna.

Rolland, R. (1959): Le voyage interieur. Songe d'une vie. Albin. Paris.

Rose, G. J. (1999): Psychoanalysis and Art: Their Mutual Relevance. Psychoanalysis and Contemporary Thought, 22(4):591–608.

Rose, G. J. (2004): Between Couch and Piano: Psychoanalysis, Music, Art, and Neuroscience. Brunner-Routledge. Hove. UK.

Rousseau, V. (2018): The Outsider Artist as Storyteller. Antiques. April 17.

Royle, N. (2003): The Uncanny, Manchester University Press, cited in Matt Ffytche (2012).

Rutter, M. (2012): Resilience as a Dynamic Concept. Dev Psychopathol. 24(2):335–44.

Sabbadini, A. (2002): Colour and Music: Voices of the Unconscious. Int J Psychoanal. 83(Pt 1): 263–6.

Sacks, O. (2017): Musicophilia. Picador. London.

Salimpoor, V. N., van den Bosch, I., Kovacevic, N., McIntosh, A. R., Dagher, A., and Zatorre, R. J. (2013): Interactions between the Nucleus Accumbens and Auditory Cortices Predict Music Reward Value. Science. 340(6129):216–9.

Salmon, D. (2008): Voices: A World Forum for Music Therapy, Vol 8, No 1: Bridging Music and Psychoanalytic Therapy.

Sartre, J. P. (1964): Les mots. Gallimard. Paris. The Words. George Braziller. New York.

Scarfone, D. (2006): A Matter of Time: Actual Time and the Production of the Past. Psychoanal Q. 75:807–34.

Scarfone, D. (2011): The Analyst at Work. Live Wires: When Is the Analyst at Work? Int J Psychoanal. 92:755–9.

Scarry, E. (1999): On Beauty and Being Just. Princeton University Press. Princeton.

Schiele, E. (2014): Mother and Child. W&K Fine Art. Vienna, New York.

Schopenhauer, A. (1819): The World as Will and Representation. Vol. I, 257. Translated by E.F.J. Payne. In: Storr, A. (1992): Music and the Mind. Ballantine Books. New York.

Schultz, W. (2013): Updating Dopamine Reward Signals. Curr Opin Neurobiol. 23(2):229–38.

Scoville, W. B., and Milner, B. (1957): Loss of Recent Memory after Bilateral Hippocampal Lesions. J Neurol Neurosurg Psychiatry. 20,11.

Segal, H. (1952): A Psycho-analytical Approach to Aesthetics. Int J Psychoanal 33: 196–207.

Segal, H. (1986): A Psychoanalytical Approach to Aesthetics. Aronson. New York.

Semprun, J., and Wiesel, E. (2019): It Is Impossible to Remain Silent. Indiana University Press. Indiana. USA.

Segal, H. (1987): Silence Is the Real Crime. International Review of Psychoanalysis, 14: 3–12.

Serres, M. (1982): Genesis. Grasset and Fasquelle. Paris.

Servaes, F. (1902): Segantini sein Leben und Werk. M. Gerlach und Co. Vienna.

Shideler, R. (2004): Introduction: Per Olov Enquist. Swedish Book Review.

Siegel, L. (1978): Caspar David Friedrich and the Age of German Romanticism. Branden Publishing Co. Boston.

Sirois, F. J. (2008): Aesthetic Experience. Int J Psychoanal 89:127–142.

Sloterdijk, P. (2012): Zeilen und Tage. Suhrkamp. Berlin.

Sloterdijk, P. (2014): Der ästhetische Imperativ. Suhrkamp Taschenbuch 4529. Berlin.

Solms, M. (2017): What is "the Unconscious" and Where Is It Located in the Brain? A Neuropsychoanalytic Perspective. Ann. N.Y. Acad. Sci. 1406 90.

Spoerri, T. (1964): Le monde imagé d'Adolf Wölfli. Psychopathologie de l'expression vol 5, Sandoz.

Spoerri, E., and Glaesemer, J. (1976): Adolf Wölfli, Austellungskatalog. Kunstmuseum. Bern.

Stang, R. (1979): The Man and His Art. Abbeyville Press. New York.

Steck, H. (1975): Psychopathology and Pictorial Expression. Aloyse. Series 22. Sandoz.

Steck, A. and Steck B. (2016): Brain and Mind. Springer. New York.

Stefana, A. (2019): Revisiting Marion Milner's Work on Creativity and Art. The International Journal of Psychoanalysis, 100:1, 128–147.

Stein, A. (1999): Well-Tempered Bagatelles—A Meditation on Listening in Psychoanalysis and Music. Amer. Imago *56*(4), 389-416.

Stein, A. (2003): Music, Mourning, and Consolation. JAPA, 52/3, 2003, 787–788, 801–802.

Stein, A. (2004): Music and Trauma in Polanski's "The Pianist" (2002). Int. J. Psycho-Anal. 85(3), 755–65.

Stein, A. (2004b): Music, Mourning, and Consolation. J. Amer. Psychoanal. Assn., 52(3), 783–811.

Steiner, J. (2015): Reflections on the Work of Hanna Segal (1918–2011). Int J Psychoanal 96:165–175.

Stern, D. N. (1994): One Way to Build a Clinically Relevant Baby. Infant Ment Health J. 1994;15(1):9–25.

Stern, D. N. (1998): The Process of Therapeutic Change Involving Implicit Knowledge: Some Implications of Developmental Observations for Adult Psychotherapy. Infant Ment Health J 19:300–8.

Stern, D. N. (2004): The Present Moment in Psychotherapy and Everyday Life. Norton. New York.

Stern, D. N., Sander, L. W., Nahum, J. P., Harrison, A. M., Lyons-Ruth, K., Morgan, A. C., et al. (1998): Non-interpretive Mechanisms in Psychoanalytic Therapy. The "Something More" Than Interpretation. Int J Psychoanal. 79 (Pt 5):903–21.

Storr, A. (1992): Music and the Mind. Ballantine Books. New York.

Szpilman, W. (1999): The Pianist: The Extraordinary Story of One Man's Survival in Warsaw, 1939–1945. Picador. New York.

Tadié, J. Y. (2008): Le songe musical. Claude Debussy Collection L'un et l'autre, Gallimard. Paris.

Tansella, C. (2007): The Long and Winding Journey of Outsider Art: An Historical Perspective. Epidemiol Psychiatr Soc. 16,133.

Tarr, B., Launay, J., and Dunbar, R.I. (2014): Music and Social Bonding: "Self-other" Merging and Neurohormonal Mechanisms. Front Psychol. 5:1096.

Terr, L. (1985): Remembered Images and Trauma: A Psychology of the Supernatural, Psychoanalytic Study of the Child, 40.

The Beatles (2012): The Beatles Anthology. Chronicle Books. San Francisco

Thévoz, M. (1975): L'Art Brut. Skira. Geneva.

Tisseron, S. (1978): Histoire de la psychiatrie en bandes dessinées. Éditions Savelli.

Tisseron, S. (1992): Tintin et les secrets de famille. Aubier. Paris.

Toadvine, T. (2016): Maurice Merleau-Ponty. Stanford Encyclopedia of Philosophy (ed.) Edward N. Zalta. Metaphysics Research Lab. Stanford.

Trehub, S. E. (2003): The Developmental Origins of Musicality. Nat Neurosci. 6(7):669–73.

Treisman, A. (1999): Solutions to the Binding Problem: Progress through Controversy and Convergence. Neuron. 1999, 24,105.

Tsao, D. Y., and Livingstone, M. S. (2008): Mechanisms of Face Perception. Annu Rev Neurosci. 31, 411.

Tulving, E. (1983): Elements of Episodic Memory. Oxford University Press. Oxford.

Turri, M. G. (2015): Transference and Katharsis: Freud to Aristotle. Int J Psychoanal 96:369–387.

Uga, V., Lemut, M. C., Zampi, C., Zilli, I., and Salzarulo, P. (2006): Music in Dreams. Conscious Cogn. 15: 351–7.

Ungerer, T. (2002): A la guerre comme à la guerre. Editions La Nuée Bleue/ DNA, Strasbourg.

Ungerleider, L. G., and Haxby, J. V. (1994): "What" and "where" in the Human Brain. Curr Opin Neurobiol. 4,157.

Välimäki, S. (2005): Subject Strategies in Music. A Psychoanalytic Approach to Musical Signification. Acta Semiotica Fennica XXII. Approaches to Musical Semiotics 9 International Semiotics Institute at Imatra Semioti. Helsinki.

Vaughan, W. (2004): Friedrich. Phaidon Press. Oxford.

Vaz, A. P., Inati, S. K., Brunel, N., et al. (2019): Coupled Ripple Oscillations between the Medial Temporal Lobe and Neocortex Retrieve Human Memory. Science. 363, 975.

Vermorel, H. (2009): The Presence of Spinoza in the Exchanges between Sigmund Freud and Romain Rolland. Int J Psychoanal 90:6,1235–1254.

Vermorel, H. (2018): Sigmund Freud et Romain Rolland. Un dialogue. Albin Michel. Paris.

Vernon, R. J., Sutherland, C. A., Young, A. W., et al. (2014): Modeling First Impressions from Highly Variable Facial Images. Proc Natl Acad Sci USA. 111,E3353.

Villari, L. (1901): Giovanni Segantini. The Story of His Life. T. Fisher Unwin Paternoster Square. London.

Vircondelet, A. (2001): Mémoires de Balthus. Editions du Rocher. Paris.

Vogelsang, L., Anold, S., Schormann, J., Wübbelman, S., and Schredl, M. (2016). The Continuity Between Waking-Life Musical Activities and Music Dreams. Dreaming. 26,132.

Volmat, R. (1956): L'Art Psychopathologique. Presses Universitaires de France. Paris.

Wakefield, J. C. (2007): Max Graf's Reminiscences of Professor Sigmund Freud Revisited: New Evidence from the Freud Archives. Library of Congress. Washington, DC.

Waldrop, M. (2017): Inside Einstein's Love Affair With "Lina"—His Cherished Violin. National Geographic. April 25.

Walker, A. (1979): Music and the Unconscious. Br Med J. 2:1641–3.

Walters, K., and Jarell, R. (2013): Blessed Peacemakers: 365 Extraordinary People Who Changed the World. Wipf and Stock Publishers. Eugene Oregon USA.

Weiner, K. S., Barnett, M. A., Lorenz, S., et al. (2017): Cytoarchitecture of Domain-specific Regions in Human High-level Visual Cortex. Cereb Cortex. 27,146.

Wiesel, E. (1983): Le Cinquième Fils. Editions Grasset et Fasquelle. Paris,

Wiesel, E. (1988): Some Questions That Remain Open. In: Asher Cohen, Joav Gelber, and Charlotte Wardi (eds). Comprehending the Holocaust. Historical and Literary Research. Frankfurt.

Wiesel, E. (2001): On Integrity. The American Academy of Achievement. London.

Wiesel, E. (2008): Night. Penguin Books Ltd. London.

Wiesel, E., and Heffner, R. D. (2001): Conversations with Elie Wiesel. Schocken Books. New York.

Wilde, O. (2007). Epigrams of Oscar Wilde. Wordsworth Editions. London.

Winnicott, D. W. (1949): Hate in the Countertransference. Int. J. Psycho-Anal., 30:69–74.

Winnicott, D. W. (1963): Communicating and not Communicating Leading to a Study of Certain Opposites. In: Winnicott, D. W. (1965): The Maturational Processes and the Facilitating Environment.

Winnicott, D. W. (1965): The Maturational Processes and the Facilitating Environment. International Universities Press. New York.

Winnicott, D. W. (1967): Mirror-Role of Mother and Family in Child Development. In: Winnicott, D. W. (1971): Playing and Reality.

Winnicott, D. W. (1970): Living Creatively. In: Winnicott, C., Shepherd, R., Davis, M., (eds) (1986): Home Is Where We Start From. Penguin Books. Harmondsworth.

Winnicott, D. W. (1971): Playing and Reality. Routledge. London. Basic Books. New York.

Winnicott, D. W. (1974): Fear of Breakdown. Int R Psychoanal. 1974; 1:103–7.

Winnicott, D. W. (1975): Through Pediatrics to Psychoanalysis. The International Psycho-Analytical Library, 100:1-325. The Hogarth Press and the Institute of Psychoanalysis. London.

Winnicott, D. W. (1986): The Concept of the Healthy Individual. In: Winnicott, D. W. (1986): Home is Where We Start From.

Winnicott, D. W. (1986): Home is Where We Start From. W.W. Norton. New York.

Woolf, V. (1891–1895): Hyde Park Gate News. Vol. I and Vol. II. Hesperus Classics.

Woolf, V. (1919–1924): On Being Ill. In: Collected Essays. Hogarth Press. London.

Woolf, V. (1925): Modern Fiction. In: The Common Reader. Harcourt, Brace and Company, Inc. New York.

Woolf, V. (1927): To the Lighthouse. Hogarth Press. London.

Woolf, V. (1929): A Room of One's Own. Morag Shiach (ed.) (1992). Oxford University Press. Oxford.

Woolf, V. (1940): Roger Fry: A Biography. Harcourt Brace. San Diego, CA.

Woolf, V. (1976): Moments of Being—a Collection of Autobiographical Writing. Jeanne Schulkind (ed.) (1985). A Harvest Book. New York.

Woolf, V. (1992): The Waves. Penguin Books. London.

Zatorre, R. J. (2015): Musical Pleasure and Reward: Mechanisms and Dysfunction. Ann N Y Acad Sci. 1337:202–11.

Zatorre, R. J., and Salimpoor, V. N. (2013): From Perception to Pleasure: Music and Its Neural Substrates. Proc Natl Acad Sci USA. 110 Suppl 2:10430–7.

Zehder-Segantini, B. (1912): Giovanni Segantinis Schriften und Briefe. Klinkhardt and Biermann. Leipzig.

Zeki, S. (1999): Inner Vision: An Exploration of Art and the Brain. Oxford University Press. Oxford.

Zeki, S. (2003): The Disunity of Consciousness. Trends Cogn Sci.7, 214.

Zeki, S., and Balthus (1995): Balthus ou la Quête de l'essentiel: Entretiens avec Semir Zeki. Les Belles Lettres. Paris.

Zirnsak, M. (2011): Anticipatory Saccade Target Processing and the Presaccadic Transfer of Visual Features. J Neurosci. 31,17887.

ILLUSTRATION CREDITS

Unless otherwise indicated, illustrations were created or adapted by Eric Bernardi.

Chapter 1

1.3 Painting titled 'The Starry Night' by Vincent van Gogh. AKG-images / WHA / World History Archive.

Chapter 3

3.1 and 3.2 Brain and Mind, Steck and Steck 2016. Permission Springer International Publishing.

Chapter 4

4.5 5.XII.1950 "Le visage de la paix" by Pablo Picasso. Succession Picasso, Prolitteris, Zürich.

Chapter 5

5.1 Brain and Mind, Steck and Steck 2016. Permission Springer International Publishing.

Chapter 6

6.1 Apollo Belvedere. Ca. 120–140. Roman copy of Greek bronze original of ca. 350-325 BC. White marble. Attributed to Leochares. Vatican Museums. Vatican City. AKG-images.

6.2 The Kiss (1908) by Gustav Klimt. Oil on canvas. Vienna, Österr. Galerie im Belve-dere. AKG-images / Erich Lessing.

6.3 Francis Bacon. Study for portrait of Lucian Freud, sideways (1971). AKG-images / Album / Joseph Martin. © The Estate of Francis Bacon. All rights reserved / 2020, Pro-Litteris, Zurich.

Chapter 7

7.1 Caspar Friedrich. Two Men Contemplating the Moon (ca.1825-1830). New York, Metropolitan Museum of Art. AKG images.

Chapter 8

8.1 Jean Dubuffet. La vision Tisserande (1976). Photo: Etienne Malapert. Musée cantonal des Beaux-Arts de Lausanne. Donation de Mireille et James Lévy. © 2020, ProLitteris, Zurich.

8.2 Louis Soutter. Volagie (1937). Stiftung Im Obersteg, Depositum im Kunstmuseum Basel. AKG-images.
8.3 Adolf Wölfli. Assiisen des Mittel Landes (1904). © Adolf Wölfli-Stiftung, Kunstmuseum Bern.
8.4 Adolf Wölfli. West Frontt des Zehntheiligen Skt. Adolf Kathedral Schiffes (1916). Schenkung Ernst und Maria Elisabeth Mumenthaler-Fischer. Depositum im Kunstmuseum Basel. Données photographiques relevant du domaine public – Kunstmuseum Basel
8.5 Adolf Wölfli. Holirod (1927). © Adolf Wölfli-Stiftung, Kunstmuseum Bern.
8.6 Aloïse. Lulu Mater dolorosa (ca. 1917-1924). Photo: Claude Bornand. Collection de l'Art Brut, Lausanne. © Association Aloïse.
8.7 Aloïse. Enlève le manteau royal de la sirène (ca. 1941-1951). Photo: Arnaud Conne, Atelier de numérisation - Ville de Lausanne. Collection de l'Art Brut, Lausanne. © Association Aloïse.
8.8 Aloïse. Le fiancé à la rose Schwilge sur son cœur (ca. 1941-1951). Musée cantonal des Beaux-Arts, Lausanne. © Association Aloïse.
8.9 Aloïse. Gloria in excelsis Deo - Singer Bornod (ca.1960-1963). Collection Jean-David Mermod, Lausanne. © Association Aloïse.

Chapter 11

11.1 Camille Claudel. L'Implorante (ca. 1898-1910). New York, Metropolitan Museum of Art. AKG-images.
11.2 Salvador Dali. Melting pocket watch, detail (1931). New York, Museum of Modern Art. AKG-images. © Salvador Dalí, Fundació Gala-Salvador Dalí / 2020, ProLitteris, Zurich.

Chapter 13

13.1 Edvard Munch. The Scream (1893). AKG-images / WHA / World History Archive.
13.2 Balthus. Le Roi des Chats (1935). Collection musée cantonal des Beaux-Arts, Lausanne. Autorisation Mme Harumi Klossowska de Rola, Rossinière.

Chapter 15

15.1 Giovanni Segantini. Two mothers (1899). Chur, Bündner Kunstmuseum. AKG images.
15.2 Egon Schiele. Tote Mutter (I) (1910). Wien, Leopold Museum - Privatstiftung. AKG-images.
15.3 Käthe Kollwitz. Pieta. Berlin, Käthe-Kollwitz-Museum Berlin. AKG-images.